Praise for *The Finance Book*

'*Reduces the time required by management to understand the essentials of accounting and finance, enabling them to spend more time focusing on their core business*'.

Nasser Abbas, Joint Managing Director, Gearhouse SA (Pty) Ltd

'*This book is set out clearly and is often transformational. This is the go-to source for clarity on how financial language and structures relate to real life business situations.*'

Derek Ion, Projects Director, Annesbrook Holdings Ltd (NZ)

'*If you need a clear introduction to the critical concepts of finance then this book delivers it. A highly intuitive structure means readers can dip in and out and learn as they go.*'

Ken Lee, Head of European Equity Research, Barclays

'*A really helpful, well organised and easy to understand primer and reference book for those who aren't accountants but still need to understand the accounts*'.

Roger Siddle, Chairman, Cordium Group

'*Language is a key to understanding any field of specialty, and in this book Warner and Hussain have managed to distill principles of finance and accounting in such a way that the language that often mystifies non-practitioners is clearly explained and meaningful. I wish I'd had access to this book when I started my career in management. The Finance Book is an excellent reference and a handy resource for any professional; it will be indispensable to aspiring managers. In the business world accountancy and finance are the ring that binds managers, and this book clarifies and explains concepts; for many it covers familiar territory, but for most non-financial professionals it will also provide the information to fill the inevitable gaps in our knowledge. Warner and Hussain explain in a straightforward and clear manner the concepts that baffle many managers from a non-financial background early in their careers. The language of business is presented unambiguously with relevant examples that enable the reader to quickly grasp and embed concepts.*'

André Snoxall, Director, Russau Consulti

'*A great book. At last, a guide that
to practically understand financi*

'This is fantastic! Full of real-time insights for business people who haven't studied accountancy.'

Daniel Feather, Partner, EY London

'I wish I'd had a book like this at the start of my career! The bite-sized summaries at the start of each chapter are a smart time saver for any busy business professional.'

Ben Grover, Finance Director, UBM EMEA

'Essential reading for any non-finance professional. This is an easy to read and practical guide to the world of finance.'

Paul Herman, Group CEO, Bluebox Corporate Finance

'As an experienced CFO I can see the business value in all employees, not just those in finance, having financial awareness and understanding. The Finance Book does an excellent job in making finance accessible and articulating clearly its relevance in practice.'

Phil Mickler, CFO, Jack Wills

'A clear, concise and straightforward introduction to the world of accounting and finance - which, to non-accountants, too often seems nothing of the sort'.

Tessa Park, Technical Partner, Kingston Smith LLP

'The financial aspect of business is so important. This invaluable book helps make finance simple and understandable and is a must-read.'

Martin Port, CEO, BigChange Apps

'The most user-friendly book for non-finance professionals I've ever seen! Finance is the lifeblood of a business. Read this book and help your business live and succeed.'

Daniel Mark, Chief Financial Officer, Adstream

'This book is a thorough and well-organised overview for the non-finance professional. Si Hussain has spent many years in the educational field, and this comes through in the clarity of explanation and the numerous practical examples. A must-have for the manager who is climbing the management mountain.'

David Parmenter, author, *Key Performance Indicators* and *The Financial Controllers and CFO Toolkit*

The Finance Book

Pearson

At Pearson, we believe in learning – all kinds of learning for all kinds of people. Whether it's at home, in the classroom or in the workplace, learning is the key to improving our life chances.

That's why we're working with leading authors to bring you the latest thinking and best practices, so you can get better at the things that are important to you. You can learn on the page or on the move, and with content that's always crafted to help you understand quickly and apply what you've learned.

If you want to upgrade your personal skills or accelerate your career, become a more effective leader or more powerful communicator, discover new opportunities or simply find more inspiration, we can help you make progress in your work and life.

Every day our work helps learning flourish, and wherever learning flourishes, so do people.

To learn more, please visit us at **www.pearson.com/uk**

The Financial Times

With a worldwide network of highly respected journalists, *The Financial Times* provides global business news, insightful opinion and expert analysis of business, finance and politics. With over 500 journalists reporting from 50 countries worldwide, our in-depth coverage of international news is objectively reported and analysed from an independent, global perspective.

To find out more, visit **www.ft.com**

The Finance Book

Stuart Warner and Si Hussain

 Pearson

Harlow, England • London • New York • Boston • San Francisco • Toronto • Sydney
Dubai • Singapore • Hong Kong • Tokyo • Seoul • Taipei • New Delhi
Cape Town • São Paulo • Mexico City • Madrid • Amsterdam • Munich • Paris • Milan

PEARSON EDUCATION LIMITED

Edinburgh Gate
Harlow CM20 2JE
United Kingdom
Tel: +44 (0)1279 623623
Web: www.pearson.com/uk

First edition published 2017 (print and electronic)

ISBN: 978-1-292-12364-6 (print)
       978-1-292-12367-7 (PDF)
       978-1-292-12365-3 (ePub)

British Library Cataloguing-in-Publication Data
A catalogue record for the print edition is available from the British Library

Library of Congress Cataloging-in-Publication Data
A catalog record for the print edition is available from the Library of Congress

11
21 20

Cover design by David Carroll & Co

Print edition typeset in Stone Serif ITC Pro by 9/13 by SPi Global
Print edition printed and bound in Great Britain by Ashford Colour Press Ltd,
Gosport, Hampshire

NOTE THAT ANY PAGE CROSS REFERENCES REFER TO THE PRINT EDITION

Contents

About the authors

Stuart Warner Bsc (Hons) FCA is the author of four books on finance, an international speaker, a teacher and a non-executive adviser. His goal is to help businesses increase productivity and profits through innovative and engaging finance training. He delivers finance based training programmes around the world across multiple sectors. Over his career, Stuart has trained over ten thousand people. He has taught accounting trainees for professional qualifications, and has delivered CPD courses for qualified accountants and interactive courses for non-finance professionals from graduate to board level. Stuart studied management sciences at UMIST and became a Chartered Accountant whilst working at PwC.

Stuart loves the fresh air and peace of the countryside, especially the scenic hills of North Wales, so he decided to live in London for ample doses of air pollution, loud noises and views of tall concrete buildings. In his spare time he can be found falling off his mountain bike or falling off walls whilst indoor rock climbing.

Saieem (Si) Hussain BSc (Hons) FCA is a chartered accountant. He trained at KPMG and qualified in 1990. Si has spent 25+ years delivering financial and business training programmes to thousands of professionals. He has held senior positions in several listed companies, including Chief Executive of BPP Professional Education.

Si runs an independent consultancy delivering financial and business training, including coaching to senior executives. He provides strategic and business advice to organisations across the training and education sectors.

Despite being vegetarian, tee-total and a fan of country and folk music, Si describes himself as an easy-to-please and entertaining dinner guest. He is a Londoner born and bred and in his spare time can be seen walking the streets of London, re-tracing the steps of Pepys, Dickens, Johnson and others.

Acknowledgements

We are grateful to Greggs plc for the use of material from Greggs plc's Annual Report and Accounts 2015, which is used with permission.

Our thanks to Nick Weller for his technical check of this book. His attention to detail and thought-provoking comments added both value and rigour to the writing process.

Dedications

Stuart Warner: To all the people I have ever taught. Thank you for your attentiveness, willingness to learn, challenging questions and occasionally laughing in the right places. You have helped me to develop, refine and fine tune my own understanding of finance, as well as my questionable sense of humour. Your contribution enabled me to write this book.

Si Hussain: To Myra, Janita, Liyana and Eliza. Your enthusiasm has been the one constant throughout. I am forever indebted.

Introduction

Why is this book different to other finance books?

Not for accountants

The overwhelming majority of finance books available that are targeted at non-finance professionals are better suited to trainee accountants because they take an academic approach to finance. While necessary for accountants, they are too focused on the detail.

The Finance Book is written for non-finance people. It is primarily aimed at those who work (or aspire to work) in business including directors, supervisors, graduates and undergraduates in any department or specialism. Students studying business at school and college will also find the book helpful.

Practitioners not academics

This is not an academic book but it is also not a simplistic book. It is a practical book because it has been written by practitioners. We include in this book our personal experiences gained through working in business in favour of replicating knowledge from academic text books.

In addition, both authors have spent countless hours instructing, teaching and training many thousands of professionals from disciplines including marketing, sales, production, administration, HR and legal. Knowledge and insights from this book have been used in boardrooms and workplaces across many industries and sectors.

Quick and easy

The book is purposefully designed to be quick and easy to use. We tell you what you need to know to quickly get 'up to speed' in core finance concepts.

A key benefit of this book is that you do not have to read it from cover to cover to make sense of finance. You can dip in and dip out of chapters, each of which has been written as a standalone chapter. No pre-study is required to comprehend the concepts. We have taken complex topics and broken them down to key concepts that are explained in concise, easy to read sections.

Within each chapter there are multiple cross references (or links) to other relevant chapters as they occur. This will enable you to review chapters and make connections relevant to you. Allow your curiosity to determine your path through the book.

A consistent structure

To make the book easy to read, we have used a consistent format in chapters.

In a nutshell

In a few simple sentences, we explain the meaning of key concepts used in finance.

This is designed for busy people who want to 'cut to the chase' and eliminate extraneous detail.

Need to know

The bare essentials of the chapter are covered under this section.

We explain:

- Why it is important
- When it is important
- 'Grey areas'
- What happens in practice.

Nice to know

If you want to know more or are interested in some of the complexities, read on to this section.

Optional detail

For those interested in the complexities and further detail.

Where to spot in company accounts

Company accounts are a helpful resource when trying to understand finance. We use this section to show you how and where concepts are reflected within a company's accounts.

Watch out for in practice

We provide some points to be on the lookout for in practice.

Terminology

This book uses terminology in everyday use (such as 'stock' and 'fixed assets') to make the book readily accessible to non-finance professionals. Alternative terminology (eg 'inventory' and 'non-current assets' used in IFRS) is introduced to show equivalence in practice (see **Chapter 19 Accounting and financial reporting standards**). For financial reporting treatment and disclosures we have used IFRS. This is consistent with Greggs plc, the example company used throughout this book.

The terms 'company', 'business', 'entity' and 'organisation' are used interchangeably. There is no distinction in meaning intended by the authors in the use of these terms.

Contents

The individual chapters are grouped in seven parts. A brief description of each part is included below:

1 Finance fundamentals
   - The finance department, key personnel and its systems.
   - The difference between cash and accruals accounting which is a fundamental concept underpinning accounting.

2 Primary financial statements
   - The main three financial statements: the P&L; the balance sheet; and the cash flow statement.

3 Key elements of financial statements
   - A number of key elements which make up financial statements are covered.

4 Financial and regulatory environment
   - The rules, regulations, responsibilities and best practice of running a company.

5 Assessing financial health
   - Key performance measures and indicators to asses a company's financial health.

6 Sources of business finance
   - The two main sources of business finance: equity and debt, plus alternative sources.

7 Financial management
   - The best practice financial management techniques employed by companies.

one

Finance fundamentals

1 Finance personnel and systems

> 'I have no use for bodyguards, but I have very specific use for two highly trained certified public accountants.'
>
> Elvis Presley, American musician and actor

In a nutshell

The finance department is the central hub of many organisations. Most areas of a business will have a relationship with finance and have some level of interaction with the finance system.

The finance team and the finance system provide essential support to the rest of the business.

Need to know

Why is this important?

Sound financial management is critical to the success of any organisation. It can be one of the key differentiators between high performance and average performance within an industry.

The most successful organisations invest in both finance personnel and management accounting systems, as they understand this pays dividends through better-quality information, which leads to improved business decisions.

An efficient and effective finance team can provide a value added service to the rest of the business.

When is this important?

The key deadline for finance is the financial year end when the statutory financial accounts are produced and subsequently published.

The annual budgeting process (see **Chapter 34 Budgeting and forecasting**) is when most non-accountants will have contact with 'finance'.

Most businesses will produce monthly management accounts (see **Chapter 31 Management accounts**) although there is a trend towards ad hoc and real-time information.

1. Finance personnel

The diagram below represents a typical structure of a finance department:

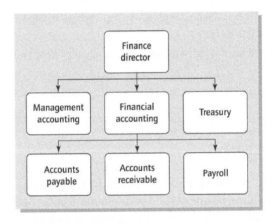

Finance director

The FD (finance director) (FD) or CFO (chief financial officer) is responsible for financial strategy and its link to business strategy and is usually a board member. FDs have overall responsibility for the financial health of a business and closely monitor KPIs (key performance indicators) such as:

- profitability performance measures (see **Chapter 23 Profitability performance measures**)
- working capital and liquidity (see **Chapter 24 Working capital and liquidity management**)

- long-term solvency performance measures (see **Chapter 26 Long-term solvency performance measures**)
- investor ratios (see **Chapter 27 Investor ratios**).

Financial accounting

The financial accounting team is responsible for processing transactions and maintaining core accounting records. The 'financial controller' heads the team.

Three key areas are:

1 *Accounts payable*: processing purchase invoices and paying suppliers (see **Chapter 12 Debtors and creditors**).
2 *Accounts receivable*: processing sales invoices and collecting payments from customers (see **Chapter 12 Debtors and creditors**).
3 *Payroll*: paying employees correctly and on time.

Other financial accounting areas include:

- bookkeeping
- fixed asset management (see **Chapter 9 Tangible fixed assets and depreciation**)
- stock control (see **Chapter 11 Stock**)
- tax accounting (see **Chapter 8 Business tax**)
- company secretariat
- investor relations (see **Chapter 29 Equity finance**)
- financial reporting (see **Chapter 19 Accounting and financial reporting standards**)
- group accounting (see **Chapter 16 Group accounting**)
- liaison with external auditors (see **Chapter 20 External financial audit**).

Treasury

The treasury team's responsibilities include:

- ensuring that the business does not run out of cash
- making the most effective use of any surplus cash

- identifying sources of medium and long-term finance
- managing the relationship with banks and monitoring covenants on any loans
- managing foreign exchange, for overseas operations.

Management accounting

The management accounting (MA) team monitor budgets, make forecasts and provide the information that supports financial decisions (see **Chapter 31 Management accounts**).

In practice

Every organisation will have its own structure. In smaller organisations many of these roles are combined. The smallest organisations may outsource their finance operations to a firm of accountants, as this is more cost effective than employing staff.

2. Finance systems

Source documents (See **Figure 1: Source documents**)

The majority of source documents are for the sales and purchase subsystems (see **Chapter 12 Debtors and creditors**) and include:

- Purchase requisitions
- Sales and purchase orders
- Delivery notes (sales)
- Goods received notes (purchases)
- Sales and purchase invoices
- Remittance advice (cash receipts and payments).

Other source documents include:

- Timesheets for payroll
- Overhead invoices, such as utilities and rent
- Capital purchase invoices (see **Chapter 7 Opex and capex**).

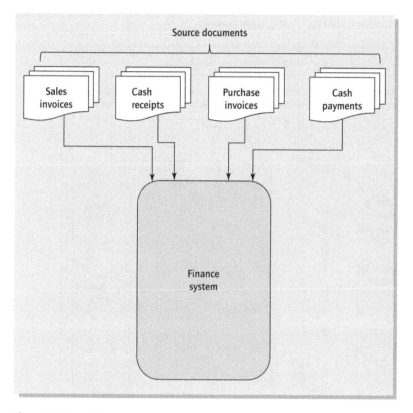

Figure 1: Source documents

Key tasks (See **Figure 2: Key tasks**)

- Sales and purchase related reporting
- Cash flow management (see **Chapter 24 Working capital and liquidity management**)
- Fixed assets management (see **Chapter 9 Tangible fixed assets and depreciation** and **Chapter 10 Goodwill and other intangibles**)
- Stock management (see **Chapter 11 Stock**)
- Tax administration, for example VAT returns (see **Chapter 8 Business tax**)
- Payroll administration will sometimes be a separate system as an additional control.

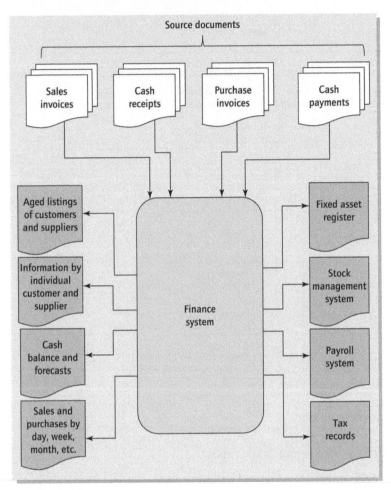

Figure 2: Key tasks

The nominal ledger (See **Figure 3: Nominal ledger, trial balance and journals**)

The *nominal ledger* is a central repository for all accounting transactions. Each transaction is allocated to a different nominal 'account' (or 'code') depending on its nature. The nominal ledger will sometimes be very detailed. For example, 'sales' may have an individual nominal account for every single product or service sold in every single geographical location. The level of detail depends on the size of company, its complexity and business requirements.

The trial balance (TB) (See **Figure 3: Nominal ledger, trial balance and journals**)

The *trial balance* is a list of every account in the nominal ledger and its associated 'balance' (or total), categorised into profit and loss account (see **Chapter 3 Profit and loss (P&L)** and balance sheet (see **Chapter 4 The balance sheet**) items.

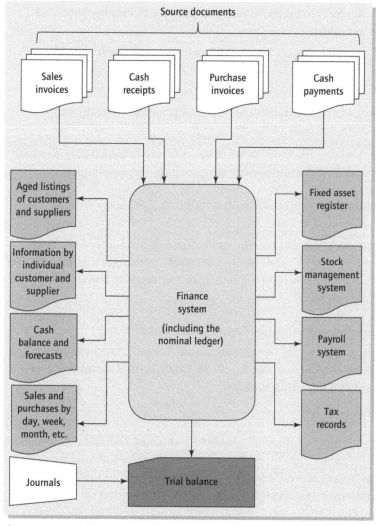

Figure 3: Nominal ledger, trial balance and journals

Journals (See **Figure 3: Nominal ledger, trial balance and journal**)

Authorised members of the financial accounting team will be responsible for making period-end *journals*. These are accounting adjustments to reflect timing differences relating to the accruals concept (see **Chapter 2 Cash versus accruals accounting**). Typical journals include:

- Depreciation (see **Chapter 9 Tangible fixed assets and depreciation**)
- Accruals and prepayments (see **Chapter 13 Prepayments and accruals**)
- Provisions (see **Chapter 14 Provisions and contingencies**).

Draft financial accounts (See **Figure 4: Accounts**)

The 'adjusted' trial balance is used to produce the profit and loss account and balance sheet.

At this stage the financial accounts may be in a format that meets the needs of the business but may not be in statutory format.

Management accounts and budgeting (See **Figure 4: Accounts**)

The MA team will use the draft financial accounts when they prepare regular management accounts packs (see **Chapter 31 Management accounts**). These will include reports of performance against budget.

Statutory accounts (See **Figure 4: Accounts**)

The draft financial accounts are adjusted to reflect accounting and financial reporting standards (see **Chapter 19 Accounting and financial reporting standards**).

In practice

Historically, in manual accounting systems, transactions were recorded in 'books' and 'ledgers'. These terms are still used despite the widespread prevalence of computerised accounting systems. Today there is a wide choice of off-the-shelf systems such as Sage and QuickBooks, most of which offer cloud-based versions.

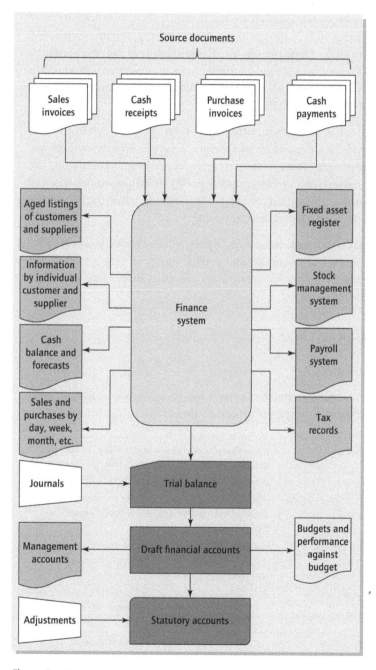

Figure 4: Accounts

Large (and increasingly some medium-sized) organisations are more likely to use ERP (enterprise resource planning) systems such as SAP and Oracle. These provide an integrated suite of subsystems which besides finance include supply chain management, production processing, customer relationship management, human resources and other areas of the business.

The growth in technology has seen 'finance' change from transaction processing and routine analysis towards more ad hoc analysis and business support roles. Many large organisations use shared service centres (a central department within a multidivisional organisation) which are used for processing transactions and the more routine aspects of accounting.

Many organisations now focus on the value added by the finance department. Accountants are increasingly seen as finance business partners who play a contributory as well as supporting role in the business.

Nice to know

System controls

All finance systems should have robust controls over human error and fraud. Examples of typical controls are:

Authorisation	All transactions and system inputs should be approved or authorised by an appropriate person. For example, purchase orders by a line manager.
Segregation of duties	Where possible, different personnel should be responsible for authorising, recording and reconciling transactions.
Access controls	Hierarchical password restricted access. For example, only appropriate personnel can input information or access output information.
Physical controls	Only authorised personnel have access to certain assets. For example, only authorised IT personnel can access the server room.
Input controls	For example, batch inputs and digit verification.

Reconciliations	Regular reconciliations, for example bank reconciliations and stock checks (see **Chapter 11 Stock**).
Budgets	Unexpected differences between budget and actual figures (known as variances) will highlight any potential errors (see **Chapter 34 Budgeting and forecasting**).
Audit trails	A system log which tracks every change and who made the change.
Backups	Regular backups kept offsite so the system can be restored to a prior state.
Contingency plans	For example, a disaster recovery plan in case of system failure or other hazards.
Internal audit	Regular independent 'internal' reviews of systems and their controls (see **Chapter 20 External financial audit**).
Audit committee	A board committee including non-executive directors responsible for ensuring the integrity of the financial statements (see **Chapter 22 Corporate governance and whistleblowing**).

As well as the obvious internal benefits of strong controls, they should also enable an auditor to reduce the amount of testing required (see **Chapter 20 External financial audit**).

Optional detail

Representative bodies

There are a number of representative bodies for accountants and other finance personnel. The six main types of 'accounting' qualification are as follows:

Type	Example body
Chartered	ICAEW (Institute of Chartered Accountants in England and Wales)
Certified	ACCA (Association of Chartered Certified Accountants)
Public Sector	CIPFA (Chartered Institute of Public Finance and Accountancy)
Management	CIMA (Chartered Institute of Management Accountants)
Technicians	AAT (Association of Accounting Technicians)
Tax	CTA (Chartered Tax Adviser)

Only members of ICAEW and ACCA in the above list can act as external auditors.

In the UK the term 'accountant' is not restricted to practitioners fulfilling professional requirements, unlike other professions such as solicitors and medical doctors. Therefore, it is wise to check which type of accountant one is dealing with and whether they have a professional qualification.

Where to spot in company accounts

1   The following note is included in the chief executive report of Greggs 2015 annual report.

Investment in systems

We have made significant progress in the second year of our major investment programme to create the integrated systems platform necessary in order to compete more effectively as a centralised business in the food-on-the-go market. The initial phases, involving workforce management and supplier relationship management, have delivered benefits in excess of our initial expectations.

In 2015 we installed the infrastructure necessary to run SAP as our core Enterprise Resource Planning system and implemented the first module of this, going live with a new customer contact system in the fourth quarter. We are well advanced with plans to bring our existing finance processes into SAP in the first half of 2016. This will provide the platform on which we will build a suite of new capabilities across logistics, procurement, product lifecycle management and centralised ranging, forecasting and replenishment. We plan to trial improved processes around shop ordering in the latter part of the year.

We continue to be encouraged by the results of the programme, which is expected to make an annual net contribution of around £6.0 million once all the key functionality is in place, as well as making us more agile in terms of our ability to adopt further change in the future.

2   Within Greggs intangible assets note are software and assets under development. The note shows that during the last two financial years Greggs has invested £9.8 million in software and assets under development.

10. Intangible assets
Group and Parent Company

	Software £'000	Assets under development £'000	Total £'000
Cost			
Balance at 29 December 2013	1,715	–	1,715
Additions	817	2,992	3,809
Balance at 3 January 2015	2,532	2,992	5,524
Balance at 4 January 2015	2,532	2,992	5,524
Additions	–	5,981	5,981
Balance at 2 January 2016	2,532	8,973	11,505
Amortisation			
Balance at 29 December 2013	703	–	703
Amortisation charge for the year	100	–	100
Balance at 3 January 2015	803	–	803
Balance at 4 January 2015	803	–	803
Amortisation charge for the year	454	–	454
Balance at 2 January 2016	1,257	–	1,257
Carrying amounts			
At 29 December 2013	1,012	–	1,012
At 3 January 2015	1,729	2,992	4,721
At 4 January 2015	1,729	2,992	4,721
At 2 January 2016	1,275	8,973	10,248

Assets under development relate to software projects arising from the investment in new systems platforms.

Watch out for in practice

→ The structure of the finance department. Are roles and responsibilities clearly defined?

→ Is the finance team integrated into the business? Are they seen as business partners who provide a value added service to support decisions?

→ The actual finance system being used. Is it a recognised system? Are there lots of disparate systems which need to be reconciled and manually integrated?

→ Does the business make use of extensive spreadsheets instead of/in addition to system reports?

→ The level of investment into maintaining and enhancing the system.

→ Are there system input controls such as segregation of duties and hierarchical access?

→ Does the finance system produce accurate and reliable information? Do managers actually use the system information?

→ Is there an internal audit function or an independent assessment of the finance system and department?

→ Do external auditors place reliance on finance systems when conducting their audit? (see **Chapter 20 External financial audit**).

2 Cash versus accruals accounting

'Remember that credit is money.'

> Benjamin Franklin, American statesman,
> diplomat, writer, scientist and inventor.

In a nutshell

'Cash accounting' simply records inflows and outflows of cash, into and out of a business. Income is recognised only when cash is 'received' and expenses are recognised only when cash is 'paid'. This risks understating or overstating a business's net worth.

Instead, the vast majority of businesses and all companies prepare their accounts on what is known as the 'accruals' or 'matching' basis.

'Accruals accounting' acknowledges the timing differences inherent in and arising from business transactions. Income and expenses should be 'matched' to the correct period. Financial transactions are recorded, whether or not a cash transfer has been made. Income is recognised when it is 'earned' and expenses are recognised when they are 'incurred', irrespective of cash movements. This gives a much better reflection of a business's actual profit and net worth.

Need to know

The key concepts to understand are 'earned' income and 'incurred' expenses:

Earned income	Incurred expenses
Income is recognised in financial accounts, when it is 'earned' versus when cash is 'received'.	Expenses are recognised in financial accounts, when they are 'incurred' versus when cash is 'paid'.
For example, a credit sale is recognised when it is made, before cash is received.	For example, a credit purchase is recognised when it is made, before cash is paid.

Sales and purchases

Business to business sales are typically made on credit, i.e. the purchaser pays the supplier after a number of agreed days.

Under accruals accounting, a sale is recognised (i.e. 'earned') by the supplier at the point of the transaction, as opposed to when the cash payment is received from the purchaser, which could be 30 or more days later.

Similarly, the purchase is recognised (i.e. 'incurred') by the purchaser at the point of the transaction, as opposed to when cash payment is made to the supplier.

The point of the transaction is typically the point when goods are delivered or a service is performed, depending on the nature of the business.

Why is this important?

Accruals accounting is required by company law and is generally accepted accounting principles (*GAAP*) (see **Chapter 19 Accounting and financial reporting standards**).

Preparing financial accounts on an 'accruals basis' gives a more accurate reflection of a business's current financial position or its net worth. Just because a business has a lot of cash in the balance sheet it doesn't mean that it is in a strong financial position. There could be a number of cash commitments in the very near future.

Example

All of ABC Ltd sales are for cash and all its purchases are made on credit. The accruals basis recognises that part of ABC Ltd's cash balance is committed to paying its supplier in the future. At the same time when calculating profit, the accruals basis matches (cash) sales with the (credit) purchases (made on credit) which generated those sales.

When is this important?

Accruals are most important at a company's financial year end, when financial accounts are prepared. The accounts should clearly reflect any future cash commitments and/or cash receipts.

For example, a sale which took place just prior to the year end should be recognised as revenue in that same year, even if the cash for that sale was not received until the following year.

If a business prepares regular management accounts (see **Chapter 31 Management accounts**), it is also important to account for any timing differences at each period end.

Watch out for in practice

Some examples of the accruals concept in practice are:

- Revenue recognition (see **Chapter 6 Revenue recognition**)
- Depreciation (see **Chapter 9 Tangible fixed assets and depreciation**)
- Debtors and creditors (see **Chapter 12 Debtors and creditors**)
- Accruals and prepayments (see **Chapter 13 Prepayments and accruals**)
- Provisions (see **Chapter 14 Provisions and contingencies**).

Auditors (see **Chapter 20 External financial audit**) will always be attentive to transactions around the year end to make sure they are reflected in the correct period. A large credit sale immediately prior to the year end, or a large credit purchase immediately following the year end will have a clear impact on profit, due to accruals accounting.

Nice to know

'Grey areas'

For most businesses involving simple products or services, establishing the point of the transaction is relatively straightforward.

However, for more complex situations, there are some grey areas which will require more thought and the input of accountants and/ or auditors. Although there are a number of established methods, depending upon the transaction there may be some discretion over which method a company chooses as its accounting policy.

Here are a couple of examples of grey areas:

Example 1: Product and service combinations

There can be grey areas where products and services are combined, for example a product which includes after-sales service. The service could be performed some months following the delivery of the product and payment for the product. The company will need to establish an accounting policy to determine the period(s) in which the sale proceeds and service expense should be allocated.

Example 2: Long-term projects

Construction companies with projects lasting several years, for example, need to have a clear revenue recognition policy. The stage of completion may not clearly reflect when the pre-agreed stage cash payments are received. This becomes even more complex where retentions (cash withheld until satisfactory completion) are involved.

(See also **Chapter 6 Revenue recognition.**)

Optional detail

It's often the word 'accrual' which confuses non-accountants. Many of the words in accounting are derived from Latin, given that bookkeeping is credited to the Italian, Luca Pacioli. The Latin derivative of accrual is accrēscere – which means to grow – and most dictionary definitions of accrual refer to accumulation. Unfortunately, this is still challenging to relate to the concept of accruals accounting, hence the simpler-phrased concept of 'matching'.

Where to spot in company accounts

All company accounts will be prepared under accruals accounting.

Specific revenue recognition policies can be found within the accounting policy note.

Greggs plc illustration

The accounting policy note on revenue can be found on **page 304** of the Appendix. It is also extracted below.

It is clear to see the accruals concept being applied. It is interesting to note the policy in relation to loyalty programmes and gift cards, which also follow the accruals concept. For example, income is only recognised when gift cards are utilised or expired.

(q) Revenue

i Retail sales – Revenue from the sale of goods is recognised as income on receipt of cash or card payment. Revenue is measured net of discounts, promotions and value added taxation.

ii Franchise sales – Franchise sales are recognised when goods are dispatched to franchisees. Any additional franchise fee income relating to franchise sales is recognised on an accruals basis in accordance with the substance of the relevant agreement. Capital fit-out costs are recharged to the franchisee and recognised when they are completed.

iii Wholesale sales – Wholesale sales are recognised when goods are dispatched to customers.

iv Loyalty programme/gift cards – Amounts received for gift cards or as part of the loyalty programme are deferred. They are recognised as revenue when the Group has fulfilled its obligation to supply products under the terms of the programme or when it is no longer probable that these amounts will be redeemed. No adjustment is made to revenue to reflect the fair value of the free items provided under the loyalty scheme as these would be immaterial to the accounts. The costs of these free items are expensed as the products are provided to the customer.

Watch out for in practice

➤ Transactions taking place around period ends, especially year ends.

➤ Year-on-year changes in debtor, creditor and accruals.

➤ Revenue recognition accounting policies (see **Chapter 6 Revenue recognition**).

Primary financial statements

3 Profit and loss (P&L)

'Business is all about solving people's problems – at a profit.'

Paul Marsden, business consultant,
writer and former politician

In a nutshell

The P&L or 'profit and loss account' or 'statement of profit or loss' or 'income statement' is one of the key financial statements prepared by a company. It shows a company's financial performance.

The purpose of a P&L is to show the profit (or loss) made by an organisation over a period of time, typically a year. The P&L shows the income generated and various expenses incurred to generate that profit (or loss).

Need to know

The P&L records the financial activities of a business over a period of time. It can be useful to think of the P&L as a video of the business's journey from one balance sheet (see **Chapter 4 The balance sheet**) date to another.

The funnel analogy, commonly used in the context of sales, can be used to represent the P&L. Sales come into a business at the top of the funnel and the output of the funnel represents the profit retained in the business.

Looking at this in more depth, the following diagram takes a cross section of a funnel to represent the various expenses or outflows as money flows through the business.

We can also use this diagram to represent the key headings seen within a P&L which will be defined shortly.

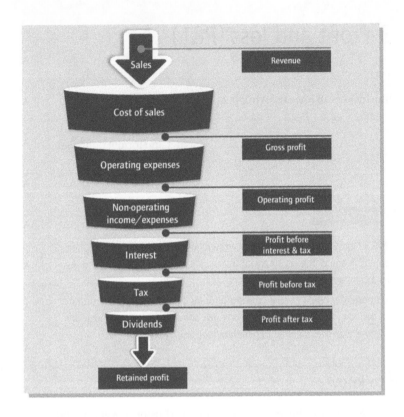

Some of the key P&L headings are explained below:

Revenue	▦ Revenue is often referred to as the 'top line'. It is the income earned during the period.
	▦ Revenue is also known as turnover, income, or sales in some organisations (see **Chapter 6 Revenue recognition**).
Cost of sales	▦ 'Cost of sales' are the direct costs associated with revenue earned in the period.
	▦ For a retailer they will be the cost of purchases, for a manufacturer the cost of production.
Gross profit	▦ *Gross profit* is calculated by deducting 'cost of sales' from revenue.
	▦ It is used to calculate gross margin, a commonly used performance measure (see **Chapter 23 Profitability performance measures**).

Operating expenses	▦ Operating expenses are the other costs of running a business during a period, for example: marketing, administration, rent, utilities and other overheads (see **Chapter 7 Opex and capex**).
Operating profit	▦ Operating profit can be seen as the profit from running a business. ▦ It is calculated by deducting both 'cost of sales' and 'operating expenses' from revenue. ▦ It excludes non-operating income (and expenses, if any) such as bank interest received.
EBIT/PBIT	▦ Earnings/profit before interest and tax. ▦ This is operating profit after adjusting for any non-operating income and/or expenses. ▦ This is a commonly used performance measure for divisions of large businesses, where both finance and tax are organised and paid centrally (see **Chapter 23 Profitability performance measures**).
EBT/PBT	▦ Earnings/profit before tax. ▦ This is EBIT after deducting finance expenses. ▦ This total is also often used as a performance measure within large businesses depending on how central finance is recharged (see **Chapter 23 Profitability performance measures**).
EAT/PAT	▦ Earnings/profit after tax. ▦ This is EBT after deducting the tax charge for the period. ▦ This is commonly known as net profit (or sometimes net income or net earnings). It is often referred to as the 'bottom line'.

Note: Retained profit is not shown in the P&L. See the **Nice to know** section for more details.

Why is this important?

Profit is the primary measure of business success and long-term survival.

Simplified P&Ls can also be prepared for individual divisions, departments, products, customers, etc. P&Ls should be commonplace throughout an organisation.

For managers it may be the most important source of their financial information and a key financial performance measure.

When is this important?

Although company accounts containing P&Ls are produced at least annually, many businesses will prepare more frequent and regular P&Ls internally. Typically, P&Ls are prepared on a monthly basis as part of a business's management accounts (see **Chapter 31 Management accounts**).

Nice to know

Some additional terms related to the P&L are explained below:

EBITDA	▦ Earnings before interest, tax, depreciation and amortisation.
	▦ This is essentially operating profit before known accounting adjustments.
	▦ It is a commonly used measure of core profits by external analysts and therefore often used as an internal performance measure for listed companies.
Exceptional items	▦ Profit is sometimes shown before and after exceptional items. These are one-off large, 'unusual' items (tightly defined by accounting regulation). For example, the sale of a division or a major restructuring programme.
	▦ Disclosing the impact of exceptional items enables users of accounts to view trends in profits, without one-off incidents which may distort the trend.
Distributable profits	▦ Distributable profit is the profit remaining in the business after all other expenses. It is available for distribution to shareholders.
	▦ It is usually the same as EAT (earnings after tax).
	▦ Distributable profit is disclosed in a separate financial statement (the statement of changes in equity), which typically appears after the P&L.
Retained profits	▦ *Retained profits* or retained earnings are calculated by deducting dividends paid to shareholders from distributable profits.
	▦ Most businesses will retain some level of funds to finance future investment and therefore retained profits are an important source of business finance.
	▦ Retained profits are disclosed together with distributable profits, in the statement of changes in equity. They can also be seen on the balance sheet (see **Chapter 4 The balance sheet** and **Chapter 15 Capital and reserves**).

Optional detail

Alternative titles

The P&L is known under a number of different titles. Here is a selection of the most common:

- The profit and loss account
- The profit and loss statement
- The statement of profit or loss and other comprehensive income
- Income statement
- Statement of comprehensive income
- Income and expenditure statement
- Earnings statement
- Statement of financial performance.

Some of these titles are defined in company law and some by accounting regulations, depending on the jurisdiction. Some are historical and many are used interchangeably.

Other income not shown in the P&L

The P&L records revenue-producing activities of a company. For some companies there are non-primary or non-revenue producing activities which cause a change in net assets. Some examples are:

- Revaluation surpluses related to property, plant and equipment (see **Chapter 17 Revaluation**)
- Actuarial gains and losses
- Gains and losses arising from translating the financial statements of a foreign operation
- Specific gains and losses from financial instruments.

These items are recorded in the 'Statement of Other Comprehensive Income'.

There is very specific accounting regulation around these areas.

Where to spot in company accounts

There will usually be a single-page P&L statement which shows values against each of the major P&L headings for the current and previous financial period.

The majority of P&L headings will have a note reference where more detail can be found within the notes to the accounts.

Greggs plc Illustration

The consolidated income statement can be found on **page 295** of the Appendix. There are detailed notes for:

- Revenue
- Finance income and expense
- Profit before tax
- Income tax
- Earnings per share.

The consolidated statement of comprehensive income can be found on **page 295** of the Appendix. This relates to actuarial gains and losses on Greggs, defined benefit pension scheme.

The statements of changes in equity can be found on **page 297** of the Appendix. These show the dividends paid to shareholders as well as other changes to equity (retained profit).

Watch out for in practice

The P&L should be benchmarked. Useful internal benchmarks are prior period, budget and forecast. Useful external benchmarks are competitors and industry averages.

The P&L is a short-term record of a business's performance. It is useful to analyse P&Ls over a number of years to establish a trend.

Be aware that profit can be distorted by timing differences. Transactions around the period end can make a particular period appear more or less profitable than usual. Hence the importance of analysing the trend.

Be aware that profit can be distorted by accounting adjustments, such as:

accruals and prepayments (see **Chapter 13 Prepayments and accruals**)

provisions (see **Chapter 14 Provisions and contingencies**)

impairments (see **Chapter 18 Impairment**).

Be aware that profit can be affected by accounting policies and decisions (see **Chapter 19 Accounting and financial reporting standards**) such as:

opex and capex (see **Chapter 7 Opex and capex**)

depreciation (see **Chapter 9 Tangible fixed assets and depreciation**).

Analysts commonly calculate percentage performance measures from the P&L. For example, gross profit margin and net profit margin (see **Chapter 23 Profitability performance measures**).

Retained profits are a potential sign of future confidence or a safety net for future years. The business could be 'saving' for a future investment opportunity (see **Chapter 15 Capital and reserves**).

4 The balance sheet

In a nutshell

The balance sheet (or statement of financial position) is one of the key financial statements prepared by a company. It shows a company's financial position at a point in time.

Values are attributed to every asset and every liability to give a net overall position or net worth of a business.

Need to know

It is useful to think of the balance sheet as a snapshot of the business's assets and liabilities. It is a static document and a business should take repeated snapshots at fixed intervals (usually annually and also more frequently) if it wishes to see how the assets and liabilities change over time.

A balance sheet is like taking a photo of the business a point in time. The profit and loss account (P&L) (see **Chapter 3 Profit and loss (P&L)**) shows the journey (or video) from one balance sheet date to another.

Assets and liabilities

Simply put, an asset is something that is 'owned' and a liability is something that is 'owed'.

The balance sheet is basically a list of a business's assets and liabilities. A balance sheet 'balances' as the value of its assets will be equal to the value of its liabilities. This is because a company must identify exactly where funds were obtained to acquire its assets.

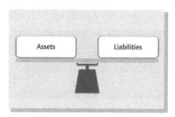

Some of the key balance sheet items are explained below:

Long-term assets	▓ Long-term assets are often referred to as fixed assets. They are kept in the business for the long term, which should be more than one year.
	▓ They consist of tangible (for example plant, property and equipment) (see **Chapter 9 Tangible fixed assets and depreciation**) and intangible (for example trademarks, patents and goodwill) (see **Chapter 10 Goodwill and other intangibles**) assets as well as investments.
Short-term assets	▓ Short-term assets are often referred to as current assets. They should usually convert back into cash quickly and mostly within 12 months.
	▓ Examples are *stock* (see **Chapter 11 Stock**), or debtors (see **Chapter 12 Debtors and creditors**), prepayments and cash.
Short-term liabilities	▓ Short-term liabilities are often referred to as current liabilities.
	▓ Examples are overdrafts, short-term loans, or creditors (see **Chapter 12 Debtors and creditors**), and accruals (see **Chapter 13 Prepayments and accruals**).
Long-term liabilities	▓ Long-term liabilities are often referred to as non-current liabilities.
	▓ Examples are bank loans (debt) and company issued bonds (see **Chapter 30 Debt finance**).
Capital and reserves	▓ Capital and reserves are sometimes referred to as shareholders' funds or owner's equity (see **Chapter 15 Capital and reserves**).
	▓ This consists of share capital (the shareholder's original investment) (see **Chapter 29 Equity finance**) plus reserves (which are largely retained profits).
	▓ Notwithstanding its separate classification under capital, *equity* is a form of liability. This is because it belongs not to the company but to the shareholder. This is because a company is a legal entity separate from its owners.

Why is this important?

The balance sheet gives an indication of the size of a business and shows its assets (what it owns), its liabilities (what it owes/how it is financed) as well as the amount invested by its shareholders. For asset-rich businesses, such as manufacturers or property companies, it is an important sign of their financial strength.

Important measures of a company's position are calculated from the balance sheet alone which mostly fall into the following two categories:

- short-term solvency and liquidity, including working capital (see **Chapter 24 Working capital and liquidity management**)
- long-term solvency and stability (see **Chapter 26 Long-term solvency performance measures**).

The balance sheet can be used as context when analysing a company's P&L. The following key performance measures (see **Chapter 23 Profitability performance measures**) are calculated from both financial statements:

- asset turnover
- return on capital employed
- return on equity.

When is this important?

As a balance sheet represents a set point in time in a company's life, it is important to consider *timing* when interpreting balance sheets. A snapshot taken a day earlier or later could potentially present a different picture of a business.

In practice

Auditors (see **Chapter 20 External financial audit**) will always be attentive to transactions around the year end. They will consider how they impact on balance sheet values and to make sure they are reflected in the correct period. Auditors may also focus on revaluations (see **Chapter 17 Revaluation**) and impairments (see **Chapter 18 Impairment**) and their impact on balance sheet asset values.

Nice to know

Other items in the balance sheet

Other balance sheet items worth noting are listed below:

- Goodwill: the difference between the purchase price from an acquisition and the value of the acquired assets (see **Chapter 10 Goodwill and other intangibles**).
- Provisions: money set aside for a known liability whose extent and timing cannot be precisely determined (see **Chapter 14 Provisions and contingencies**).
- Deferred tax: timing differences between accounting and tax regulations (see **Chapter 8 Business tax**).
- Capital reserves: surpluses which have not arisen from trading (see **Chapter 15 Capital and reserves**).
- Revenue reserves: trading profit retained in the business for future investment (see **Chapter 15 Capital and reserves**).

Balance sheet valuation

Asset values within a balance sheet are typically stated at historic cost (known by accountants as 'book value'). Under certain accounting regulations, such as UK GAAP, assets can be revalued (see **Chapter 17 Revaluation**). For example, investments or property (which is one of the largest asset values in the balance sheet).

The question if asset values should be adjusted to reflect current market values is an ongoing contentious issue, especially in periods of high inflation.

Sometimes a balance sheet can contain a mixture of historic and current values. This is influenced by the accounting policies chosen by a company (see **Chapter 19 Accounting and financial reporting standards**).

Liabilities are typically stated at the amount 'owed' to third parties.

It is important to be aware of the impact of fluctuating asset and liability values on the overall balance sheet value and its related performance measures.

It is also important to note that the balance sheet is unlikely to reflect the market values of either its individual assets or the total company (see **Chapter 28 Business valuation**).

Optional detail

Different perspectives on the balance sheet

All balance sheets show the assets and liabilities of a business. Some balance sheets simply show all a company's assets in one section and all a company's liabilities in another. The two sections will always be equal. Total assets will always equal total liabilities.

However, it is possible to arrange the two sections or halves in different ways. For example, it can be useful to show some of the liabilities next to the assets. Given that the liabilities are netted from assets, the two halves will remain equal.

Two examples of alternative presentations are below:

1 Shareholders' funds/net assets

The shareholder is the primary user of financial statements and this balance sheet presentation is designed to present the business from their perspective.

Shareholders' funds (equity) is shown on the right of the diagram, balanced by *net assets* (fixed assets + current assets − current liabilities − debt) on the left hand side.

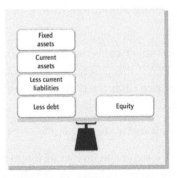

A common performance measure is ROE (return on equity) or RONA (return on *net assets*) (see **Chapter 23 Profitability performance measures**), which utilises this presentation of the balance sheet. The total of each half of the balance sheet represents the 'value' of the shareholders' investment in the business.

2 Source and use of funds

Cash brought into a business is a source of funds and all cash paid out is a use of funds. A balance sheet can therefore be seen as a statement of sources and uses of funds.

The source of a business's finance or funds (equity and debt) (see **Chapter 29 Equity finance** and **Chapter 30 Debt finance**) are shown on the right of the diagram, balanced by the use of funds or 'capital employed' in the business (fixed assets + current assets − current liabilities) on the left hand side.

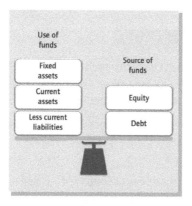

Capital employed also known as *TALCL* (total assets less current liabilities) represents how finance is utilised by a business. It is a commonly used total by internal and external analysts.

A common performance measure is ROCE (return on capital employed), which utilises this presentation of the balance sheet (see **Chapter 23 Profitability performance measures**).

This form of presentation shows the business from the perspective of the providers of business finance, both equity and debt.

Where to spot in company accounts

The balance sheet is one of the three primary financial statements included in a set of company accounts, the others being the P&L and the cash flow statement.

There will usually be a one- or two-page balance sheet which shows values against each of the major headings for the current and previous financial period.

The majority of balance sheet headings will have a note reference where more detail can be found within the notes to the accounts.

Greggs plc illustration

The balance sheet can be found on **page 296** of the Appendix. Greggs balance sheet is presented as total assets and total liabilities. There are detailed notes for almost every balance sheet item.

Watch out for in practice

→ The balance sheet should be benchmarked. There should always be a previous period included for comparison. Useful internal benchmarks are budget and forecast. Useful external benchmarks are competitors.

→ The balance sheet is a record of a business's financial position at a single point in time. It is useful to analyse balance sheets over a number of years to establish the trend.

→ Be aware that balance sheets can be distorted by timing differences, hence the importance of applying the accruals concept correctly (see **Chapter 2 Cash versus accruals accounting**). Transactions around the period end can make the balance sheet for a particular period appear stronger or weaker than usual. Therefore, it is important to analyse the trend.

→ Be aware that balance sheet values can be distorted by accounting adjustments.

→ Trends in a company's position, for example liquidity and gearing ratios (see **Chapter 24 Working capital and liquidity management**).

→ Trends in a company's performance, for example return on capital employed and return on equity (see **Chapter 23 Profitability performance measures**).

5 Cash flow statement

> 'Cash is king. Get every drop of cash you can get and hold onto it.'
>
> Jack Welch, author and chairman/CEO of
> General Electric between 1981 and 2001

In a nutshell

The CFS (cash flow statement or statement of cash flows) is one of the primary financial statements in a set of accounts.

The CFS shows the inflows and outflows of cash during a reporting period. It explains how the cash balance shown in the balance sheet has increased or decreased from the previous reporting period.

The CFS contains three major headings, under which inflows and outflows of cash are categorised:

- Operating activities
- Investing activities
- Financing activities.

For a business, 'cash is king' and analysing the CFS is a highly informative way to assess a company's ability to generate and utilise its cash.

Need to know

Why is this important?

The CFS is one of the most useful financial statements to analyse a company's performance and its cash management. It provides a number of insights not available from the more familiar P&L (see **Chapter 33 Profit and loss (P&L)**) and balance sheet (see **Chapter 4 The balance sheet**).

Cash is a matter of fact. The P&L and balance sheet incorporate accounting adjustments which are subject to judgement such as accruals (see **Chapter 13 Prepayments and accruals**), provisions (see **Chapter 14 Provisions and contingencies**) and depreciation (see **Chapter 9 Tangible fixed assets and depreciation**). There is no judgement in a CFS.

The CFS reveals how a company has:

- managed its short-term liquidity, for example balancing debtors and creditors (see **Chapter 24 Working capital and liquidity management**);
- controlled its long-term solvency and adapted its financing to prepare for its future (see **Chapter 26 Long-term solvency performance measures**);
- invested in assets for its future.

For an established business, the CFS can be used to give an indication of the amount, timing and certainty of future cash flows. It also enables comparability of a company's year-to-year cash position, as cash flows are not affected by accounting policies.

Operating activities

Operating activities are the principal revenue generating activities of the business.

In the CFS, they also include interest and tax payments.

This is the key section of the CFS as it shows whether the business is generating a positive cash flow from its operations. A company that is not generating cash has to borrow or deplete short-term cash reserves. Ultimately, cash from operations must support the rest of the business in the long run.

The main operating activities are:

- cash received from customers
- cash paid to suppliers
- cash paid to and on behalf of employees
- interest and taxes paid.

As there will be a difference between the cash from operating activities and the operating profit (see the **In practice** section), the CFS has a supporting note which shows how the cash flow from operating activities is calculated (see the **Nice to know** section).

Investing activities

Investing activities are typically the acquisition and disposal of long-term assets and other investments.

They also include returns from investments such as bank deposits and dividends from other companies in which the business holds shares.

Investing activities are important to the long-term success of a business and show the extent of new investment in assets. These investments will hopefully support future cash flows and generate profit.

Financing activities

Financing activities are changes (increases or decreases) to funding from either equity finance (see **Chapter 29 Equity finance**) or debt finance (see **Chapter 30 Debt finance**).

They include dividends paid to shareholders. Although, interest paid to debtholders, such as banks, is shown under operating activities.

Financing activities indicate how well a company is managing its financing by balancing its gearing (the amount of debt versus equity – see **Chapter 26 Long-term solvency performance measures**).

They also provide an indication of future interest and dividend payments.

In practice – cash versus profit

Cash is not the same as profit (see **Chapter 2 Cash versus accruals accounting**) and in practice this is clearly demonstrated in the CFS.

The year-on-year change in a company's operating profits may not correlate to its change in cash generated from operating activities.

For example, Tesco reported its worst ever results during 2015. Its accounts showed an operating loss of £5.8 billion compared with an operating profit of £2.6 billion in 2014. Its CFS, however, showed that the business still generated £1.5 billion of cash from operations during the year (£4.3 billion in 2014).

In the long run the cash flow from operating activities and operating results should move in the same direction. However, it's the short-term differences which may reveal insights into performance which can't be identified from the other financial statements.

Nice to know

Calculating cash flows from operating activities

There are two permitted methods under IAS 7 (statement of cash flows) to calculate cash flows from operating activities:

- the direct method, and
- the indirect method.

Whichever method is used; it is shown either following or as a supporting note to the CFS.

Direct method

This method provides the most clarity over where cash flows have been derived and spent.

	£
Cash received from customers	X
Cash paid to suppliers	(X)
Cash paid to and on behalf of employees	(X)
Interest and taxes paid	(X)
Cash flows from operating activities	X

Indirect method

This method is more popular in practice as it is simpler to calculate the figures required. It shows the impact of accounting adjustments and movements in working capital.

	£
Operating profits	X
Adjust for:	
Depreciation/amortisation	X
(Profit)/loss on the sale of assets	(X)
(Increase)/decrease in stock	(X)
(Increase)/decrease in debtors	X)
Increase/(decrease) in creditors	(X)
Interest and taxes paid	(X)
Net cash flows from operating activities	X

Optional detail

Cash and cash equivalents

The CFS analyses the change in 'cash and cash equivalents' from one reporting period to another.

- 'Cash' means physical cash held in the company (e.g. petty cash) plus cash held in instant access, i.e. current bank accounts.

- 'Cash equivalents' are short-term (three months or less to maturity), highly liquid investments which are readily convertible to cash and do not significantly fluctuate in value (e.g. commercial paper and marketable securities). These are held to meet short-term cash commitments and not for investment purposes.

The CFS does not look at movements between 'cash' and different types of 'cash equivalents'.

Where to spot in company accounts

The CFS follows the other primary statements (the P&L and balance sheet) in a company's annual report.

Small companies (see **Chapter 21 Information in the public domain**) that are not subsidiaries are exempt from preparing a CFS.

Greggs plc illustration

The Greggs statement of cashflows can be found on **page 299** of the Appendix. There are detailed notes for many items within the statement.

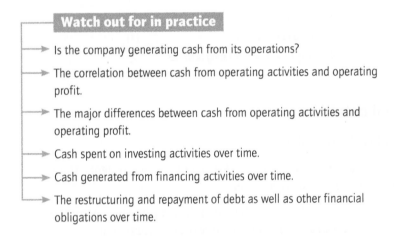

Watch out for in practice

- Is the company generating cash from its operations?
- The correlation between cash from operating activities and operating profit.
- The major differences between cash from operating activities and operating profit.
- Cash spent on investing activities over time.
- Cash generated from financing activities over time.
- The restructuring and repayment of debt as well as other financial obligations over time.

Key elements of financial statements

6 Revenue recognition

> 'The sweeping revisions in revenue-recognition rules will represent a change for many industries.'
>
> Christine Klimek, spokeswoman for the Financial Accounting Standards Board as reported in *The Wall Street Journal*

In a nutshell

Revenue recognition determines both *when* and *how much* revenue can be recognised in a company's accounts.

For most companies, revenue is recognised at the *point of sale* in business transactions. This is usually the point at which legal title to goods passes from a seller to a buyer. In complex transactions or those that involve judgement there is scope for error or manipulation of revenue numbers.

Every company will need to determine (and disclose) its revenue recognition policies. For companies requiring external audit (see **Chapter 20 External financial audit**), these policies are subject to careful scrutiny.

Need to know

A company's revenue recognition policy is critical to understanding its performance.

Why is this important?

Mistakes in revenue recognition can significantly impact a company's reported results and reputation. Tesco's announcement in 2015 that it had overstated revenue by around £250 million caused the company's market value to fall by £2 billion (an 11.5% fall in share price) and led to significant boardroom changes.

Revenue (known also as turnover, sales or income) is a 'headline' number that attracts investor attention as it signals how a business is performing in its markets and against competitors. It is typically the largest number in a company's financial statements.

Investors, analysts, employees and others are interested in the revenue number. Year-on-year revenue growth is a key metric used to assess company growth. Revenue data is widely used at industry and government level to understand trends and in policy formulation. Directors' performance rewards can also be linked to revenue.

When is this important?

Determining the point of sale should be straightforward for most business transactions. Revenue should only be recognised when it has been *earned*. This application of the accruals concept (see **Chapter 13 Prepayments and accruals**) typically results in a sale being recognised at the point at which goods are transferred to the buyer.

In the case of sellers of *goods* such as fashion clothing retailers, revenue should be recognised at the point of sale, which is when the buyer takes the goods (or accepts delivery) having committed to paying for them.

In the case of *service* providers such as mobile operators, revenue should be recognised in the period over which the service is provided.

In cases where a product/service is combined and sold together (such as mobile contracts comprising handset and service) the product revenue element should be recognised at the point of sale while the service revenue element should be deferred and recognised over the period during which the service is provided.

Example

A pay-monthly two-year phone contract package was sold on 1 July for £720. The price of the handset could be purchased separately for £400.

In this example, revenue for the service would amount to £320 (£720 minus £400 handset price). Revenue would be earned by the company over 24 months, i.e. the period over which the service is provided.

Assuming the vendor has a year end of 31 December, it would recognise revenue as follows:

Year one

Handset	£400 (revenue recognised immediately at *point of sale*)
Service	£ 80 (6 months/24 months × £320)
	£480

Year two (onwards)

Service revenue for the remainder of the contract would be recognised as follows:

Year 2	£160 (12 months/24 months × £320)
Year 3	£ 80 (the remainder of the period, 6 months)

Profit (the difference between revenue and cost) in each year would be calculated by matching related costs against revenue (see **Chapter 3 Profit and loss (P&L)**). In this example, the 'cost' of the handset would be recognised at the point of sale, i.e. in year one, whereas the costs of providing the ongoing service would be matched against revenue over the contract term.

In practice

Despite the requirement for a company to follow clear revenue recognition policies, revenue is, perhaps surprisingly, still open to manipulation. The temptation to misstate is particularly high in listed companies, where company (and directors') success is measured against market expectations.

In Tesco plc, revenue recognition policies allegedly enabled the company to misstate a key component of revenue known as 'commercial income' (essentially rebates from suppliers) by 'estimating' the revenue due from likely future sales of products in its stores. Tesco overstated its commercial income by aggressively estimating future sales on which rebate was calculated.

It is interesting that Tesco's company financial statements hadbeen externally audited and received no criticism from its auditors on its recognition of commercial income (see **Chapter 20 External financial audit**).

Nice to know

Revenue is reported in the financial statements net of VAT and other sales taxes. Because a company collects taxes on behalf of tax authorities (see **Chapter 8 Business tax**) these monies do not represent income for the company.

Revenue is also reported *net* of trade and volume discounts.

For companies operating as agents, revenue is calculated as the commission receivable for providing a service rather than the full value of the goods sold. For example, eBay provides a shop window for thousands of retailers in its role as agent. While normal accrual principles apply to determine at what point a sale is made, only the value of commissions is recognised as revenue in the accounts of the agent (eBay).

Revenue is also recognised *net* of *anticipated sales returns* (see below).

Optional detail

Revenue is reported net of anticipated sales returns. In situations where a company expects returns, such as following the launch of a new product, sales would be recognised net of anticipated returns.

Where a sale is made but monies are not due until a future date (in excess of one year) it may be necessary to *discount* future monies to present value. Discounting reflects the reality that tomorrow's pound is worth less than a pound today due to inflation (see **Chapter 35 Investment appraisal**). Discounting is particularly relevant in accounting for 'buy now pay later' deals, e.g. four-year (or other term) interest free credit payment terms, prevalent in furniture retailing. In such arrangements, the sales price is split into an equivalent price for goods (revenue) if sold for cash today plus an amount for interest receivable.

Buyback agreements can artificially inflate a company's reported turnover. Revenue is recognised in the year a business sells goods only to be reversed in a future year when it buys the same goods back. In fact, these arrangements do not create genuine 'sales' and should therefore be removed (excluded) from revenue. In practice, however, they are very difficult to spot because the reversing of the transaction can only be identified at a later date, i.e. in a future year's accounts.

Further detail on the accounting treatment and disclosures for revenue recognition are set out in IAS 18 with a new standard, IFRS 15, due to replace IAS 18 from 2018.

Globally, a new US standard issued on revenue recognition and closely aligned with IFRS 15 will make it easier for investors to compare companies internationally see **Chapter 19 Accounting and financial reporting standards**).

Where to spot in company accounts

Read the Accounting Policy note in any set of accounts. This should summarise clearly a company's revenue recognition policies and include explanations of significant judgements required in reporting the revenue number.

The audit report should highlight significant judgements associated with revenue.

Extract from Greggs plc (2015), page 306

(q) Revenue

(i) Retail sales
Revenue from the sale of goods is recognised as income on receipt of cash or card payment. Revenue is measured net of discounts, promotions and value added taxation.

(ii) Franchise sales
Franchise sales are recognised when goods are dispatched to franchisees. Any additional franchise fee income relating to franchise sales is recognised on an accruals basis in accordance with the substance of the relevant agreement. Capital fit-out costs are recharged to the franchisee and recognised when they are completed.

(iii) Wholesale sales
Wholesale sales are recognised when goods are dispatched to customers.

(iv) Loyalty programme/gift cards
Amounts received for gift cards or as part of the loyalty programme are deferred. They are recognised as revenue when the Group has fulfilled its obligation to supply products under the terms of the programme or when it is no longer probable that these amounts will be redeemed. No adjustment is made to revenue to reflect the fair value of the free items provided under the loyalty scheme as these would be immaterial to the accounts. The costs of these free items are expensed as the products are provided to the customer.

Watch out for in practice

- Revenue recognition policy in the notes to the accounts and changes to policy.

- Risks of revenue recognition misstatement highlighted in the audit report.

- The nature of the product/service sold and if this is reflected in the revenue recognition policy.

- Sales returns and how they are calculated. Changes to how a business estimates sales returns can reduce/boost reported turnover and provide scope for manipulation or error.

- Buyback agreements in which a company sells an asset only to buy it back at a higher price in the future.

7 Opex and capex

> 'Control your expenses better than your competition. This is where you can always find the competitive advantage.'
>
> Sam Walton, founder of Walmart
> (10 Rules for Building a Business)

In a nutshell

Opex (operating expenditure) is money spent on running a business. It is recognised in the profit and loss account.

Capex (capital expenditure) is money spent on 'long-term investments'. It is recognised in the balance sheet.

Need to know

The key differences between opex and capex are shown in the table below:

Opex	Capex
Definition	*Definition*
Expenses incurred in running a business. Also referred to as revenue expenditure.	Payments to purchase or improve long-term assets.
Examples	*Examples*
Salaries, administration costs, marketing, utilities, repairs and maintenance.	Buildings, machines, cars, computers, office furniture, refurbishments.
Impact	*Impact*
Expenses in the P&L account which reduce current year profit.	Increase in asset values recorded in the balance sheet.
	No immediate impact on profit, only a gradual impact over time through depreciation (see **Chapter 9 Tangible fixed assets and depreciation**).

Why is this important?

Both annual profit and the 'size' of the balance sheet are important performance measures for both businesses and managers (see **Chapter 23 Profitability performance measures** and **Chapter 26 Long-term solvency performance measures**).

The decision to categorise an item of expenditure as either opex or capex will impact on both the profit and loss account and the balance sheet.

'Grey areas'

The opex versus capex distinction becomes relevant for items of expenditure which could potentially fall into either opex or capex.

A typical grey area is repairs and refurbishments. General repairs and maintenance are usually opex. Refurbishments are mostly capex. However, there could be repairs or refurbishments which can fall into either category. For example, repairing a broken window could clearly be categorised as opex under 'repairs and maintenance'. However, if the new window is an improvement on the old window, such as being polarised, then it could be argued that it should be categorised as capex.

When is this important?

Businesses may be tempted to categorise expenditure as capex instead of opex when:

- rewards are based on profit targets – recognising an expense as capex as opposed to opex will have a favourable impact on the current year's profits;
- there are separate organisational budgets for opex and capex and the opex budget has been fully spent;
- financing is available for expenditure on 'investments' (capex) but not 'running costs' (opex).

In practice

The majority of companies will have a clear and consistent policy. The same items of expenditure should be treated the same way over time.

However, two otherwise identical companies could have different treatments and hence show different profits from the same transaction.

Nice to know

In practice, companies should use clear and persuasive reasoning to make distinctions between opex and capex classifications. Their decisions should not be motivated by a desire to present particular pictures of profit and asset values.

Capex spent on improving a long-term asset should actually increase the assets' value as opposed to just maintaining the economic benefits expected from the asset.

Accounting standards

There are a number of accounting and financial reporting standards (see **Chapter 19 Accounting and financial reporting standards**) which give guidance to accountants and auditors, covering some common grey areas between opex and capex classification. For example:

1 Expenditure on development costs is allowed to be capitalised (treated as capex) if a company can demonstrate future benefits from the development.
2 Certain costs of 'borrowing' to purchase a fixed asset can be capitalised.

In practice

Most companies will have a set capex limit. For example, any expense under £1,000 will be 'expensed', i.e. treated as opex. The key reason for a capex limit is to reduce the administration burden. Capex requires further record keeping (within a fixed asset register) and depreciation calculations (see **Chapter 9 Tangible fixed assets and depreciation**).

Optional detail

In financial statements there is a degree of discretion over opex and capex classification. However, under tax law the difference between opex and capex is tightly defined. Therefore, the treatment of opex and capex can often be different in the 'tax accounts' (essentially a separate profit calculation upon which the tax charge is based) to the financial accounts (see **Chapter 8 Business tax**).

Where to spot in company accounts

All administration expenses will be opex.

Capex, however, is easier to spot and can usually be spotted in two places:

1 The fixed asset note(s).

2 The cash flow statement.

Greggs plc illustration

The intangible assets note can be found on **page 311** of the Appendix.

The property, plant and equipment note can be found on **page 312** of the Appendix.

The statements of cash flows can be found on **page 299** of the Appendix.

An extract from the intangible assets note follows:

	Software	Assets under development	Total
	£'000	£'000	£'000
Additions	817	2,992	3,809

An extract from the property, plant and equipment note follows:

	Land and buildings	Plant and equipment	Fixtures and fittings	Assets under construction	Total
	£'000	£'000	£'000	£'000	£'000
Additions	429	10,121	34,278	278	45,106

Extracts from the financial review relating to capex follows:

Capital expenditure

We invested a total of £71.7 million (2014: £48.9 million) on capital expenditure in the business during 2015. This included £36.3 million on 202 shop refurbishments, the conversion of 20 existing bakery cafés and the opening of 61 new shops (excluding franchises). We continued to invest in shop equipment to support further growth in sales of coffee and hot sandwiches, totalling £6.9 million, and also invested £7.0 million in our programme of process and systems improvement. Investment in our supply chain of £17.8 million included £8.9 million in the year in respect of the acquisition of our new distribution facility in Enfield. Depreciation and amortisation in the year was £40.1 million (2014: £38.0 million).

Following the success of our 2015 capital investment programme we plan capital expenditure of around £85 million in 2016. This will support further conversion of our core shops to the bakery food-on-the-go format, continued growth and diversification of the estate and more work on the upgrading of our process and systems platform. We plan to refurbish around 200 shops in 2016 and expect to invest in 80-90 new Company-managed shops, with further openings funded by franchise partners. The 2016 capital expenditure plan also includes the first phase of the proposed programme of investment in our supply chain.

Watch out for in practice

➤ Internal discussions about the classification of expenditure as opex or capex.

➤ The type and nature of capex and how it aligns to strategy.

➤ Year-on-year changes in capex.

➤ The ratio of capex to depreciation (see **Chapter 9 Tangible fixed assets and depreciation**) and amortisation (see **Chapter 10 Goodwill and other intangibles**).

➤ The ratio of cash flow to capex.

8 Business tax

> '...in this world nothing can be said to be certain, except death and taxes.'
>
> Benjamin Franklin, polymath and
> one of the USA's founding fathers

In a nutshell

The main activities which give rise to a business tax charge are:

- Profits on sales of goods or services and returns from investments
- Capital gains from the disposal of assets and investments.

A business is also responsible for administering and collecting certain taxes relating to sales and employment. The latter also carries an additional tax charge. Examples are included later in this chapter.

In the UK, *HMRC* (Her Majesty's Revenue and Customs) is the appointed tax authority and enforcement agency to which taxes must be paid.

Need to know

This chapter provides a high-level overview of key business taxes. Professional advice is always required for tax matters. Taxation is a large and complex discipline, it is unique to each company and depends upon business structure. There are also differences between and within countries.

Why is this important?

Tax is a major business cost both in terms of the actual cash cost and the time involved in compliance and administration.

There is also a legal requirement to pay tax, keep detailed tax records and steep penalties for making mistakes or deliberate misstatement.

Tax on profits

Although the profit and loss account is the official record of a company's profit, the reported profit will often be different from the profit used to calculate tax. This is because certain expenses are not allowable deductions for tax purposes. Examples include:

- depreciation (see the **Nice to know** section below) (also see **Chapter 9 Tangible fixed assets and depreciation**)
- formation and acquisition costs
- donations to political parties
- entertaining clients.

Accounting profit is also adjusted for:

- non-taxable income, for example government grants
- tax allowances on certain asset purchases (see the **Nice to know** section below).

Returns from investments such as bank interest and dividends from other companies in which the business holds shares (see **Chapter 16 Group accounting**) are also included in taxable profit.

On an annual basis, the adjusted profit figure is multiplied by the 'tax rate' (20% in the UK at the time of publication) to arrive at the 'tax charge'.

In the UK, tax on a company's profits is known as *corporation tax* (CT).

Losses are covered in the **Nice to know** section below.

Tax on capital gains

If a company sells an asset or investment for more than its original cost, it is subject to tax on the *capital gain* which arises.

In the UK the capital gain is calculated as the disposal proceeds less the following:

- the original cost
- initial purchase-related costs

- improvements and enhancement costs (but not repairs and maintenance)
- selling costs.

The UK also allows the original cost to be adjusted for the effect of inflation. This is known as 'indexation allowance'. However, this allowance cannot create or increase a capital loss. It can only reduce a gain.

In the UK, capital gains are taxed at the same tax rate as other profits.

If a company replaces an asset, the capital gain on disposal of the original asset can be deferred until the replacement asset is disposed. This is known as 'rollover relief' in the UK.

If a company makes a capital loss, it can only usually be set against gains of the current and future years. The relief available is therefore far more limited than for trading losses (covered in the **Nice to know** section below).

Employment taxes

Employers act as tax collectors and deduct employees' income tax and other contributions directly from their pay. This is subsequently paid across to tax authorities. In the UK, this system is known as *PAYE* (Pay As You Earn).

The costs of administering the system are borne by employers.

PAYE includes:

- income tax on cash payments such as basic pay, overtime, bonuses and commissions;
- income tax on non-cash items (benefits in kind) such as company cars and private health insurance;
- social security contributions towards state benefits such as public health services, pensions and welfare benefits. These are known as National Insurance Contributions (NIC) in the UK and are paid by both employees and employers.

Value added tax (VAT)

Value added tax (*VAT*) or sales tax is an indirect tax levied on the final consumer of certain goods and services.

In the UK and most other OECD (Organisation for Economic Co-operation and Development) countries, VAT is applied at multiple stages in the supply chain. In this system, every time a sale is made, VAT is charged (output VAT). However, a business can also claim back the VAT it has paid on purchases to make or sell the product (input VAT). The business pays back the difference to the tax authorities on a regular basis.

Example

ABC Ltd sells furniture and buys its raw materials (such as wood, glue and nails) from XYZ Ltd. In a typical month ABC purchases £50,000 of raw materials and sells £100,000 of furniture. This example uses a VAT rate of 20% (which is the standard rate of VAT in the UK at the time of publication).

	Net of VAT	VAT @ 20%	Total
	£	£	£
XYZ Ltd			
Sales of raw materials	50,000	10,000	60,000
ABC Ltd			
Sales of furniture	100,000	20,000	120,000
Purchases of raw materials	(50,000)	(10,000)	(60,000)
	50,000	10,000	

In this example, XYZ and ABC have both 'collected' and paid £10,000 of VAT. Both companies have added £50,000 of value. The difference is that ABC has deducted £10,000 of input VAT on its purchases to calculate the net £10,000.

The end 'retail' consumers of the furniture have paid the full VAT burden of £20,000. The £20,000 has been collected at two stages in the supply chain, when value has been added to the furniture.

Therefore, in summary, VAT is not technically a cost to a business, as it can reclaim input VAT on its purchases. The business is merely a collecting agent on behalf of the tax authorities.

Exceptions

1   Certain items (for example children's clothing and books in the UK) are zero rated for VAT. This means that no output VAT is charged on sales, although input VAT can be reclaimed on purchases made to make those items.

2   Certain items (for example domestic fuel and mobility aids for the elderly in the UK) are taxable at different rates (e.g. 5%) from standard goods and services.

3   Certain activities (for example charitable fundraising events and lottery ticket sales in the UK) are exempt from VAT. No output VAT is charged on sales and no related input VAT can be reclaimed on those activities.

When is this important?

There are multiple deadlines for both reporting and paying tax. Penalties and interest may be charged for being late and reporting incorrect amounts.

The UK has the following deadlines:

- Corporation tax:
  - For small and medium companies – payment is due nine months and one day after the year end.
  - For large companies – payment is due in four instalments (two within the financial year and two after).
  - All companies must submit a tax return within 12 months of the year end.
- Employment taxes:
  - Tax and NI contributions must be paid on set dates each month.
  - An EPS (Employer Payment Summary) must be filed using RTI (Real Time Information) every time employees are paid.
  - Annual summaries must be submitted at the same time every year.
- Value added tax:

- Most VAT-registered businesses need to pay the net VAT collected quarterly and submit a quarterly return.

- There are a number of schemes designed to ease the administration burden on small businesses, which have different deadlines and requirements.

In addition, UK businesses are required to keep tax records for a minimum of six years for most taxes.

In practice

In the tax year 2015–16, HMRC collected £534 billion in taxes. Total receipts are split as follows (10-year average):[1]

- 56% income tax, capital gains tax and NIC
- 20% VAT
- 10% corporation tax
- 14% other taxes.

Tax evasion and avoidance

'Tax evasion' is deceiving the tax authorities by not paying tax that is rightfully payable – for example, deliberate misrepresentation of profits. Tax evasion is subject to substantial penalties. 'Tax avoidance' is the use of legal methods to reduce the amount of tax payable. This is usually achieved by claiming permissible tax deductions and tax credits.

Tax authorities can introduce anti-avoidance legislation if they become aware of many businesses using perceived legal loopholes.

In December 2013 the UK's Public Accounts Committee criticised HMRC for not using 'the full range of sanctions at its disposal to pursue vigorously all unpaid tax'.[2]

---

1 www.gov.uk/government/collections/hm-revenue-customs-receipts

2 www.publications.parliament.uk/pa/cm201314/cmselect/cmpubacc/666/66602.htm

The same report recommended that 'HMRC should be explicit about the limitations of its current measure of the tax gap and gather intelligence about the value of tax lost through aggressive tax avoidance schemes'.[2]

The *tax gap* is a measure of the difference between the amount of tax collected by a country's tax authorities and the amount that should be collected.

In November 2014 the Public Accounts Committee criticised HMRC for overstating its compliance yield (the additional revenue it generates through its activities to identify and prevent tax losses, arising from avoidance, evasion and criminal attack) baseline targets. In the tax year 2013–14 HMRC reported a compliance yield of £23.9 billion.[3]

In August 2016, the UK government announced proposals that accountants, tax planners and advisers may also face penalties for inappropriate tax avoidance advice.[4]

Nice to know

Capital allowances

In the UK businesses deduct *capital allowances* instead of depreciation (see **Chapter 9 Tangible fixed assets and depreciation**) to calculate taxable profit. Capital allowances are similar in principle to depreciation, in that they apportion the cost of an asset over its life, but use specific tax rules.

Capital allowances are typically permitted on assets such as machinery, computer equipment and certain items in buildings, but not usually on land or the buildings themselves.

To encourage investment, accelerated capital allowances (for example a 100% first-year allowance) are allowed on certain assets such as environmentally friendly vehicles.

---

3 www.publications.parliament.uk/pa/cm201415/cmselect/cmpubacc/458/45802.htm

4 www.gov.uk/government/news/tax-avoidance-enablers-to-face-tough-new-penalties

Tax relief for losses

If a company makes a loss instead of a taxable profit, no tax is payable for that particular year and a tax relief is created. The UK offers the following reliefs for trading losses:

- carry the loss forward against future trading profits of the same trade;
- offset the loss against other income or capital gains of the same period;
- carry the loss back against profits of previous periods;
- offset the loss against the profits of another group company ('group loss relief') (see **Chapter 16 Group accounting**).

Optional detail

International taxation

Residence

Globalisation and the growth in multinational corporations, with operations in multiple countries, have increased the relevance of international taxation.

Companies pay tax on their worldwide income to the country in which they are 'resident' for tax purposes. Residence is determined by a company's:

- Place of incorporation (domicile)
- Place of effective management and control
- Place of permanent establishment.

To be resident a company must demonstrate that a degree of trade is undertaken or decisions are made in a particular country. A warehouse on its own, for example, is simply a storage area. A registered office does not mean that actual office work takes place.

Double taxation

Where a company is resident in two (or more) countries, it is potentially subject to tax in both those countries and could theoretically suffer *double taxation*.

The OECD suggests that a company can only have one place of effective management, which is where it should be deemed resident and pay tax. The place of effective management is:

- The place where key management and commercial decisions are made

- The place where the board or senior management meets.

Most countries have established double tax treaties with their international trading partners. These treaties determine which country will tax profits and the methods of double tax relief for companies which trade in both countries.

For example, dividends are paid from post-tax profits, i.e. they will have already 'suffered' tax in the paying country. When a parent company receives a dividend from a foreign subsidiary, the dividend must be included in the parent company's income and once again be taxed, this time in the receiving parent company's country of residence (see **Chapter 16 Group accounting**). Depending on the country and treaty, double tax relief is often available for the overseas tax paid.

The decision to establish an overseas subsidiary (a separate legal entity) or simply a branch, may be influenced by the 'local' tax rate and the respective double tax treaty.

Where to spot in company accounts

Tax can be found in both the profit and loss account (the current year's tax charge) and balance sheet (the amount of tax owed to tax authorities). This will usually be supported by detailed notes to explain any adjustments made in calculating the tax charge and liability.

Employers' contributions to NI (or equivalent) are usually detailed in the note under employment costs.

In Greggs 2015 annual report, the supporting tax notes calculate an effective tax rate. This is the rate of tax paid based on accounting profits, as opposed to taxable profits. This gives a more accurate picture of a company's tax liability than a country's headline tax rate. In the report, Greggs effective tax rate was 21 % (compared to a headline rate of 20 %). In the associated 'financial review' the effective rate was forecast to be 2% above the headline rate in future years, mainly due to non-deductible expenses.

The 2015 annual report also shows a 'deferred tax' asset. Deferred tax is an accounting adjustment which arises because the accounting treatment of a transaction is different from the tax treatment. It is essentially a temporary timing difference. The asset has arisen from taxable deductions (principally in relation to employee benefits) which have been deducted from accounting profit in the current year and will be deductible from taxable profit in future years (providing there is sufficient taxable profit).

Watch out for in practice

- The effective rate of tax paid and how it compares to the headline tax rate.
- The nature of adjustments to the taxable profit.
- The nature of any non-deductible expenses.
- The reason for any deferred tax assets or liabilities.
- Tax losses carried forward, as these give an indication of historic trading activity.
- Tax in relation to capital gains. This indicates a disposal of assets. It is useful to know why a company is disposing of assets and if they are being replaced.

9 Tangible fixed assets and depreciation

'Nothing lasts forever...'

Arnold H. Glasow, American author

In a nutshell

Tangible fixed assets (TFA) are assets that possess physical substance. Examples include land, property, equipment, motor vehicles, etc.

The term fixed denotes an intention by the company to use the asset within the business over the long term (in excess of one year), i.e. to generate revenues over many years. This is in contrast to current assets like stock, where speed of sale is often considered a key objective (see **Chapter 11 Stock**).

The cost of using TFA is recognised through *depreciation*. *Depreciation* is an accounting expense which attempts to spread the cost of TFA over their life in the business. In effect, it reflects the usage, wearing-out or 'consumption' of TFA.

Need to know

Why is this important?

The value of TFA held by a business can be a useful indicator of a company's capability.

- They affect performance measures such as gearing and return on capital employed (see **Chapter 26 Long-term solvency performance measures**).
- They provide security to lenders of finance against any loans made to the company (see **Chapter 30 Debt finance**).

In certain industries, TFA are also a reflection of productive capacity. For example, the size of a manufacturing company's TFA may reflect its ability to meet additional demand.

Depreciation is important as it directly affects accounting profits (it is an expense which reduces profit) as well as the value of assets in the balance sheet.

Companies have a choice over their depreciation policies (see **Chapter 19 Accounting and financial reporting standards**). While these policies must be reasonable and consistent, they allow an element of discretion which directly affects financial results.

Net book value

In a balance sheet TFA are stated at *NBV* (net book value). NBV is the cost of TFA less accumulated depreciation (cumulative depreciation expense over time).

For example, ABC Ltd's NBV is calculated as follows:

	£
TFA cost	100,000
Accumulated depreciation	(30,000)
NBV	70,000

It is important not to confuse NBV with market value, which is determined by external economic factors. There is often little correlation between NBV and market value. This is relevant when performing a balance sheet based valuation of a company (see **Chapter 28 Business valuation**).

Calculating depreciation

Depreciation is calculated as follows:

$$\text{Annual depreciation expense} = \frac{\text{Asset cost } less \text{ estimated residual value}}{\text{Estimated useful life}}$$

This method of depreciation is known as the *straight line* method. See the **Nice to know** section below for alternative methods.

Example

XYZ Ltd purchases a new delivery van during the year for £20,000. Vans are used for an average of four years, after which the company replaces them with newer models. The estimated residual value of the van in four years' time is £8,000.

$$\text{Annual depreciation expense} = \frac{£20,000 - £8,000}{4 \text{ years}} = £3,000 \text{ p.a.}$$

The van's net cost of £12,000 (£20,000 less £8,000) is charged against revenues on a systematic basis over the asset's useful life (£3,000 per year over four years).

The van's NBV will change over the next four years as follows:

	Year 1	Year 2	Year 3	Year 4
	£	£	£	£
Cost	20,000	20,000	20,000	20,000
Accumulated depreciation	(3,000)	(6,000)	(9,000)	(12,000)
NBV	17,000	14,000	11,000	8,000

At the end of year 4 the van's NBV of £8,000 should equate to its residual value of £8,000.

Profit/loss on disposal

- If the actual residual value is more than £8,000 there will be a profit on disposal.
- If the actual residual value is less than £8,000 there will be a loss on disposal.

Note that this is only a 'paper' profit or loss. It effectively adjusts the cumulative depreciation expense, which was based on an estimate made four years earlier. It does not reflect cash flows (see **Chapter 2 Cash versus accruals accounting**). It is common for there to be small differences from estimates in reality.

Any profit or loss on disposal will be included under other operating income or expenses in the profit and loss account (see **Chapter 3 Profit and loss (P&L)**).

Revaluations

Companies have a choice of whether to revalue tangible fixed assets or keep them at historic cost less accumulated depreciation.

If a business chooses a policy of revaluing tangible fixed assets they must keep valuations 'up to date' (see **Chapter 17 Revaluation**).

Impairment

Tangible fixed assets must also be assessed annually for indications of impairment to ensure they are not overvalued in the balance sheet. Where indications of impairment exist, the recoverable amount is calculated with any loss reflected in the profit and loss account (see **Chapter 18 Impairment**).

When is this important?

TFA are recorded ('recognised') in the balance sheet when a company has the right to earn economic benefits from the assets. This most typically happens when the company pays to acquire or construct assets.

The annual depreciation will usually be apportioned from the date of purchase, depending on the company's accounting policy. As depreciation directly affects the profit and loss account and balance sheet, the timing of asset purchases will have an impact on financial results.

In practice

As companies have discretion over their depreciation policies and 'estimates', this can directly affect short-term financial results as follows:

'Short' estimations of useful asset life (a.k.a. aggressive depreciation)	Higher annual depreciation charge (lower profits) and lower NBV.
'Long' estimations of useful asset life	Lower annual depreciation charge (higher profits) and higher NBV.
Low estimations of residual value	Higher annual depreciation charge (lower profits), lower NBV and profits on disposal.
High estimations of residual value	Lower annual depreciation charge (higher profits), higher NBV and losses on disposal.

It is not uncommon to find companies continuing to utilise assets beyond the end of their estimated useful economic lives, i.e. after they have been fully depreciated. This is sometimes evidence of an 'aggressive' depreciation policy. It may also be a result of a change in replacement policy or cash flow planning by delaying capital expenditure.

While changes in depreciation assumptions may appear to be an easy way to boost reported performance, these changes would be disclosed in a company's accounting policy note and scrutinised internally, e.g. by an audit committee (see **Chapter 22 Corporate governance and whistleblowing**) and by a company's auditors (see **Chapter 20 External financial audit**).

Nice to know

Alternative methods of depreciation

The straight line method is perhaps the most common method of depreciation. Adopting this method results in an even charge to each accounting period as illustrated above.

Several alternative methods exist including *reducing balance* and *sum of digits*. The annual depreciation charge will vary according to the method chosen.

The reducing balance method is based on calculating depreciation as a fixed percentage of an asset's NBV every year. The depreciation charge will reduce each year in proportion to the declining net book value of the asset with higher depreciation in early years of an asset's life and reducing depreciation charges in later years.

The cost of fixed assets

According to accounting standards, the 'cost' of fixed assets includes:

- the cost of purchase, plus
- any costs directly attributable to bringing the asset to the location and condition necessary for it to be capable of operating in a manner intended by management.

Whereas costs such as 'delivery' and 'installation' may be considered necessary to 'bringing the asset to the location and condition', other related costs such as 'training' and 'borrowing' may not be as clear cut.

Training expenditure, for example, is usually an ongoing business cost and treated as operating expenditure (see **Chapter 7 Opex and capex**). However, certain training costs may be 'capitalised' and included as part of TFA, if the training is considered necessary to be able to operate the new asset.

Similarly, where an asset is financed specifically by borrowings then the actual finance cost can be capitalised as part of the cost of the asset rather than expensed.

Amortisation

Depreciation and *amortisation* are synonymous concepts. Amortisation is to intangible assets as depreciation is to tangible assets. Tangible means physical in nature whereas intangible assets are non-physical. Examples of intangible assets include patents and licenses (see **Chapter 10 Goodwill and other intangibles**).

Optional detail

Indefinite (or infinite) life assets

Freehold land is not depreciated. Land is a unique tangible asset that is considered to have an indefinite/infinite life. The concept of 'usage' over a period of time therefore does not apply unless there is some aspect of the land that is actually used up, for example, minerals that can be extracted

Goodwill is a special class of intangible asset that is not subject to amortisation as it is considered to have an indefinite life (See **Chapter 10 Goodwill and other intangibles**).

Fixed versus current?

The classification between fixed and current assets is not always obvious. Land and buildings could be correctly classified as current or fixed depending upon business activity.

For example, a housebuilder is likely to want to sell rather than hold properties for the long term. Houses are therefore classified as 'stock' or work in progress (for assets still in the construction phase) and would be included under Current Assets in the balance sheet (see **Chapter 11 Stock**).

If the asset was owned by a property management company intending to generate income from the asset over the long term, the property would be a fixed asset.

Fixed asset register (FAR)

A fixed asset register (FAR) is maintained by most businesses. It provides a written record (or database) that enables a company to keep track of the location of every fixed asset. The FAR records the location of fixed assets physically present at the company premises as well as fixed assets held at third party locations and will also include assets owned by the company but loaned or leased to others.

The FAR also records the value of assets and is used as a source document for the calculation of depreciation and tax calculations.

Where to spot in company accounts

The accounting policy note will explain the treatment of fixed assets including depreciation and revaluation policies.

The profit and loss note will categorise depreciation under distribution costs or administration expenses.

Tangible fixed assets are shown on the face of the balance sheet under fixed (or non-current) assets.

The fixed asset note shows separately the carrying amount and accumulated depreciation for fixed assets and intangibles. Movements for the year are shown by category of asset.

Contractual commitments to buy or construct fixed assets at the year end need to be separately disclosed in the 'capital commitments' note. This provides readers with information of the monies committed to the purchase of assets not yet in use by the company and an indication of future productive capacity and growth prospects.

Extract from Greggs plc 2015 annual report (Note 25)

25 Capital commitments

During the year ended 2 January 2016, the Group entered into contracts to purchase property, plant and equipment and intangible assets for £2,010,000 (2014: £6,454,000). These commitments are expected to be settled in the following financial year.

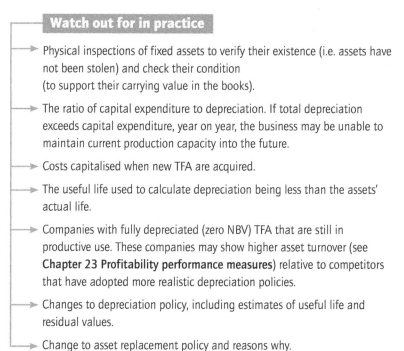

Watch out for in practice

➤ Physical inspections of fixed assets to verify their existence (i.e. assets have not been stolen) and check their condition
(to support their carrying value in the books).

➤ The ratio of capital expenditure to depreciation. If total depreciation exceeds capital expenditure, year on year, the business may be unable to maintain current production capacity into the future.

➤ Costs capitalised when new TFA are acquired.

➤ The useful life used to calculate depreciation being less than the assets' actual life.

➤ Companies with fully depreciated (zero NBV) TFA that are still in productive use. These companies may show higher asset turnover (see **Chapter 23 Profitability performance measures**) relative to competitors that have adopted more realistic depreciation policies.

➤ Changes to depreciation policy, including estimates of useful life and residual values.

➤ Change to asset replacement policy and reasons why.

10 Goodwill and other intangibles

> 'There's a crazy amount of goodwill, and I don't know where it came from...'
>
> Feist, Canadian musician

In a nutshell

A company is typically worth more than the sum of its parts and this difference is due to *goodwill*. Goodwill (also referred to as 'inherent goodwill') is a hidden asset in most businesses and exists because of factors such as reputation, location, market position, customer and employee loyalty, etc.

What makes goodwill unique and distinguishes it from other assets is that it cannot be separated from the business to which it relates, i.e. it cannot be sold or transferred, or exist separately from the business. It can be thought of as DNA value in a business.

Given its rather nebulous nature, accounting rules prohibit recording (inherent) goodwill in a company's own accounts.

However, where one company buys another, *purchased goodwill* is created. It is calculated as the difference between the price paid for a business and the fair value of net assets bought.

Purchased goodwill, unlike *inherent* goodwill, is calculated and recorded in a company's group accounts (see **Chapter 16 Group accounting**).

Goodwill is an 'intangible' asset. Other intangibles commonly found in business include patents, trademarks and development costs.

Need to know

A company's own (i.e. inherent) goodwill is *never* recorded in its accounts due to the uncertainty and volatility in calculating its value.

Consider for example a car manufacturer that has built its reputation (i.e. goodwill) for the quality of its products, including the environmental attributes of its engines. The company's future sales would likely suffer if it materialised that it had been misleading customers about its 'green' credentials. The value of its (inherent) goodwill would be affected as a result. Because of the risks of potential volatility, inherent goodwill remains 'invisible', i.e. it is never accounted for.

Why is it important?

Valuing any business can be complex and typically involves creating cash flow and profit forecasts to establish the potential worth of the business (see **Chapter 28 Business valuation**). From a shareholder perspective, any premium (i.e. goodwill) paid to buy a business should be justified through future earnings expected to be generated by the acquired business.

When is it important?

Where one company buys another (for a sum higher than its balance sheet value) goodwill will exist as an accounting 'difference'. From an accounting perspective, the value for goodwill has been reliably calculated because it is based on the amount actually paid by a company to buy another.

In such situations, purchased goodwill is recorded as an intangible asset in the group accounts of the buyer (see **Chapter 16 Group accounting**).

Example – purchased goodwill

A clothing retailer purchases another shop in a nearby town to keep it out of a competitor's hands. The net assets of the shop are valued at £200,000.

The clothing retailer pays £300,000 to acquire the business. This represents a premium of £100,000 to the net asset value. In the buyer's eyes the excess is a payment to reflect goodwill in the business over and above the identified assets of the business. There may be inherent value in the location or customer base that is expected to support revenues into the future. Control over the site location may also enable the buyer preventing a competitor from trading on the site.

In accounting terms, the identifiable net assets of £200,000 have been acquired for £300,000. The difference of £100,000 (£300,000 − £200,000) is purchased goodwill and would be recognised as an intangible asset in the books of the buyer.

In practice

The 'value' of goodwill must be agreed through negotiation between a buyer and a seller. In deciding whether to pay any premium the acquirer might consider factors including past earnings, future earnings potential and 'synergies' (cost savings or benefits that could arise from combining both companies such as improved supplier volume discounts).

In reality it is not always the case that the goodwill paid is justified. Corporate history is littered with examples of the (over) exuberance of chief executives paying to acquire businesses.

For example, the Time Warner/AOL deal in 2001 resulted in goodwill of £128 billion, i.e. this was the premium (i.e. excess) paid by AOL to buy the Time Warner business. Two years on, £60 billion of the goodwill 'asset' was written off when the overoptimistic earnings forecasts originally used to justify the premium payment failed to materialise. At the time the acquisition was dubbed 'the biggest mistake in corporate history' by an executive closely associated with the deal.

The goodwill written-off resulted in a significant fall in the share price of AOL Time Warner, destroying value for shareholders.

Cynics often argue that goodwill simply serves as a number on the balance sheet to reflect the extravagance of the buyer!

Nice to know

Fair value

Goodwill is calculated as the difference between the fair value of what is paid for the purchase and the fair value of net assets acquired. Fair value should not be confused with book value.

The fair value of assets often bears little relationship to the book value if businesses choose to record their fixed assets at their original purchase (historic) cost rather than revalue (see **Chapter 17 Revaluation**). Over time fixed assets (in particular land and buildings) are likely to increase in value leading to a growing divide between fair values and book values. A revaluation of fixed assets to fair value is therefore typically required to calculate goodwill.

Other intangibles

Intangible assets are fixed assets that have no physical form and include development costs, patents, trademarks and software. Intangibles are nevertheless 'assets' because they can generate benefits for a business. Consider for example a drug patent. The patent owner has the right to generate revenues exclusively from the sale of the patented drug for a period of time.

Intangibles are recognised in the *individual* accounts of the purchaser.

Amortisation

(See also **Chapter 9 Tangible fixed assets and depreciation.**)

Unlike tangible fixed assets which have a limited or *finite* useful life, there is a presumption that goodwill will have an *indefinite* life. This means that purchased goodwill is expected to remain an asset on the balance sheet of the buying company indefinitely. Because of this, the value of goodwill is not 'amortised' or spread over future accounting periods. Amortisation and depreciation are synonymous concepts. Amortisation is to intangible assets as depreciation is to tangible assets.

Unlike goodwill, an intangible asset will typically have a finite life and will be amortised over its expected useful life in the business.

Impairment

Because of the indefinite life presumption, goodwill is subject to an annual impairment test to validate its carrying value. Essentially this involves comparing forecast assumptions that supported any goodwill calculation with the outturn, i.e. reality (see **Chapter 18 Impairment**).

Intangibles with a finite life are subject to impairment testing only when there are indications of impairment (see **Chapter 18 Impairment**).

Optional detail

Negative goodwill

Goodwill can be negative as well as positive.

Intuitively negative goodwill implies that the buyer has secured a bargain as the sum paid to acquire the business is less than the assets bought. This could be the result of a distress sale on the part of the buyer. Unlike goodwill, which is held on the balance sheet as an asset, negative goodwill is treated as profit in the books of the buying company.

Accounting standards

Further details on the treatment and accounting for depreciation can be found in IFRS 3, business combinations.

Where to spot in company accounts

Goodwill is shown under non-current assets in the group accounts of the buying company.

Goodwill impaired is shown as a cost against profits and explained in a separate disclosure in the notes to the financial statements.

Inherent goodwill never appears in a company's own accounts.

Watch out for in practice

➤ Goodwill included in group accounts.

➤ Increases/decreases in goodwill and the reasons for changes (acquisitions, disposals, impairments).

➤ Indicators of possible goodwill impairment, e.g:

➤ Revenues/profit of the acquired business failing to meet original forecasts

➤ For quoted companies, share price declines during or post-acquisition, perhaps suggesting the 'market' is not convinced by the logic of the deal.

➤ Negative goodwill in the accounts, which suggest a 'bargain' purchase. These transactions may attract greater attention because they will result in goodwill being recognised as profit.

➤ Whether the company has adopted IFRS or UK GAAP. UK GAAP accounting treatment of goodwill requires annual amortisation.

11 Stock

In a nutshell

Stock (or inventory) is normally one of the largest assets in the balance sheet
of manufacturing/retailing businesses. It is through the sale of stock that a
business earns revenue.

Stock carries significant commercial risks for a business. Excessive stock can
result in liquidity problems and risks of non-saleability. Too little and a
business may miss out on sales opportunities or lose customers.

Stock must be counted at least annually. It is included in the balance sheet as
a current asset.

Need to know

Stock can comprise inventory in various stages of production, i.e.
raw materials, work in progress and finished goods. Exactly how
stock is classified depends on a company's business activities. For
example, supermarkets classify uncooked meat as 'finished goods'
as it is 'ready for sale' by the business even though it is not 'ready
for consumption' by the consumer. In contrast, a pie manufacturer
would classify its stock of frozen meat as raw materials.

Why is this important?

Efficient stock management is critical to the running of any business.

Companies buying too much stock will suffer loss if they are unable to sell their stock. Holding too little stock will result in potential sales lost as the company will be unable to respond to customer demand.

Holding stock utilises a company's cash resources that could be invested more profitably elsewhere (see **Chapter 24 Working capital and liquidity management**).

To minimise risks, businesses use various techniques to help manage their stock holdings.

A JIT (just in time) approach to stock ordering involves ordering and receiving goods only as they are needed. This helps to minimise the risk of 'stock-outs' while at the same time avoiding overstocking. JIT requires a business to have accurate stock tracking and demand forecasting systems.

Monitoring key stock ratios can help a business identify problems of overstocking and improve operational efficiency.

Stock days

The commercial success of a company depends in part on how quickly it can sell stock to realise cash.

Stock days is a ratio that shows the time taken to sell stock:

$$\frac{\text{Stock}}{\text{Cost of sales}} \times 365$$

There is no 'right' number for stock days/stock turnover. Instead companies will typically compare their metrics to industry and sector averages to assess their relative efficiency.

Greggs plc versus Kingfisher plc (owner of B&Q)

Stock days	2015	2014
Greggs	18.5	18.3
Kingfisher (B&Q)	106.6	107.0

Stock for Greggs comprises raw materials (flour) and work in progress (snacks at various stages of production). Stock for Kingfisher comprises non-perishable DIY items such as paint and lawnmowers.

Stock days calculated shows that Greggs holds stock for about 18 days before it is sold. In contrast, Kingfisher holds stock for much longer periods. This shorter period should be unsurprising given the perishable nature of items sold by Greggs.

A longer stock cycle ties up cash for longer periods so management will continuously focus on ways to reduce stock days. Releasing cash more quickly enables a business to re-stock more quickly or utilise the released cash elsewhere in the business.

Stock turnover

Stock turnover is a complementary measure and shows the number of times stock held is sold during the year.

Stock turnover (Cost of sales/Stock)	2015	2014
Greggs plc	19.8	19.9
Kingfisher plc	3.4	3.4

When is this important?

A commercial objective for businesses is to *optimise* their stock holding. This involves avoiding any unnecessary build up in stock while at the same time eliminating the risk of a 'stock-out' (i.e. running out of stock).

Optimising stock holding is a continuous (some might say impossible) challenge due to the uncertainty of demand patterns. In response, however, supermarkets for example have highly responsive

JIT supply chains that enable them to hold appropriate levels of stock and respond to unexpected spikes in demand. For example, when celebrity chef Delia Smith caused a 'run' on rhubarb following the screening of a television advert in 2010, Waitrose switched to importing supplies to meet the surge in demand. Stocking up in anticipation of higher sales is an alternative but more costly way of achieving the same objective.

In practice, businesses are frequently wrong-footed. For example Lord Wolfson, Chief Executive of Next plc, admitted when explaining the reasons for the company's poor financial performance in 2015 that 'we ordered too much for the lines in the big main catalogue that runs throughout the season, and not enough stock from the newer brochures ... and it was completely our fault to be under-stocked'.

Year-end accounting

Stock must be counted and valued accurately for inclusion in the financial statements. Stock purchased but unsold at the end of each accounting period is shown as (closing) stock in the accounts.

All but the smallest businesses are likely to have a stock system that shows the 'book' quantity of each line of stock the business holds. Stock-takes verify physical quantities held and highlight discrepancies with book records. Inspecting the condition of stock during the count also helps to identify obsolete or damaged stock which will affect valuation.

'Valuing' stock is complicated for two reasons:

1 Stock may be purchased at different prices throughout the year. As a result, arriving at an accurate year-end stock cost unsold may require detailed tracking of purchase cost invoices. First-In-First-Out and Average Cost are costing methods used to arrive at the year-end cost of stock (see **Optional detail** section below).

2 Even when the cost of stock is calculated, there is no guarantee it can be sold for that amount. Businesses should write down stock likely to be sold at a loss (see **Optional detail** section below).

Nice to know

Costing methods (see also **Optional detail** section below)

A business that buys stock at differing prices will need to track costs carefully, to identify the cost of stock that remains unsold at the year end. Accounting standards (see **Chapter 19 Accounting and financial reporting standards**) have established costing methods to be applied by companies when accounting for stock.

For perishable items with an expiry date, such as cheese, first-in-first-out (FIFO) reflects the order in which stock will physically be sold by the business. For homogeneous or identical products typically without a short shelf life, such as paint, average cost (AVCO) is a simpler method of recording and calculating year-end stock cost as it is based on averages.

The important point to note is that, while accounting standards permit both methods, the costing method adopted should reflect the reality of how stock 'flows through' (i.e. is bought and sold by) the company as the method chosen will impact the profit reported by a business.

Work in progress (WIP)

WIP is a term applied to goods in various stages of manufacture, the provision of services and long-term (construction) contracts.

Goods

Valuing work in progress and finished goods can be particularly complex for manufacturing businesses as production costs include labour, materials and overheads. This requires a company to keep detailed cost and time records.

Services

For service businesses (which do not have a physical output) 'stock' is work in progress and is calculated as the value of time spent not billed.

Long-term contracts

For businesses such as housebuilders engaged in long duration construction projects, stock is recorded as long-term 'work in progress' because construction typically stretches over several years. The accounting for long-term contracts requires regular calculation of the stage of completion.

Optional detail

Companies buying stock will inevitably face price rises over time (inflation). Calculating the cost of unsold stock (bought at different prices) at each year end is a complication for business. It requires a company to identify the order in which stock is sold by the business.

First-in-first-out (FIFO)

A supermarket aims to sell foods with the earliest sell by date first (think of milk on supermarket shelves, the nearest-to-expiry date milk is placed at the front of the shelves).

For year-end costing purposes therefore, the cost of stock still on the shelves will relate to the most recent stock purchased from suppliers (as this should have the longest sell by date).

Average cost (AVCO)

In contrast, retailers like B&Q have little need to sell items in order of purchase because the items they typically sell are non-perishable so the concept of a 'sell by date' is largely irrelevant. Items may be sold in any order so an 'average cost' (of all items purchased) can be calculated to value stock unsold at the year end.

The choice of costing method is relevant because it impacts a company's reported profitability and balance sheet numbers. Because of inflation, adopting FIFO reports higher stock balances than AVCO because the most recent stock items held will most likely have been brought at the highest cost (assuming inflation). FIFO will therefore also report a higher profit (because the *cost of sales* will comprise the lowest cost items purchased relative to AVCO, which uses the *average* cost of all items purchased).

A company can apply both FIFO and AVCO methods if they are relevant to differing stock lines held by the business. For example, supermarkets typically stock both food *and* non-food items.

Cost versus net realisable value (NRV)

A company with stock carries a commercial risk that it may not be sold. This risk is assessed at every year end and, where there is a likelihood of non-sale, the cost of stock is 'written down' to the best estimate of what it might sell for. This is known as the net realisable value (NRV).

Where to spot in company accounts

The accounting policy note explains the policies adopted by the company.

Stock is included on the balance sheet under 'current assets' and in the profit and loss account within 'cost of sales'.

Greggs plc

Accounting policy note:

(i) Inventories

Inventories are stated at the lower of cost and net realisable value. Net realisable value is the estimated selling price in the ordinary course of business, less the estimated costs of completion and selling expenses. The cost of inventories includes expenditure incurred in acquiring the inventories and direct production labour costs.

14. Inventories

	Group and Parent Company	
	2015 £'000	2014 £'000
Raw materials and consumables	12,213	11,833
Work in progress	3,231	3,457
	15,444	15,290

Watch out for in practice

→ Significant year-on-year increases in stock balances indicating an obsolescence problem, unless matched by a year-on-year increase in sales.

→ An increase in stock days or a fall in stock turnover.

→ Stock as a percentage of current assets, to see the value tied up in non-liquid current assets.

→ Stock as a percentage of total assets to see the value tied up in stock.

→ It is common practice for businesses to undertake stock counts on an unscheduled basis through a publicised policy of undertaking 'spot checks' These can also serve as a deterrent against theft.

→ Auditors will attend stock counts and seek to verify 'cut off' procedures, to ensure that stock is correctly recorded in cost of sales and inventory balances at the year end.

12 Debtors and creditors

'Creditors have better memories than debtors; creditors are a superstitious sect, great observers of set days and times.'

Benjamin Franklin, scientist, inventor, author and American politician

In a nutshell

Credit is one of the cornerstones of modern business. The majority of companies offer and receive credit.

Customers who receive credit are known as debtors (or receivables). Suppliers who offer credit are known as creditors (or payables).

Debtors are assets as they will be a future cash inflow or 'benefit'. Creditors are liabilities as they will be a future cash outflow or cost.

Need to know

Why is this important?

Debtors are an important source of future cash inflows. They enable a business to predict with some degree of certainty the cash that will be received in the following days and weeks.

However, debtors are not yet cash and cannot be used to fund immediate cash demands faced by a business.

Creditors, on the other hand, may be an important source of short-term business finance. They will help an organisation's cash flow considerably, if the period of credit offered by suppliers closely matches the period of credit offered to customers.

Debtors and creditors form part of a business's working capital. The other main component of working capital is stock (see **Chapter 24 Working capital and liquidity management**).

When is this important?

The management of debtors and creditors is a continuous task for the majority of businesses. Managing the timing of cash inflows and cash outflows is essential for a business to survive. It is important to regularly monitor and sometimes remind debtors that their payment is due (see **Credit control** below).

In practice

Businesses invest sizable resources into managing debtors and creditors. Examples of typical management tools are:

Credit control	▪ A credit control department is responsible for managing and collecting amounts owed by credit customers.
	▪ In a small organisation this may be the part time job of the accountant or can constitute a whole team of people in larger organisation (see **Chapter 1 Finance personnel and systems**).
	▪ Credit control is one of the functions that usually adds value to a business as inevitably some debtors do not pay unless they are continually chased.
Ledgers	▪ The debtor and creditor ledgers record the detailed financial transactions relating to every credit customer and supplier.
	▪ Debtor and creditor balances can also be prepared in the form of an 'aged report' which shows for example:
	▪ all balances due now
	▪ all balances which are one month past their due date
	▪ all balances which are two months past their due date (see **Chapter 1 Finance personnel and systems**).
Debtor and creditor days	▪ A common performance measure is to calculate the average number of days of outstanding debtors and creditors for all customers and suppliers. This is known as *debtor and creditor days*. The formulas are shown in the **Optional detail** section (see **Chapter 24 Working capital and liquidity management**).

(continued)

- Senior management and external analysts are able to quickly assess a business's liquidity by calculating these ratios.

- For example, if a business is known to offer 30 days credit to its customers but its debtor days are 60 days, this would indicate a potential liquidity problem. The business is taking 30 days longer to collect its debt than expected. The problem can be analysed to see if it is an issue across a large number of debtors or caused by a few isolated debtors who have distorted the average.

Nice to know

Alternative terminology

Debtors and creditors have a number of interchangeable terms. This chapter uses 'debtors' and 'creditors' as these are generally the most widely used and known.

Debtors	Creditors
Credit customers	Credit suppliers
Account receivables	Account payables
Trade receivables	Trade payables
Receivables	Payables

Credit control procedures

To collect cash from customers it is important to follow procedures and be organised in collecting customer debts. The following steps should be followed, where applicable:

1	Review the customer's ability to pay and check their credit reference. Consider asking for payments in advance from new customers.
2	Form a contract or agreement which clearly states payment terms.
3	Obtain evidence of delivery or confirm that the customer has received the product or service.
4	Invoice for every delivery and avoid part deliveries to avoid confusion.
5	Invoice promptly and ideally at the same time as delivery. Most customers take credit from the date of invoice not delivery.
6	Invoice clearly and include clear payment terms to avoid ambiguity.

7	Confirm the customer has received the invoice.
8	Regularly review outstanding customer debts.
9	Implement a procedure for overdue customers. For example – an email, followed by a phone call, followed by a letter, followed by a legal letter.
10	Reduce the risk of bad debts through credit insurance or outsourcing debt collection to a factoring agency.

Bad debts

Bad debts are a fact of life for many businesses. Many companies will have a bad debt provision (see **Chapter 30 Debt finance**) in their accounts made up of two elements:

1 A specific bad debt provision:

  ▪ This is for specific known debtors. For example, those which have become insolvent or where there is a potentially unresolvable dispute.

2 A general bad debt provision:

  ▪ Through experience the business typically suffers a number of unanticipated bad debts for a variety of reasons. A general bad debt provision is set a percentage of the overall debtors' balance to reflect this, for example 2 %.

Debtors are quoted net of bad debt provisions in a company's balance sheet.

Other ways to manage bad debts:

▪ *Debt factoring*:

  This is where a business outsources the collection of debt to a third party, who has specific expertise in managing and collecting debts (see **Chapter 30 Debt finance**). Debt factoring has a number of advantages (for example freeing staff to concentrate on running the business and cash advances issued by some factoring companies) but there are also a number of disadvantages (for example loss of contact with customers and reliance on the factoring company).

- *Invoice factoring*:

  Useful for cash advances on specific high-value invoices, as opposed to debt factoring all customer debts (see **Chapter 30 Debt finance**).

- *Insurance*:

  For a premium it is possible to insure against certain risky debts. This is useful for exporters.

- *Sale of debts*:

  There are specialist debt collection companies who will purchase bad debts from organisations. However, they will only pay a proportion of the amount the debtors owe for such debts.

Managing suppliers

Although this chapter has largely focused on managing debtor payments, it is also important to manage supplier payments.

Suppliers are not only an important source of credit; they are also essential to the success of a business as they often provide the key inputs. While it is acceptable to ask for credit from suppliers, it is important not to abuse their goodwill. Healthy supplier relationships are important to ensure continued future supply.

Computerised accounting systems will produce aged supplier listings which enable payments to be planned and scheduled (see **Chapter 1 Finance personnel and systems**). This should be integrated into a cash flow forecast to ensure sufficient funds are available to meet payment deadlines. Most businesses will take full advantage of the credit offered by suppliers (see **Chapter 24 Working capital and liquidity management**).

It is often a question of relative 'power', which dictates who determines payment terms, which is why many businesses prefer to do business with similar-sized partners.

Optional detail

Debtor and creditor days

Debtor and creditor days can be calculated by using the following formulas:

$$\text{Debtor collection period} = \frac{\text{Debtors}}{\text{Sales}} \times 365$$

$$\text{Creditor collection period} = \frac{\text{Creditors}}{\text{Cost of sales}} \times 365$$

(See **Chapter 24 Working capital and liquidity management**).

The debit and credit confusion

The terms 'debtors' and 'creditors' are derived from the terms 'debits' and 'credits'. Debits and credits are part of the system of double entry bookkeeping underpinning accounting.

It's the perspective which is confusing to many.

■ As we saw earlier, debtors are business assets because cash will be received in the future. However, the word debtors is related to the word 'debt', which has negative connotations. This is also because banks use the term 'debit' to refer to overdrawn cash balances.

■ Conversely, creditors are business liabilities because cash will be paid out in the future. However, banks use the term 'credit' to refer to positive cash balances.

Hence, the confusion arises because banks use the terms from their own perspective (as opposed to their customer's perspective).

■ An overdrawn customer (in debit) is their debtor. However, this is a liability (a credit) for their customer.

■ A customer with a positive cash balance (in credit) is their creditor. However, this is an asset (a debit) for their customer.

Where to spot in company accounts

Debtors and creditors can be found on the face of the balance sheet under current assets and current liabilities respectively.

Greggs plc illustration

Debtors are included under the heading 'Trade and other receivables' on Greggs balance sheet, which is supported by Note 15.

It is interesting to note the reference to Greggs bad debts provision under Note 15. It is particularly interesting that this provision is larger than the net amount outstanding.

There is also an analysis of the ageing of trade receivables within Note 15.

Creditors are included under the heading 'Trade and other payables' on Greggs balance sheet, which is supported by Note 15.

Watch out for in practice

Review the value of both debtors and creditors over time to assess if they are moving in line with the growth or decline of the business.

It is useful to analyse debtor days over time. This gives an indication of a business's exposure to debtors. It is also a reflection of credit control and any change in practice.

Similarly, it is useful to analyse creditor days over time. This gives an indication of a business's reliance on supplier's credit. It is also a reflection of any change in practice.

As part of analysing working capital (see **Chapter 24 Working capital and liquidity management**), it is useful to compare the level of debtors compared to the level of creditors as a quick and simple measure of a business's liquidity exposure.

Transactions around the year end, either sales, receipts, purchases or payments may result in a distortion of year-end balances of either debtors or creditors and in turn profit.

13 Prepayments and accruals

> 'Accounting is accrual profession.'
>
> Anonymous

In a nutshell

Prepayments	Accruals
Goods or services which have been invoiced and paid, but not yet received.	Goods or services which have been received, but not yet invoiced or paid.

Prepayments and accruals are both examples of the 'matching' concept (somewhat confusingly also known as the 'accruals' concept) (see **Chapter 2 Cash versus accruals accounting**). The objective is to match expenses to the period in which they are incurred, as opposed to paid.

One of the key things to be aware of is the dual impact of accruals on a business's financial statements.

It's useful to explore prepayments (or prepaid expenses) and accruals (or accrued expenses) at the same time, as they are related concepts which have quite different impacts on a company's accounts.

Need to know

Essentially prepayments and accruals can arise where there is a timing difference, overlapping a period end, between receiving a good or service and its associated invoice/payment. A list of typical prepayments and accruals is provided below.

Prepayments	Accruals
■ Rent and rates	■ Stock delivered not invoiced
■ Insurance	■ Contractors' and consultants' bills
■ Subscriptions	■ Accountants' and lawyers' fees
■ Software licences	■ Energy usage
■ Prepaid charge cards	■ Vacation pay

Example

ABC Ltd's accounting year is based on calendar years, whereas its insurance bill (which it pays annually in advance) runs from 1st July to 30th June. At 31st December, there will be six months of prepaid insurance which is not yet 'used'. Therefore, there will be a prepayment equal to half of the amount paid.

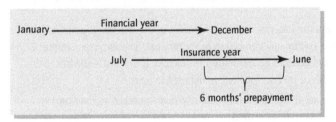

Impact on the financial statements

	Prepayments	Accruals
P&L	■ No impact (following period-end accounting adjustments).	■ An expense. ■ Therefore, a reduction in profit.
Balance sheet	■ An effective reduction in one current asset (cash) and increase in another current asset (prepayments). (This is the net effect of the bookkeeping treatment.) ■ Therefore, no impact on net assets.	■ An increase in a current liability (accruals). ■ Therefore, a reduction in net assets.
Cash flow	■ A cash outflow for the amount of the prepayment.	■ No impact as the expense has not yet been paid.

Why is this important?

Accruals are important as they impact on both the profit and loss (P&L) and balance sheet (see the table above).

The financial impact of accruals on profit is not always certain as accruals are often estimated. There should, however, be a sensible basis to their estimation. For example, a company which needs to estimate its electricity bill may look at meter usage compared to the previous quarterly bill, or simply use last year's estimate as the basis for the accrual (if there has been no significant change in operating activity).

It's important to be aware that accruals must be based on actual incurred expenditure, i.e. goods or services which have actually been received.

When is this important?

Businesses which prepare regular management accounts (see **Chapter 31 Management accounts**) may calculate accruals and prepayments on a monthly as well as an annual basis. The most important time, however, is at the financial year end as the final accrual will have an impact on year-end profit and the year-end tax calculation.

Accruals can affect levels of profit between different years. Take the example of a particularly prudent accrual for legal fees in year one, which is overestimated by £1,000. This will have the impact of reducing year one's profit by £1,000 and increasing year two's profit by £1,000. This is because the over accrual is adjusted the following year to reflect actual expenditure, once the actual invoice is received.

In practice

Prepayments	Accruals
Some services such as insurance, licences and rent will require upfront payment as a matter of course.	Accruals are effectively free credit for a business. For example, Contractor X takes one month to raise their invoice
However, there are other times when it may be advantageous to prepay for goods or services. For example:	and Business Y pays its suppliers one month after receiving invoices. In this example Business Y has received two months' credit as opposed to its usual one month. For one month the debt will be classified as an accrual, and then once the invoice is raised the debt will be classified as a trade creditor.
■ Taking advantage of a volume purchase discount.	
■ Hedging against inflation by purchasing earlier rather than later.	In practice, however, accruals result in more work. The finance department will know the value of its creditors, as the accounting system will have a record of invoices received from suppliers (see **Chapter 1 Finance personnel and systems**).
■ Building a relationship with a new supplier.	
On the other hand, prepayments represent a cash outflow which has an associated capital cost. There is also the risk of becoming an unsecured creditor if the business in receipt of the prepayment becomes insolvent.	However, the finance department may not know about goods or services received which have not yet been invoiced. It will need to rely on information from budget holders at the period end to be aware of the full extent of its liabilities.
	Most well controlled, established businesses will in practice have systems in place to identify where accruals are necessary.

Nice to know

Accounting for prepayments and accruals

Accruals and prepayments are one of a number of period-end adjustments. Other typical adjustments include depreciation (see **Chapter 9 Tangible fixed assets and depreciation**), amortisation (see **Chapter 10 Good will and other intangibles**) and bad debt provisioning (see **Debtors and creditors**). A manual journal entry is typically made by an accountant to adjust the balances in the accounting records (see **Chapter 1 Finance personnel and systems**).

Prepayments	Accruals
Only the proportion of the prepayment which straddles the period end is adjusted for.	The amount of the accrual is recorded as both an expense and an accrual (liability).
For example, ABC Ltd (see example in the **Need to know** section above) will make a journal entry at its year end which effectively records half the insurance bill as a prepayment (asset).	

Alternative terminology

Prepayments	Accruals
Deferred expense	Accrued expense
A prepayment is also known as a deferred expense.	Accruals is simply a commonly used abbreviation for an accrued expense.
Although cash has left the business the associated good or service has been deferred to a future period.	
	GRNYIs
	In some businesses, especially those involving physical goods such as retailers and manufacturers, accruals are often referred to as 'GRNYIs' (pronounced gurneys).
	This is just an acronym for 'Goods Received Not Yet Invoiced'.
	Sometimes this acronym is further abbreviated to GRNI.

Optional detail

The income perspective

So far this chapter has considered *expenditure*, both deferred (prepayments) and accrued (accruals). We will now look at deferrals and accruals of *income*.

Deferred income	Accrued income
Where a business receives prepayments (or deposits) from a third party this is treated as *deferred income* (or revenue).	Where a business has provided goods or services to a third party but not yet sent an invoice, this is treated as *accrued income* (or revenue).
In other words, income has been received (in the form of cash) but not yet earned (as the goods have not yet been delivered or the service has not yet been performed).	As income has been earned, but not yet invoiced (or received), it is recognised as a short-term debtor (asset) on the business's balance sheet.
As the income is not yet earned, this is recognised as a short-term creditor on the business's balance sheet. There is a liability to the third party.	Professional service firms, such as lawyers, often have challenges managing working capital due to large volumes of 'unbilled work-in-progress' or accrued income.
Deferred income, however, is good for cash flow.	In practice, businesses should aim to minimise accrued income and turn it into debtors instead by invoicing promptly, thus giving the debtors a set time to pay.

Summary

	Assets	Liabilities
Income	Accrued income *Earned, not yet invoiced*	Deferred income *Received, not yet earned*
Expenditure	Prepayment (Deferred expenditure) *Paid, not yet incurred*	Accrual (Accrued expense) *Incurred, not yet paid (or invoiced)* *

* Note that by comparison a creditor (see **Chapter 12 Debtors and creditors**) is an incurred expense which has been invoiced, not yet paid.

Rule of thumb

An accrual often occurs before a receipt or payment. A deferral occurs after a receipt or payment.

Where to spot in company accounts

Prepayments and accruals can be found in the notes to the balance sheet.

- Prepayments will be included within the total for 'other receivables'.
- Accruals will be included within the total for 'other payables'.

Therefore, unless there is something specific to disclose, it is challenging to know the exact value of prepayments and accruals from an external analysis alone.

Watch out for in practice

Liabilities/expenses for goods or services received close to the year end will need to be accounted for and due to their timing will often have to be accrued. Requesting prompt invoices or estimates from suppliers will aid the accruals process.

An analysis of supplier invoices received early in the financial year may be for goods or services received in the previous financial year, which should have been accrued.

Unexpected differences in the year-on-year trend for prepayments and accruals.

14 Provisions and contingencies

In a nutshell

Provisions and contingencies are liabilities arising from past activities, which a company may have to pay in the future.

To present a realistic and prudent picture of financial performance, company accounts may include provisions for liabilities, even where the extent and timing of these liabilities cannot be precisely determined.

Need to know

Provisions

A *provision* is a known yet imprecise liability, i.e. we know it exists but we may not know exactly when it will have to be paid or how much.

A provision has to be made when each of the following occurs:

- There is a present obligation (i.e. a duty to make a future payment – see the **Nice to know** section below for more detail) resulting from a past event.
- It is probable that there will be a future cost (or outflow of resources).
- The amount of the obligation can be reliably estimated.

Contingent liabilities

In contrast, a 'contingent' liability arises when there is uncertainty over one or more of the above (hence the use of the term 'contingent'). Typically, the uncertainties are around:

- the likelihood of the obligation (where it is possible but not probable); and
- the reliability.

Contingent liabilities become actual liabilities only if one or more uncertain events actually happen. It is prudent to make shareholders aware of the possible liabilities that may crystallise rather than ignore them.

In these situations, the company should disclose the presence of a 'contingent' liability, however, unlike a provision, the financial impact of the liability should not be recognised in the financial statements.

Why is this important?

Provisions are recognised as a cost to a business. They reduce both profit and net assets and adversely impact key performance measures (see **Chapter 23 Profitability performance measures** and **Chapter 26 Long term solvency performance measures**) including:

- net profit margin;
- return on capital employment;
- gearing.

One of the hidden challenges of provisions is actually identifying them, compared to more identifiable liabilities such as payables and accruals, which will be part of an accounting system (see **Chapter 1 Finance personnel and systems**).

Once identified there is an element of judgement and potential subjectivity involved when making a provision. In contrast to payables (which are certain, as they are invoiced - see **Chapter 12 Debtors and creditors**) and accruals (which can be traced to a transaction with perhaps a degree of estimation - see **Chapter 13 Prepayments and accruals**), there is more uncertainty with provisions.

When is this important?

At the end of each reporting period a company should consider if any provisions need to be made and existing provisions should be reviewed to see if they should be increased, reduced or removed.

Provisions directly impact profit at the following times, in the following ways:

- On creation → increases expenses → reduces profit.
- If increasing → increases expenses → reduces profit.
- If reducing → reduces expenses → increases profit.
- On removal → reduces expenses → increases profit.

In practice

Provisions

Some well-known examples of provisions are:

- **BP's Deepwater Horizon disaster (2015).** BP made a US$10.8 billion provision in 2015 to cover costs relating to the disaster. This brought the total cost for BP since 2010 to US$54.6 billion. Shares in BP rose 1.4% following the announcement.
- **Volkswagen's diesel emissions scandal (2016).** Volkswagen almost tripled its provisions for the scandal to Euro €16.2 billion in 2016. In 2015 Volkswagen had previously made a provision of Euro €6.7 billion for potential costs or recalls. The increased provision in 2016 included legal costs as well as the cost of fixing and buying back affected vehicles. The provision caused Volkswagen's biggest annual loss in its 79-year history.

Other examples of typical provisions made by companies are:

- **Onerous contracts:**
  - If a company which rents property has to relocate before the end of the lease term, they will still be committed to the lease. If they are unable to re-let the property they may become an onerous lease.

- In this case the company could make a provision for future lease rentals and exit costs for properties which are no longer occupied but have remaining lease terms. See the **Where to spot in company accounts** section below for an example relevant to Greggs.

- **Restructuring:**
  - If, prior to the year end, a company has made a decision to close part of its business, relocate or fundamentally reorganise its operations it may be necessary to make a provision. The accounting treatment depends on whether there is a constructive obligation (see the **Nice to know** section below) at the reporting date.
  - Companies should only make restructuring provisions where a formal plan has been publicly communicated to stakeholders.

Contingent liabilities

Typical examples of contingent liabilities are provisions which are either improbable or cannot be reliably estimated. These will often include legal claims and product warranties which are unlikely to be exercised.

In BP's 2015 annual report, details were given of contingent liabilities in relation to the Gulf of Mexico oil spill, in addition to the provisions referred to above. The following is extracted from their financial statements:

> BP has provided for its best estimate of amounts expected to be paid that can be measured reliably. It is not possible, at this time, to measure reliably other obligations arising from the incident, nor is it practicable to estimate their magnitude or possible timing of payment. Therefore, no amounts have been provided for these obligations as at 31 December 2015.

Nice to know

IAS 37 (Provisions, Contingent Liabilities and Contingent Assets) requires that a provision is only recognised where all the following three conditions are met:

1 Present obligation as a result of a past event

- The obligation (see legal and constructive obligations in the table below) must have already occurred by the end of the reporting period. Provisions cannot be made for future obligations.

- The obligations must be independent of future actions. If they can be avoided by future decisions, such as exiting a particular line of business or stopping the provision of a particular service, then no provision should be made.

- Unless a management decision has been communicated and hence committed (for example a decision to restructure a business), then no provision should be made, as the decision could still be reversed.

Legal obligations	Constructive obligations
A service warranty issued with the sale of a product is an example of a legal obligation and therefore should result in a provision.	A well-known and established refund policy (for example those offered by retailers such as Marks and Spencer and John Lewis) is an example of a constructive obligation. A breach of this policy, even where there is no legal or contractual obligation, may cause damage to the company's reputation. This therefore has the same commercial impact as a legal obligation and should result in a provision.

2 Payment is probable

In practice if there is a greater than 50% probability of a future cost then a provision should be made.

3 The amount can be reliably estimated

A provision should only be recognised if the obligation can be reliably estimated. This amount, however, is still an estimate based on the information available at the time and can involve judgement based on experience.

Optional detail

Single obligation

For a single obligation a provision is made for the full future obligation.

For example, ABC Ltd has calculated there is a 60% probability of receiving a £25,000 fine from a legal proceeding. It should nevertheless make a provision for the full £25,000 fine.

Multiple obligations

Where a business has multiple probable obligations, its provision can be based on the probability of the outcome.

For example, XYZ Ltd offers a money back guarantee on £10 million worth of its sales. It knows from experience that 5% of customers will take up the guarantee. It should make a provision for £500,000 (being 5% of £10 million).

Contingent assets

The converse to a contingent liability is a contingent asset.

A contingent asset arises where there is an uncertain asset resulting from a past event which will only be confirmed by the occurrence or non-occurrence of one or more uncertain future events not wholly within the control of the company.

As with a contingent liability, a contingent asset should not be recognised in the financial statements. Instead it should be disclosed in the notes to the accounts if the inflow of economic benefits is probable, unless it is virtually certain in which case it should be recognised.

Contingent assets should be continually assessed to see if they become probable versus just possible and if their financial benefit can be reliably estimated.

Typical examples are insurance and legal claims.

It is worth noting that in accounting there is a principle of 'no netting off'. For example, under an insurance claim a company is required to account for the cost once incurred and only disclose the potential recovery as a contingent asset, which may arise sometime later.

Bad debt provisions

It is common for companies to make provisions against bad debts (see **Chapter 12 Debtors and creditors**).

The accounting treatment for bad debt provisions is, however, different to the other provisions outlined in this chapter. Bad debt provisions are deducted from the total debtor balance and are treated therefore as a reduction in asset values.

Where to spot in company accounts

Accounting policies

A company's treatment of provisions will be found in its accounting policy notes.

For example, Greggs provision policy is as follows:

> Provisions have been estimated for onerous leases and dilapidations. These provisions represent the best estimate of the liability at the balance sheet date, the actual liability being dependent on future events such as trading conditions at a particular shop or the ability of the Group to exit from the lease commitment. Expectations will be revised each period until the actual liability arises, with any difference accounted for in the period in which the revision is made.

Provisions notes

Where provisions are applicable IAS 37 requires the following disclosures in the notes:

- Carrying amounts at the beginning and end of the period.
- Movements during the period, including:
  - amounts provided;
  - amounts used (i.e. incurred and charged against the provision);
  - unused amounts reversed.

For each class of provision, the company should provide:

- A brief description including expected timing of any outflows.
- An indication of the uncertainties involved.

Gregg's provisions note is shown below:

22. Provisions

	Group and Parent Company					
	2015 Dilapidations £'000	2015 Onerous leases £'000	2015 Total £'000	2014 Dilapidations £'000	2014 Onerous leases £'000	2014 Total £'000
Balance at start of year	3,456	3,155	6,611	1,689	3,672	5,361
Additional provision in the year	1,422	581	2,003	3,330	1,232	4,562
Utilised in year	(1,135)	(1,059)	(2,194)	(1,249)	(1,369)	(2,618)
Provisions reversed during the year	(400)	(388)	(788)	(314)	(380)	(694)
Balance at end of year	3,343	2,289	5,632	3,456	3,155	6,611
Included in current liabilities	2,632	1,043	3,675	2,474	1,635	4,109
Included in non-current liabilities	711	1,246	1,957	982	1,520	2,502
	3,343	2,289	5,632	3,456	3,155	6,611

Provisions relate to onerous leases, dilapidations and other commitments associated with properties. Included within the provision is £704,000 in respect of possible recourse on leases which have been conditionally assigned.

The provision for onerous leases is held in respect of leasehold properties for which the Group is liable to fulfil rent and other property commitments for shops from which either the Group no longer trades or for which future trading cash flows are projected to be insufficient to cover these costs. Amounts have been provided for the shortfall between projected cashflows and property costs up to the lease expiry date or other appropriate estimated date. The majority of this provision is expected to be utilised within four years such that the impact of discounting would not be material.

The Group provides for property dilapidations, where appropriate, based on estimated costs of the dilapidation repairs. £2,078,000 of the additional provision made in the prior year in respect of dilapidations was exceptional and relates to the dilapidation costs arising from the removal of in-store bakeries from shops as described in Note 4. £555,000 of this is expected to be utilised after more than one year. The remainder of the dilapidations provision is expected to be utilised within one year.

The provisions reversed or utilised during the year do not contain any items that were included as exceptional costs in the prior year.

Contingent liabilities should not be recognised in the financial statements, but may require disclosure in the notes. For each contingent liability, unless extremely unlikely (i.e. the probability is so small that it can be ignored), the company should disclose:

- A brief description; and
- Where practicable:
  - an estimate of the financial effect;
  - an indication of the uncertainties; and
  - the possibility of any reimbursement.

There are no contingent liabilities disclosed by Greggs in its 2015 annual report.

Watch out for in practice

- New provisions made by a company and what they relate to. Do they relate to normal business practice, for example onerous leases or are they an indication of a larger long-term problem?

- Changes to existing provisions, including provisions that have been released and the reasons why.

- The amount of provisions in total.

- Year-on-year movement in provisions, as these can have a significant impact on profit.

- Provisions as a percentage of total liabilities and year-on-year changes in this percentage.

- Any contingent liabilities and what they relate to. For example, losing a large legal claim could force a company out of business (see **Chapter 25 Insolvency and going concern risk**).

15 Capital and reserves

> 'I love the creativity. I love the ability to create a capital structure that is appropriate for a company, no matter what field it happens to be in.'
>
> Henry Kravis, US businessman and
> co-founder KKR & Co.

In a nutshell

Capital and reserves is the owners' 'equity' in a business. It is equivalent to net assets in a balance sheet.

(Share) capital reflects capital contributions made by investors.

Reserves can be of two types:

1 'Revenue' reserves - profits set aside for specific or general purposes.

2 'Capital' reserves - balances set aside because of regulatory or accounting requirements.

The distinction between *capital* and *revenue* reserves is important in law. Share capital plus capital reserves represent the creditors' 'buffer' or statutory capital of a company. The creditors' buffer cannot be reduced or distributed except with special permission.

Need to know

Share capital

To raise finance, a company can issue different types of shares (see below). Only ordinary share capital confers the rights of ownership in the company. Ordinary shareholders are 'equity' owners in the business (see **Chapter 29 Equity finance**). Only ordinary shareholders have voting rights.

When a company issues ordinary shares in exchange for consideration (typically cash), the sums are recorded as share capital and *cannot* be paid back to shareholders except by court approval, e.g. on liquidation of a business.

Individual shareholders can sell shares, e.g. through a stock exchange (for listed companies) or to a private buyer. From a *company* perspective, however, this has no effect on the capital invested in the company as shareholders are re-selling shares previously issued by the company.

Reserves

Reserves belong to shareholders and are classified as *revenue* or *capital*. The distinction determines whether or not the reserve is distributable, i.e. can be paid out to shareholders as dividends. Revenue reserves are distributable and are created by a company's trading and operating activities. Profits can be distributed as dividends to shareholders. Any profits not distributed accumulate in a 'retained earnings' reserve available for future distribution.

In contrast, capital reserves are not distributable. They exist to protect creditors. Capital reserves can be created through the issue of shares or as a result of accounting measurement changes – see below.

Capital reserve created (or added to)	Example situation
Share premium reserve	Shares issued to shareholders at a premium to nominal value
Revaluation reserve (see **Chapter 17 Revaluation**)	Accounting measurement change e.g. upward revaluation of company assets

Why is this important?

A company's 'capital and reserves' balance is an indicator of its financial strength (see **Chapter 4 The balance sheet**). Creditors and providers of finance may base their lending decisions in part on this information.

When is this important?

A company planning to pay dividends to its shareholders can only do so from its revenue reserves. It cannot legally pay a dividend if the payment would have the effect of reducing its net assets to below its *capital* reserves (plus share capital) balance. These regulations are known as *capital maintenance rules* and prevent shareholders extracting too much cash from the company.

Creditors have priority in a winding up and capital maintenance rules help give 'substance' to this prioritisation, i.e. there would be no point in creditors having priority over shareholders on a winding up if there were no restrictions on a company's ability to pay dividends to shareholders (see **Chapter 25 Insolvency and going concern risk**).

While legal protection exists, it is important for creditors and lenders to note that capital reserves may nevertheless be depleted where a company is making losses.

Example

Company A Year 1		
Net assets	900	
Equity		
Share capital	300	(capital reserve)
Share premium	600	(capital reserve)
	900	

Company A has net assets of £900 equivalent to capital reserves (comprising share capital and premium). The company is not legally permitted to distribute this sum.

Year 2

Company A made losses of £100. Net assets have fallen to £800 (£900 less £100).

	£	
Net assets	<u>800</u>	
Equity		
Share capital	300	(capital reserve)
Share premium	600	(capital reserve)
Retained earnings	(100)	(revenue reserve)
	<u>800</u>	

Net assets in the company have fallen to £800. As a result protection for creditors has fallen to £800. This is because the company has suffered losses and *not* because of any distribution of profits (dividend).

If the company continues to make losses it could become 'insolvent' (see **Chapter 25 Insolvency and going concern risk** and **Chapter 10 Goodwill and other intangibles**).

In practice

It is unusual for profitable companies to pay out all profits earned as dividends to shareholders. Companies typically set aside some of their profits to build up their reserves. This has the following benefits:

1   It provides additional security to creditors. Keeping reserves in the company helps to prevent depletion of the capital reserve (see the example above).

2   It provides an internal source of finance, i.e. working capital is available to a business. Profits not paid out as dividends are a source of cash for the business.

3   It provides greater certainty that the company can maintain its dividend levels. Some listed companies have what are known as 'progressive' dividend payment policies (see **Chapter 27 Investor ratios**). Where earnings fall in a year, having a reserves can prevent dividends from being reduced.

4 To finance a specific need. For example, a Debenture Redemption Reserve is created to set aside (distributable) profits to redeem debentures at a premium in the future.

Nice to know

Share capital

While different types of shares may be issued by a company only ordinary shares carry rights of ownership:

- Ordinary shareholders are owners of the business. Ordinary shares carry the highest risk as there is no guarantee of return. Ordinary shareholders are the last to be paid if the company is wound up (see **Chapter 25 Insolvency and going concern risk**). However, they also have the potential to obtain the highest financial gains (see **Chapter 29 Equity finance**).

- Preference shares give holders 'preferential' rights. Shareholders typically receive a fixed dividend but there is no guarantee of this. If the business is wound up, they would rank ahead of ordinary shareholders in any pay out (see **Chapter 25 Insolvency and going concern risk**). Preference shareholders are not owners in the business which means that they do not benefit from an increase in the profits or value of the business.

- Cumulative preference shares have similar rights to ordinary preference shares plus the right that, if a dividend cannot be paid one year, it will accumulate into the next year. Dividends on cumulative preference shares have to be paid provided the company has sufficient distributable profits.

- Redeemable shares give the right to the company to buy them back at a future date (fixed or flexible, at the behest of the business). Note a company can only have redeemable shares if it has ordinary (non-redeemable) shares in issue also.

Capital reserves

Capital reserves are created in a variety of ways:

1 Shareholder contributions

The share premium reserve is created when shares are issued by a company at a price in excess of the nominal value of shares. The share premium reserve is a non-distributable legal reserve and an example of what is known as a 'capital reserve'.

2 Statute

Companies may be required to maintain certain types of reserves by legislation. For example there is a requirement to create a *capital redemption reserve* consisting of the nominal value of shares repurchased and cancelled by a company. This reserve maintains capital in the business providing protection for creditors.

3 Accounting requirements

Most other reserves result from accounting requirements and reflect *measurement changes* in equity rather than profit and loss. Some common examples are given below.

a   Revaluation reserve (see **Chapter 9 Revaluation**). Fixed assets may be revalued to fair value. A revaluation surplus is a capital reserve and therefore cannot be distributed, although a surplus may be transferred periodically to the profit and loss reserve and distributed as a dividend. The amount that can be transferred is based on the difference between depreciation on the revalued carrying amount of the asset and depreciation based on the asset's original cost.

   When a revalued asset is sold, any balance in the reserve (relating to the asset sold) may be transferred to retained earnings and distributed as a dividend.

b   Foreign currency translation reserve. Foreign currency differences arising from converting ('translating') assets, liabilities, income and expenses from an entity's functional currency to the reporting currency result in a foreign currency reserve. The reserve arises only in group situations in consolidated accounts. It is only on disposal of a foreign entity that any accumulated translation differences can be recognised as part of the profit on sale of the entity.

Optional detail

Reserves are amounts set aside out of profits and are not required to meet a particular liability at the balance sheet date.

Provisions (see **Chapter 14 Provisions and contingencies**) are costs deducted in arriving at distributable profits.

Companies may 'hide' profit by increasing provisions. Increasing a provision has the effect of *reducing* profit, which is a distributable reserve.

By building up the level of provisions in years when profits are good (i.e. better than expected) a company is effectively holding back profit which can be taken to profit in bad years, by releasing the built-up provision. This can enable a company to 'smooth' its profile of reported results. While accounting standards have to a large extent helped to eliminate or minimise profit manipulation opportunities there still remain limited opportunities to do so (see **Chapter 19 Accounting and financial reporting standards**).

Examples of profit manipulation opportunities include:

a Excessive provisions against the value of stock.

b Over provisioning to reduce the value of debtors, by creating an excessive provision for doubtful debts (see **Chapter 12 Debtors and creditors**).

c Classifying contingent liabilities as actual liabilities (see **Chapter 14 Provisions and contingencies**).

d Reclassifying capital expenditure as revenue expenditure (see **Chapter 7 Opex and capex**).

Provisions can be difficult to identify as they are typically 'netted off' in the balance sheet asset to which they relate.

Understated reserves

A company may also report an understated reserves position as a result of 'hidden' assets, i.e. assets not reflected in the balance sheet. Hidden assets include:

- The value of inherent goodwill (brand, customer base, location) not included within the balance sheet (see **Chapter 10 Goodwill and other intangibles**).

- The market value of fixed assets where a company uses historic cost accounting for fixed assets (see **Chapter 17 Revaluation**).

These assets may provide additional protection to creditors in insolvency situations (see **Chapter 25 Insolvency and going concern risk**).

Where to spot in company accounts

Capital and reserves should be clearly identifiable in the balance sheet.

The 'statement of changes in equity' will provide details of movements in capital and reserves from one year to the next.

Extract from Greggs plc

Statement of changes in equity (extract)
52 weeks ended 2 January 2016

			Attributable to equity holders of the Company		
	Note	Issued capital £'000	Share premium £'000	Capital redemption reserve £'000	Retained earnings £'000	Total £'000
Balance at 4 January 2015		2,023	13,533	416	230,731	246,703
Total comprehensive income for the year						
Profit for the financial year		–	–	–	57,600	57,600
Other comprehensive income		–	–	–	4,030	4,030
Total comprehensive income for the year		–	–	–	61,630	61,630
Transactions with owners, recorded directly in equity						
Sale of own shares		–	–	–	3,876	3,876
Purchase of own shares		–	–	–	(11,125)	(11,125)
Share-based payment transactions	21	–	–	–	3,662	3,662
Dividends to equity holders	23	–	–	–	(43,714)	(43,714)
Tax items taken directly to reserves	8	–	–	–	5,242	5,242
Total transactions with owners		–	–	–	(42,059)	(42,059)
Balance at 2 January 2016		2,023	13,533	416	250,302	266,274

23. Capital and reserves (extract)

Capital redemption reserve

The capital redemption reserve relates to the nominal value of issued share capital bought back by the Company and cancelled.

Watch out for in practice

→ Number and type of reserve categories and what they are used for.

→ Relative size of distributable and non-distributable reserves.

→ Existence of a share premium account (indicating the company has raised further capital).

→ Existence of preference shares.

→ Year-on-year movement in reserves.

16 Group accounting

> 'I think a lot can be said for consolidation, but I think it should be done for the right reasons.'
>
> Margrethe Vestager, Danish politician

In a nutshell

A *group* comprises a parent company and at least one subsidiary.

Company law (and accounting standards) requires a parent company to combine its results with those of its subsidiaries to present accounts as if it were a single entity. These combined accounts are referred to as *group accounts* or 'consolidated accounts'.

Group accounting, at its simplest, involves adding together income and expenses from the profit and loss account of each company to produce a group profit and loss account, and the assets and liabilities from each balance sheet to produce a group balance sheet. These accounts are presented, together with other required disclosures, in a single set of financial statements.

Investments in other entities can only be consolidated into group accounts when they are 'controlled' by a parent. Control typically arises when a parent owns a majority of shares in a subsidiary although it is the ability to direct decisions made by a subsidiary that ultimately determines control.

Need to know

Why is this important?

Companies normally prepare financial statements annually to report performance (profit and loss) and balance sheet assets and liabilities of the business. Financial statements should reflect transactions undertaken on an arm's-length basis, i.e. with the business acting *independently* in its own self-interest and *without influence* from any other party.

There is no reason why a parent and its subsidiaries should have to act independently, however, because the parent owns and controls each subsidiary. The impact of transactions, if any, between group companies is, however, always eliminated in the group accounts to only show the performance of the group 'with the outside world' and avoid giving a misleading impression of business performance.

Note that the *individual* accounts of a company in the group will disclose the financial effect of any transactions undertaken within the group.

Example

Parent company A recently acquired 100% of subsidiary company B.

Company A is a well-established and profitable company whereas company B is a smaller company that has made losses historically. By virtue of its shareholding, company A is able to control the activities of company B and therefore influence the performance of company B. This includes setting prices for goods and services traded between the companies.

During the year company B sells goods to company A at an uncommercial (high) price. As a result company B reports profits and a net asset growth after acquisition by company A.

The profit and loss account of company B, looked at in isolation, would now show an improved (profitable) performance. In the absence of the disclosure of transactions between group companies, a lender (bank) or creditor might form an overly positive (i.e. wrong) impression of company B based on its reported performance.

Company B is required to disclose the financial effect of group transactions on its performance as well as the identity of a parent preparing group accounts that incorporate the results of the subsidiary.

When is this important?

Suppliers and lenders typically review financial statements as part of due diligence before extending credit to a company. Looking at a company in isolation, i.e. without understanding the influence exerted by a parent may give a misleading view of its underlying performance.

Creditors/banks may therefore seek additional parent company guarantees before advancing credit/monies to a subsidiary that is reliant on intra-group trading for its success.

In practice

Companies are separate legal entities. A company therefore has no legal obligation to make good the debts of any other company in a group. Lenders requiring additional security over debts will have to register a legal charge over one or more assets of group companies as security for lending to a company in the group. Legal guarantees may also be sought from the parent company.

Nice to know

Related parties

Parent and subsidiaries are 'related parties' because the parent controls the subsidiary. Transactions between these companies may not be undertaken on an arm's length basis because the parent has the power to determine trading terms between companies. Trading on a non-arm's-length basis is not illegal but it creates the risk that *individual* company performance can be manipulated or misunderstood, which could give a misleading impression of the success (or otherwise) of a company.

Disclosure of related party transactions in the accounts of the subsidiary helps ensure underlying company performance is understood.

Ownership versus control

51% (or more) ownership (i.e. a majority of shares) does not necessarily result in control. Similarly 49% (or less) does not imply that a controlling relationship does not exist. What matters in deciding whether or not control exists is the degree of power to direct a company's operations.

Example

Company A owns 60% of company B. The remaining 40% is held by company C. By virtue of a legal agreement between the parties, company A has the right to appoint (only) 2 of 5 directors onto the board while company C appoints the remainder. Company C controls the company irrespective of A's majority shareholding. Company A's directors do not hold majority voting rights on the board.

Significant influence (associate relationships)

A company that owns between 20% and 50% is more likely to have *significant influence* over another rather than 'control'. The investing company will have voting rights and can influence decisions but cannot, in its own right, determine them.

Associate relationships are not consolidated, i.e. the results are not added together (line by line). The relevant % share of profits (or losses) and relevant % share of net assets owned are included in the consolidated accounts of the investing company. This is known as *equity accounting*. Note that equity accounting is only used in consolidated accounts and will not be used if the investing company has no subsidiaries and does not prepare consolidated accounts.

Optional detail

Consolidation accounting

To prepare a consolidated balance sheet, the assets and liabilities of parent and every subsidiary are added together on a line by line basis and adjustments made for goodwill and non-controlling (minority) interest (see 1 and 3 below).

To prepare the consolidated profit and loss account, the income and expenses of parent and each subsidiary are summated on a line by line basis. Group income is reduced by the non-controlling interest in profits (see 3 below).

The accounting involved in consolidation can be quite complex. However, the basic steps in every consolidation involve a number of *permanent adjustments*, to recognise the following:

1 Identification of goodwill

Compare the 'cost of investment' (included in the parent company balance sheet under fixed assets) against 'share capital and reserves', i.e. equity in the subsidiary at the time of acquisition (and including any fair value adjustments such as revaluation of assets):

1 Where the cost of investment is identical to equity, just cancel out i.e. there is no goodwill.

2 Where a company pays more (or less) than the equity in the subsidiary (at the time of acquisition), recognise this difference as positive (or negative) goodwill.

Goodwill is as an intangible asset under fixed assets in the consolidated balance sheet (see **Chapter 10 Goodwill and other intangibles**).

2 Non-controlling interest (NCI) – liability

Where a subsidiary is less than 100% owned a *non-controlling interest* exists. NCI (also known as minority interest) refers to the financial interests of third party shareholders.

In situations of less than full ownership, while the assets and liabilities fall under the *control* of the parent, it does not *own* 100% of those assets and liabilities. NCI reflects the proportion of net assets owned by third parties and shown as a long-term liability of the business in the consolidated balance sheet. For a company that was 60% owned by a parent, NCI would be calculated as 40% of balance sheet net assets.

3 Non-controlling interest (NCI) – profit

Where a subsidiary is less than 100% owned a share of annual profits will belong to non-controlling interests also.

NCI in profits are deducted from group income, to show the net income that belongs solely to (the shareholders of) the parent company. For a company that was 60% owned by a parent, NCI would be calculated as 40% of the company's post tax profit.

Additional considerations

Different accounting policies or year ends will need to be adjusted for. For example, a subsidiary that has a different year end to its parent will prepare additional financial information that covers the intervening period.

Group accounting - exemptions

A company with subsidiaries may not have to prepare group accounts in the following circumstances:

1   Small group exemption. A group is small if its combined revenue, total assets and employees are below certain thresholds (see **Chapter 21 Information in the public domain**).

2   Where the parent forms part of a larger group. In this situation its results would be consolidated into the results of that (larger) group.

Where to spot in company accounts

Disclosure of the existence of a parent company is required in a subsidiary's accounts.

Where related party transactions have taken place during the year, disclosure is required of the effect of those transactions, where they have not been undertaken on an arm's length basis.

Group accounting policies disclose how intragroup transactions have been accounted for (see extract from Greggs plc consolidated accounts, below).

Greggs plc 2015 annual report and accounts

Relevant extracts from accounting policies note

(c) Basis of consolidation

(i) Subsidiaries
Subsidiaries are entities controlled by the Company. The Company controls an entity when it is exposed to, or has rights to, variable returns from its involvement with the entity and has the ability to affect those returns through its power over the entity. The accounts of subsidiaries are included in the consolidated accounts from the date on which control commences until the date on which control ceases.

(ii) Associates
Associates are those entities in which the Group has significant influence, but not control, over the financial and operating policies. Significant influence is presumed to exist when the Group holds between 20 and 50 % of the voting power of another entity. At the year end the Group has one associate which has not been consolidated on grounds of materiality (see Note 12).

(iii) Transactions eliminated on consolidation
Intragroup balances, and any unrealised gains and losses or income and expenses arising from intragroup transactions, are eliminated in preparing the consolidated accounts.

Watch out for in practice

- Goodwill in group accounts (see **Chapter 10 Goodwill and other intangibles**).

- Impairment testing (see **Chapter 18 Impairment**) and goodwill written off in year.

- Interest free loans to subsidiary companies to fund working capital and/ or growth.

- Significant intra-group trading activity affecting financial performance, e.g. buying/selling stock at uncommercial prices. This can significantly distort the underlying ('true') performance and position of a company.

- Dramatic improvement/deterioration in financial performance of a company following acquisition. Group may have access to markets or improved commercial terms from third party suppliers.

17 Revaluation

In a nutshell

Revaluations are carried out to reflect the current value of fixed assets
included in a company's balance sheet.

The effect of revaluing fixed assets is to increase (or decrease) their values,
from their original purchase cost to market (fair) value.

The positive (or negative) difference is typically reflected as a gain (or loss) in
a *revaluation reserve*. The gain is not profit, i.e. it is not reflected in the profit
and loss account.

Land and buildings are most likely to be revalued by a business.

Need to know

A company can decide whether or not to revalue its fixed assets, i.e. it is
an accounting policy *choice* (see **Chapter 19 Accounting and financial
reporting standards**). Where it chooses to revalue it must do so
regularly to ensure asset valuations are kept up to date. In the case of
land and buildings, 'up to date' means revaluing at least every three
years.

Valuations should be carried out by experts such as qualified
surveyors.

Example 1– Revaluation of building

ABC Ltd originally purchased a building at a cost of £100,000. The
company revalues its assets. At the end of the year, the building had
a value of £250,000.

Ignoring depreciation, the 'gain' in value is calculated as the difference between valuation and original cost, i.e. £150,000 (£250,000 − £100,000).

This would be reflected in the financial statements as follows:

Fixed assets (Building)   £250,000 (£100,000 + £150,000)

Revaluation reserve   £150,000

The gain of £150,000 is recorded in a revaluation reserve, not in the profit and loss account (see **Chapter 15 Capital and reserves**).

Why and when is this important?

Companies typically adopt a revaluation policy in order to improve their balance sheet net asset position. Where asset values are rising, this can have commercial benefits for the business:

- A business in merger or acquisition talks with another company will show higher balance sheet net assets. This may strengthen its negotiating position.

- Revaluations can increase the asset base of the business and therefore security available against which to borrow. What would otherwise be 'hidden' value is brought onto the balance sheet providing additional security against which to borrow.

- For companies already laden with debt finance, revaluing assets may provide more headroom against which to secure further loans (see **Chapter 30 Debt finance**).

Where revaluation is the norm in an industry, companies may feel inclined to adopt a revaluation policy. A consistent policy helps to create comparability with other companies in the industry. However, revaluation is a policy *choice* and this can lead to comparison difficulties where companies adopt different policies. Financial statements should, however, disclose sufficient information to enable comparison of business performance (see **Chapter 19 Accounting and financial reporting standards**). Companies choosing a policy of revaluation are therefore required to also disclose historical cost information to enable comparison on a like-for-like basis with companies that choose not to revalue.

Gain versus profit

Revaluations (upwards) result in (unrealised) gains. Gains are different to profit. *Profit* arises from *trading or operating* activities not accounting measurement changes like a policy of revaluation. An increased value of assets is reflected in a capital (non-distributable) revaluation reserve.

To understand the distinction between *gain* and *profit* consider the property you live in. If the property has increased in value over the period since it was purchased then this is a capital *gain*. However, the gain cannot be considered a *profit*. It is a notional or 'paper gain' because, until or unless the property is sold any benefit (in the form of cash proceeds) cannot be realised by the property owner.

(Unrealised) *gains* turn into *profit* when a fixed asset is sold. At this point the gain *is* 'realised' and therefore distributable, i.e. they can be paid out as dividends (see **Chapter 15 Capital and reserves**).

Downward revaluation

Asset values go down as well as up. Decreases in valuation will reverse previous (upward) revaluations.

Example 2a

Using information from Example 1:

Three years later, a revaluation of the property results in a fall in value to £200,000.

Ignoring depreciation, the asset's value has fallen by £50,000 since the previous valuation, i.e. from £250,000 to £200,000.

The latest valuation is reflected as follows:

Fixed assets (Building)	£200,000	(£50,000 lower than the previous valuation)
Revaluation reserve	£100,000	(£150,000 − £50,000)

Note that, despite the lower valuation, the asset is still valued at above its original cost, i.e. there is an (unrealised) gain of £100,000 relating to the asset (as shown in the revaluation reserve).

Example 2b - losses

If a revaluation results in a valuation *below* the original purchase cost, the difference to be 'expensed', i.e.charged as a cost in the profit and loss account.

Continuing the example, a few years later the asset is revalued (downwards) to £60,000.

Asset cost £100,000

Previous valuation £200,000

The latest valuation of £60,000 is below the original cost (£100,000).

Cost	Valuation	Difference (loss)
£100,000	£60, 000	£40,000 (£100,000 − £60,000)

The asset has fallen in value by £140,000 since the previous valuation. The asset value is reduced by £140,000 to a new value of £60,000. The revaluation reserve is eliminated (£100,000 - £100,000) and the remaining difference of £40,000 would be charged against a company's profits. The loss is recognised even though the asset has not been sold and reflects 'prudent' accounting. The revaluation reserve (£100,000) would be eliminated.

In practice

Despite the potential commercial advantages, not every company chooses to revalue its assets. A company may prefer to keep its assets at cost as a policy of revaluation can require significant management time and cost, e.g. professional fees of independent valuers.

Revaluations also impact key profitability ratios adversely. For example, return on capital employed or ROCE (see **Chapter 23 Profitability performance measures**) will worsen because upward revaluations result in a higher net asset value.

Example 3

Using the same information from example 1 (ignoring example 2), assume the company's profit was £10,000.

Ignoring depreciation, ROCE would be calculated as follows:

$$\text{ROCE} \quad = \quad \frac{\text{Profit}}{\text{Capital employed}}$$

Cost

$$\text{ROCE} = \frac{£10,000}{£100,000} = 10\%$$

Revaluation

$$\text{ROCE} = \frac{£10,000}{£250,000} = 4\%$$

Higher asset values will also result in a higher depreciation charge and therefore reduce profit (see **example 4** in the **Optional detail** section below). This would further impact ROCE negatively.

Nice to know

Subjectivity and manipulation

Interestingly, a business choosing a policy of revaluation does not have to revalue *all* of its fixed assets under that policy.

Revaluation policy can be applied by 'class of asset' and the definition of 'class' is open to some interpretation. 'Land and buildings' is typically considered to be a class of asset, 'plant and machinery' another. It could, however, equally be argued that 'office buildings' and 'manufacturing buildings' are each a class of asset within land and buildings.

This subjectivity may enable a business to 'cherry pick' (only) those classes of assets most likely to benefit from rising values.

Valuation methods

Market values have to be used wherever possible when carrying out revaluations. However, some assets such as specialised machinery may not have a market to determine their value. Where no market exists, *depreciated replacement cost* can be used as an alternative. Essentially this method is used to estimate the current cost of replacing the asset with one that is in a similar state and condition.

Optional detail

Depreciation

(See also **Chapter 9 Tangible fixed assets and depreciation**)

Revalued assets have to be depreciated in the same way as fixed assets included at original cost.

Depreciation is calculated on the new (higher or lower) revalued amount.

Example 4

Company A and company B both own an identical asset. Company A does not revalue its assets. Company B does.

Assets are depreciated 4% per annum.

Asset cost = £100,000

Latest valuation (company B only) = £200,000

The annual depreciation and net book value in each balance sheet after 5 years will be as follows:

Depreciation

	Company A	Company B
Annual depreciation charge	£4,000 (£100,000 × 4%)	£8,000 (£100,000 × 4%)

Net book value

	Company A	Company B
After 5 years	£80, 000	£160,000
	(£100,000 − £20,000)	(£200,000 − £40,000)
Basis of calculation	Purchase cost less 5 years' depreciation	Valuation less 5 years' depreciation

Depreciation is higher in company B as it has revalued its assets. A higher annual depreciation charge will have the effect of reducing profit (and therefore distributable earnings) in company B.

Although reported profits are lower in company B, this has the advantage that it 'forces' the company into retaining adequate funds, by limiting the amounts that can be paid out as dividends. Funds will likely be needed for eventual asset replacement and a higher depreciation charge based on revaluation (which is a more realistic reflection of replacement value) will reduce distributable profits and help a company to retain adequate funds. In contrast, depreciation based on purchase cost could result in payment of (excessive) dividends and risk leaving a company with insufficient cash reserves to buy a replacement asset (most likely at a higher price) in the future.

In reality, company directors adopting revaluation often still have to maintain dividend payouts because of shareholder expectations to deliver a *progressive* dividend policy (see **Chapter 27 Investor ratios**). Accounting rules therefore permit an *adjustment* to reserves for companies that choose to revalue their assets. A transfer equal to the *excess* depreciation incurred is permitted, from the revaluation reserve *to* distributable profits. In the above example, £4,000 can be transferred annually *from* the revaluation reserve *to* distributable reserves. The effect of this adjustment is that company B would not be at any disadvantage to company A in the amount it could pay as dividends under law.

Where to spot in company accounts

The accounting policy note will include the basis of revaluation, if any, adopted.

There should be sufficient information included in the *notes* to the accounts to identify the financial effects of a revaluation. This enables users to compare performance with businesses using historical cost accounting by removing the effects of revaluation.

The balance sheet (or supporting notes) should include details of:

▦ Assets held at revaluation (included in fixed assets).

▦ Revaluation reserve (included within capital and reserves).

Revaluation movements explained in the 'Statement of changes in equity' (cross referenced from the balance sheet). Greggs plc prepares accounts on a historical cost basis and therefore does not revalue fixed assets.

Watch out for in practice

➤ The size of any revaluations to assess their likely impact on key financial ratios.

➤ The definition of class of assets. Is this different to other companies in the same sector? This may affect ratio comparisons. Consider the classes of assets each business has chosen to revalue.

➤ Direction of revaluations – are they all up? Have there been any downward revaluations?

➤ An in-year change of policy, from cost to revaluation. This could indicate impending corporate activity (a potential takeover or merger) or the need to show a higher capital base against which additional debt finance might be secured.

Evidence of selective assets (only) revalued. A company can selectively revalue asset types, i.e. those most likely to rise in value. This may provide scope for distorting the financial performance of the business as a whole.

➤ Significant risks of material misstatement in the financial statements due to revaluations. Read the audit report to identify critical areas reviewed by external auditors in arriving at their opinion.

18 Impairment

'Chevron has reported impairment charges of almost $5bn in the past two years.'

Gillian Tett, US managing editor and columnist,
Financial Times

In a nutshell

Impairment refers to a permanent loss in the income-generating potential of an asset.

A fixed asset is considered impaired when its worth to the business (known as 'recoverable' value) falls below its 'carrying' value (also known as 'book' value).

Tangible fixed assets are assessed for indications of impairment annually to ensure they are not overvalued in the balance sheet. Where there are indications of impairment, the recoverable amount is calculated and the impairment loss (if any) is reflected in the profit and loss account.

Indefinite life assets such as goodwill (see **Chapter 10 Goodwill and other intangibles**) and trademarks are treated differently. The recoverable amount has to be calculated annually whether or not there is any indication of impairment.

It is not easy (or always possible) to identify whether or when an asset suffers impairment.

Need to know

Impairment testing is not a matter of choice. Assets' values *must* be reduced whenever there is a reduction in the carrying value of assets.

Impairments are conceptually different to downward revaluations as revaluation is a matter of policy choice. All companies, including those that hold their assets at cost, must adjust for market value changes to their assets.

Why is it important?

Impairment results in the value of the asset being written down (to its lower value). The loss is recognised in the profit and loss account.

When is it important?

Impairment must be considered at the end of every reporting period, e.g. annually. Directors will need to assess whether there are any indicators of impairment such as technological developments, legal or environment changes or evidence of physical damage to assets. The presence of indicators doesn't *prove* that the carrying value of an asset needs to be written down, however. It only points to the *possibility* that the asset value may be impaired. In the case of tangible fixed assets, it is the possibility that triggers a more detailed investigation to find out the asset's fair value.

Common indicators of impairment may include:

- Changes in laws, e.g. the introduction of tighter fuel emission regulations that prohibit non-compliant delivery vehicles from entering cities could impair the value of fleet vehicles.
- Material adverse events, such as the Smiler ride safety failure at Alton Towers in 2015.
- Physical damage or destruction of an asset, e.g. the grounding of the Costa Concordia cruise ship in 2012.
- Technological advances that make using existing assets uncompetitive or obsolete.

The list is not exhaustive.

Illustration

Take the example of the iconic Concorde supersonic plane. Following a fatal crash in the early 2000s the plane had to be consigned to the scrapyard because safety concerns meant the plane was no longer financially viable even though BA had originally intended for the plane to remain in service. This asset suffered 'impairment' not because it had reached the end of its planned useful life but because of damage to its reputation, largely caused by safety concerns.

Calculating impairment

Impairment is the amount by which the carrying (book) value of an asset exceeds its 'recoverable amount'. The value of the asset must be written down to its recoverable amount and the impairment loss reflected in the profit and loss account.

Example 1

A company's asset has a carrying value in the balance sheet of £1,000. The recoverable amount of the asset is £900.

Therefore, the asset must be written down to the (lower) recoverable amount.

Carrying value (balance sheet) is reduced to £900 (£1,000 − £100).

Impairment loss (profit and loss) is recognised as £100 (£1,000 − £900).

Recoverable amount

Recoverable amount is the worth of an asset to the business. In this context, 'worth' will be the *higher* of the asset's sale value (i.e. market or fair value) or its earnings potential to the business through continued use (known as 'Value in Use' or 'VIU').

Example 2

A landlord owns a property currently worth £300,000 (market value). The rental inflow (VIU) expected from continued use of the property is projected to be £350,000. The recoverable amount is £350,000 (the higher of these amounts).

If in this example the property's carrying value was previously £400,000 then the property will have suffered an impairment of £50,000 (£400,000 − £350,000).

Purchased goodwill and other indefinite life assets

Unlike tangible fixed assets, purchased goodwill is subjected to annual impairment testing because it is considered to have an indefinite life and therefore not subject to amortisation (see **Chapter 10 Goodwill and other intangibles**).

Because goodwill only arises on the purchase of one business by another, goodwill impairment testing involves the comparison of the latest cash flows for the acquired business to the cash flow forecasts prepared to support the carrying value of goodwill at the time of acquisition.

Should there be an impairment in the value of the acquired business, the goodwill asset is eliminated first with any further amount to be written down allocated on a pro-rata basis against remaining assets.

Example 3

D Ltd acquired the ABC business at the start of the year for £250,000. The fair value of the assets at acquisition was £200,000. Goodwill on acquisition is £50,000 recognised in the books of the buyer.

Following the latest impairment test, the VIU of ABC is estimated at £180,000.

The impairment loss of £70,000 (£250,000 − £180,000) is allocated first to goodwill and then to the remaining assets, as follows:

Goodwill = £0 (£50,000 − £50,000)

Other assets = £180,000 (£200,000 − £20,000).

Nice to know

Because impairment results in a lower carrying value of an asset, depreciation or amortisation charges are based on the (lower) carrying value in the balance sheet and will be lower following any impairment.

In practice

Impairment tests compare the carrying value of an individual asset to the recoverable amount of that asset. VIU forecasts should be based on cash flows generated by that asset. In practice it is very difficult to assign future earnings or cash flows to a *single* asset. Even a small business such as a car repair centre, whose assets might only comprise a garage, plant and equipment would find it difficult to identify the cash flows generated by each asset individually, i.e. to the exclusion of other assets of the business. The VIU of assets are typically considered together as a 'cash generating unit' (CGU).

Impairment testing is typically carried out on a CGU basis because this represents the smallest collection of assets that generate an income stream.

Any resulting impairment is allocated to the CGU's assets *proportionately.*

Example 4

ABC is a motor garage with assets totaling £200,000 (comprising building £180,000, plant and equipment £20,000). The value in use (recoverable amount) is estimated at £180,000.

The impairment loss is £20,000 (£200,000 − £180,000).

The impairment is allocated against assets in *proportion* to their carrying value, as follows:

Asset	Carrying value	Impairment loss	Recoverable amount (i.e. net of impairment loss)
Building (90 %)	£180,000	£18,000	£162,000
Plant and equipment (10 %)	£20,000	£2,000	£18,000
Total	£200,000	£20,000	£180,000

Optional detail

If an asset subsequently recovers in value then impairment losses can be reversed (although these are subject to certain limits).

In the case of goodwill, any impairment loss, once recognised, can never be reversed.

Where to spot in company accounts

See the basis of preparation note (under accounting policies).

Extract from Greggs plc accounts 2015

> **(b) Basis of preparation (continued)**
>
> *Impairment of property, plant and equipment*
>
> Property, plant and equipment is reviewed for impairment if events or changes in circumstances indicate that the carrying value may not be recoverable. For example, bakery equipment may be impaired if it is no longer in use and/or shop fittings may be impaired if sales in that shop fall. When a review for impairment is conducted the recoverable amount is estimated based on value-in-use calculations which include management's estimates of future cash flows generated by the assets and an appropriate discount rate. Consideration is also given to whether the impairment assessments made in prior years remain appropriate based on the latest expectations in respect of value-in-use and recoverable value. Where it is concluded that the impairment has reduced a reversal of the impairment is recorded. The sensitivities for growth rate, discount rate and lease term have been considered and are deemed not significant. For instance, a two% change in the growth rate would result in a £43,000 change in the impairment charge.

Watch out for in practice

- By their very nature, forecasts and discount rates are subject to uncertainty. Forecasts cannot be verified and are therefore open to potential manipulation by management. A small change in the discount rate used can significantly impact VIU calculations and therefore impairment.

- Discount rates and sensitivity to changes in discount rates.

- Forecast cash flows and assumptions underlying preparation.

- Changes in key assumptions from year-to-year forecast turnover.

- Amount of annual and cumulative impairments.

- Reasons stated in annual report for impairments.

- If goodwill has been impaired (indicates the success of acquisitions).

four

Financial and regulatory environment

19 Accounting and financial reporting standards

'There are no accounting issues, no trading issues, no reserve issues, no previously unknown problem issues.'

Kenneth Lay, former chairman, Enron LLC

In a nutshell

Accounting standards, also known as financial reporting standards, are rules and guidelines that set out how transactions should be recorded and presented in financial statements. 'Standard' means the expected or preferred way of accounting.

To interpret or compare company performance requires an understanding of the accounting treatments used in preparing financial statements. The accounting policy note included in financial statements typically summarises the accounting standards applied by a company in preparing its financial statements.

Comparing company performance without first understanding the accounting policies applied by each may lead to wrong conclusions about relative performance. For example, a company revaluing its fixed assets will have a lower gearing ratio to one recording fixed assets at purchase cost even where the companies have similar assets.

There is currently no single set of standards in use around the world, which makes international company comparisons more difficult. Attempts have been made in the past to converge standards globally, but this objective still remains elusive.

Need to know

The requirement for companies to apply accounting standards can best be understood within the context of director responsibilities. In the UK directors have an overall responsibility to ensure the 'truth and fairness' of financial statements (see **Chapter 20 External financial audit**). While this term is not defined in law, it would almost certainly be the case that a failure to comply with accounting standards, without adequate explanation, would raise concerns about whether accounts were true and fair. Where directors do not comply with accounting standards, they must as a minimum explain their reasons for not doing so. Failure to comply could result in a qualified audit report (see **Chapter 20 External financial audit**).

Why is this important?

Investors and financiers need to make informed assessments about a company's financial health. Financial information (historic and current profits, dividends, cash flows, etc.) helps investors and lenders to make decisions of whether to invest, how much to invest, etc. Accounting standards provide the financial ground rules for how transactions should be recorded.

Standards help to ensure companies provide *comparable* information and in a manner that fairly represents their performance and financial strength. Standards limit the freedom and flexibility of companies to use 'clever' accounting techniques that might otherwise enable them to hide or be creative with how to record transactions.

Companies can get involved in quite complex transactions and therefore standards are highly unlikely to eliminate entirely the risk of clever accounting or fraud. In the case of Enron (a US energy company) for example, loopholes in the US accounting standards framework in the early 2000s enabled the company to hide the extent of the company's debt and borrowings through a complex web of transactions. The failure to disclose the extent of the company's debt resulted in one of the biggest corporate failures of all time.

When is this important?

UK standards have been developed over many decades as regulators have continuously sought to improve the quality of financial reporting.

In the UK non-listed companies can adopt local (i.e. national) UK financial reporting standards (FRS) or international accounting/ financial reporting standards (IFRS). Listed companies *must* apply IFRS when preparing group accounts (see **Chapter 16 Group accounting**). The requirement to use IFRS makes international comparisons simpler as many countries around the world mandate the use of IFRS.

Interestingly only a minority of non-listed companies in the UK have chosen to adopt IFRS despite the advantage of comparability that a single set of global standards should bring about. It is thought the costs of switching to IFRS (including technically retraining accountants, auditors and re-educating readers) are the main reason for continuing with local standards

Nevertheless, since 2009, all new or revised FRS have been issued with an explicit objective of closer alignment ('convergence') with IFRS.

'Standards' versus choice

Perhaps surprisingly, many standards still permit choice over how to reflect accounting transactions even though this may appear to contradict the very notion of creating a 'standard' in the first place. The justification is that companies should have the choice of alternative accounting treatments where they are *equally meaningful* to users of accounts, provided there is appropriate disclosure of the impact of the accounting treatment adopted. For example, IAS 16 gives the choice of including land and buildings at (original) cost *or* market valuation. Two companies could own similar fixed assets but hold them at different values in the balance sheet, i.e. one company adopts *historic cost* and the second uses *market values*. Where choice is permitted standards require sufficient disclosures to enable direct comparisons to be made. In this case, the financial impact of adopting market values would need to be disclosed by the second company.

Companies are required to state their compliance or otherwise with accounting standards. Where a company does *not* comply with one or more standards, the reasons for departure have to be explained. Where the auditors concur with the directors' reasons for departure and disclosures, there is no audit qualification (see **Chapter 20 External financial audit**).

Nice to know

Over the past decade or so, 140+ countries, including the UK, have signed up to using international accounting standards commonly referred to as IFRS or IAS (International Accounting Standards). There are currently around 40 international standards. IFRS are developed and issued by the IASB (International Accounting Standards Board). IAS were issued by a predecessor body and a number of these standards continue to be relevant.

IFRS adoption in many countries around the world has enhanced comparability and understandability of company performance. However, and most notably, US companies adopt local US GAAP (Generally Accepted Accounting Principles). Interpreting financial performance and making international company comparisons with US companies remains a challenge. For example, Exxon Mobil (a US company) applies US GAAP whereas Shell plc (an Anglo-Dutch company) uses IFRS. Despite both operating in the oil industry, a comparison between these companies requires extensive adjustments to enable meaningful performance comparisons.

Convergence to a single set of worldwide standards is driven by the view that having a single set of accounting requirements will increase the comparability of company performance and help contribute to the flow of international investment.

Since 2002, the IASB and FASB (Financial Accounting Standards Board) in the US have been working together towards 'convergence' of IFRS and US GAAP standards although this process has notably stalled somewhat since 2012.

Optional detail

IFRS versus US GAAP

IFRS and US GAAP differ in their underlying conceptual frameworks: IFRS is *principles*-based whereas US GAAP is *rules*-based.

In a principles-based framework, different treatments of similar transactions may be permitted where they are considered appropriate. A principles-based approach therefore requires disclosures to enable a reader to understand the impact of applying an alternative to the standard treatment proposed.

A rules-based approach is based on having a comprehensive rulebook. More rules are added to respond to new or emerging accounting issues or to permit exceptions to standard accounting treatments.

Where to spot in company accounts

The *accounting policies* note is included in the financial statements and typically shown after the primary statements (profit and loss, balance sheet and cash flow statement).

The notes to the accounts may provide further detail of the accounting treatments adopted.

Watch out for in practice

The accounting standards adopted, e.g. US GAAP, IFRS or UK GAAP, other local country GAAP. Reported profit will be directly influenced by the standards regime adopted.

Differences in accounting policies adopted by companies operating in the same industry, e.g. cost versus revaluation accounting for fixed assets. The accounts should contain sufficient disclosures to make performance comparisons between companies adopting different policies.

Changes in accounting policy and impact on performance reward targets set for managers, e.g. costs of 'borrowing' to buy a fixed asset are capitalised instead of expensed. This treatment would improve profitability and ROCE ratios (see **Chapter 23 Profitability performance measures**).

The impact of new or revised accounting standards on key financial ratios or performance reward targets set for managers, e.g. a new standard on lease accounting (IFRS 16, issued January 2016) will likely have a significant (adverse) impact on a company's gearing ratios and ROCE. IFRS 16 requires all leases to be capitalised with the result that companies will have to recognise the liability (and asset) in respect of all leases.

For companies with loan covenants calculated on debt levels, the introduction of IFRS 16 could lead to covenant breaches.

20 External financial audit

'They were auditing us, and if something was wrong I figured somebody would say something to me.'

Kelvin Sampson, head coach, Houston Cougars

In a nutshell

An *external audit* is an external examination of a company's financial statements carried out by independent auditors. Auditors are qualified professionals, appointed annually by shareholders to provide an independent opinion on whether the financial statements present a true and fair view.

An audit gives shareholders confidence that the numbers reported in the balance sheet and profit and loss account are true and fair. Auditors must be independent not only of the directors (who have responsibility for the financial statements) but also they must have no vested interest in the performance of the business, for example through holding shares.

An 'unqualified' audit report confirms that the financial statements are, in the opinion of auditors, true and fair. Modified reports highlight auditor issues or concerns with the numbers and/or disclosures made within the financial statements.

Need to know

All UK companies except dormant companies (see **Chapter 21 Information in the public domain**) must prepare financial statements. However, not all require an audit. As part of the government's drive to reduce the administrative burden on business, companies defined as 'small' (other than public limited companies (plcs) or those involved in banking and insurance) are exempt from requiring an audit (see **Chapter 21 Information in the public domain**).

According to UK Government statistics, small businesses accounted for over 99% of all private sector businesses at the start of 2016. Despite this, many small companies still have an audit each year, even though they are not legally required to be audited. In fact, considerably more than 2 % of companies are audited annually. Commercial requirements, imposed for example by banks as part of their lending criteria, result in companies having to engage auditors even where there is no legal requirement to do so.

Why and when is this important?

While an audit provides no guarantee that the numbers are correct, it gives credibility to financial statements by providing independent assurance on the numbers and disclosures.

The audit report is prepared solely for a company's shareholders ('members') as a body rather than any individual shareholder. Other interested parties known as 'stakeholders' (lenders, creditors, etc.) need to be aware of the limitations the audit.

Misunderstandings relating to the statutory audit are commonplace and collectively referred to as the 'expectations gap', the gap between what readers consider to be the purpose of an audit and the reality. Some of the common misconceptions are covered below.

Fraud

Fraud is intentional deception with a view to gaining personal advantage.

If company directors (or other employees) wish to perpetrate fraud by, say, hiding or manipulating transactions then they will probably have a good chance of success as the auditors are unlikely to be able to uncover carefully concealed frauds. Directors have *primary* responsibility to report company results faithfully and are responsible for preventing or detecting fraud and error in the company.

Auditors can be held legally liable where they have conspired with company directors to defraud investors. They may also be sued for breach of contract where they have not carried out the audit properly, i.e. in accordance with relevant auditing standards and guidelines. Auditors can face civil liability for negligence if they do not exercise due care in the conduct of the audit. As regulated professionals, they can also face disciplinary action by their Institute (regulator) where they have failed to demonstrate competence and due care.

Errors

Errors are the result of unintentional mistakes, for example a bank crediting the wrong customer account with a receipt. A statutory audit provides only 'reasonable assurance' that the financial statements do not contain errors, i.e. an audit provides no *guarantee* against fraud or errors.

This is because auditors typically only sample-check transactions when forming their opinions, which means that there is always a risk of errors remaining undetected. Consider the volume of transactions (loans, deposits, cash withdrawals, inter-branch and worldwide activity) relating to Barclays during the course of a single *day* (let alone a year!) and it should be quite clear why it would be impossible to check the authenticity of every transaction occurring at every branch of Barclays bank for the year.

Going concern

Financial statements are prepared on the (default) assumption that a company will continue into the future, known as *going concern*, a period of at least 12 months from the date the accounts are signed. An audit, however, does not guarantee the future financial health of the company.

An audit primarily focuses on checking transactions relating to *past* activity with only a limited focus on the future. It is the responsibility of the directors of companies to satisfy themselves that their strategy is appropriate and that the business is financed adequately to deliver that strategy into the future.

The auditor will review the assumptions used by directors in drawing their conclusion that the going concern basis of preparation is appropriate. Where the auditor concludes that these assumptions are reasonable then no further action is taken (see **Chapter 25 Insolvency and going concern risk**).

In practice

Banks, lenders, creditors and shareholders evidently still place value on independently audited financial statements, despite the limitations of an audit. Banks for example will typically require audited company accounts as a condition of a loan agreement. Where an organisation is seeking to obtain new loan funding, a history of audited financial statements provides a higher level of assurance than unaudited statements.

If an investor is considering which of a number of potential companies to invest in, a company with a history of audited accounts may make it a more credible investment opportunity. An independent review of the financial statements may also provide comfort to directors especially where they have not been involved in the detailed preparation of the numbers. Accounts prepared by a company's internal finance team reviewed by an impartial auditor could highlight errors or system weaknesses that might otherwise go undetected. Companies looking to supply services into the public sector have to follow a strict government tender process, with a higher weighting or score typically attributed to audited accounts.

Nice to know

There is no formal definition of *true and fair* even though it is a legal term. It is interpreted to mean that the accounts are free from material misstatements and faithfully represent the financial performance and position of the entity. Determining whether financial statements are true and fair is ultimately a professional judgement left to auditors although checking that financial statements comply with accounting standards and company law are relevant considerations.

Larger companies typically also have an internal audit function. Internal audits differ in nature, purpose and scope to an external audit. The scope and purpose of an internal audit is determined by the company and work may be undertaken by staff employed by the company. The focus of internal audit includes testing (and making recommendations for improvements to) systems and controls in a business, fraud investigations or looking for efficiency improvements. External auditors may seek to rely on work carried by internal audit although this is typically restricted to non-judgemental areas or areas considered low risk by the external auditor.

Optional detail

Audit modifications

Modifications comprise audit report 'qualifications', 'adverse' or 'disclaimer' opinions.

Qualifications

With a qualified opinion the auditor is basically stating that there are, or could be, material misstatements, but they are confined to a specific element (e.g. number or disclosure) of the financial statements.

An auditor will issue a qualification in their audit report because of:

1 *Disagreement*: when the financial statements include a matter that does not comply with generally accepted accounting principles but the rest of the financial statements are fairly stated. For example, if the accounts do not include the depreciation expense related to its motor vehicles, the profit and loss account will overstate profit.

2 *Uncertainty*: where the auditor has been *unable* to obtain sufficient appropriate evidence about a matter in the financial statements but this limitation does not apply to the rest of the audit. For example, if the auditor was unable to obtain sufficient evidence to confirm physical quantities of stock held by the business at its year end there will be uncertainty over the stock balance included in the accounts.

The auditor qualifies their opinion by including a 'Basis for Modification' section in the audit report to explain the matter(s) giving rise to the modification.

The audit opinion paragraph will include the words 'except for' or 'except for ... might', to highlight the disagreement or uncertainty in each specific area of the financial statements. These words are used to indicate that, but for the matters raised, the financial statements give a true and fair view.

Adverse opinion

An adverse opinion is a very severe (pervasive) disagreement and is issued when the disagreement is so significant that the financial statements are *not* true and fair. For example, where a company has prepared accounts on a going concern basis but the auditor has concluded that the basis of preparation is not appropriate, they will state in their opinion that the financial statements 'do not give a true and fair view'.

Disclaimer

A disclaimer is a very severe (pervasive) form of uncertainty. It results in an auditor being unable to form an audit opinion. For example, where directors refuse to provide the auditor with information and explanations they require to undertake the audit. In this situation, the auditor is unable to complete the audit and therefore does not express an opinion on the financial statements.

Going concern

(See also **Chapter 25 Insolvency and going concern risk**)

Company accounts must include a statement setting out the directors' judgements about the ability of the company to continue operating into the foreseeable future (a period defined as being at least 12 months after the date the financial statements are signed by the directors). Directors state whether it is considered appropriate to continue preparing the financial statements on the basis that the company is a going concern.

This statement is reviewed by auditors and referenced in the audit report. Where the auditor concurs with the directors' disclosure then there are no changes necessary to the audit report.

However, where directors raise doubts about the viability of the business, the directors need to explain the uncertainty in the financial statements. For example, a company may be subject to a significant lawsuit and this could affect its future ability to continue in business. In this situation the directors would be required to make further disclosures including details of the lawsuit and its potential adverse impact on the continuity of the business. Where the auditor agrees with the adequacy and accuracy of these disclosures the audit report would be unqualified. However, it would contain an additional 'emphasis of matter' paragraph to highlight the existence of the uncertainty. The inclusion of this paragraph within the audit report is designed to draw the readers' attention to the material uncertainty.

Should the auditors *disagree* with the directors' disclosures regarding going concern, they will issue an adverse opinion (see above).

Where to spot in company accounts

The audit report is included in the annual report and accounts:

Independent auditor's report to the members of Greggs plc only (extract, see appendix)

Opinions and conclusions arising from our audit

1 Our opinion on the accounts is unmodified.

We have audited the accounts of Greggs plc for the 52 weeks ended 2 January 2016 set out on pages 70 to 99. In our opinion:

- the accounts give a true and fair view of the state of the Group's and of the Parent Company's affairs as at 2 January 2016 and of the Group's profit for the year then ended;
- the Group accounts have been properly prepared in accordance with International Financial Reporting Standards as adopted by the European Union (IFRSs as adopted by the EU);
- the Parent Company accounts have been properly prepared in accordance with IFRSs as adopted by the EU and as applied in accordance with the provisions of the Companies Act 2006; and
- the accounts have been prepared in accordance with the requirements of the Companies Act 2006 and, as regards the Group accounts, Article 4 of the IAS Regulation.

Watch out for in practice

Qualified audit opinions and reason(s) for qualifying.

Note, audit qualifications are quite rare in practice as errors identified during the audit will be corrected by directors by making appropriate adjustments to the financial statements.

Where an audit report for a company is qualified, it is important to read through the audit report to understand the reasons for the qualification, i.e. whether the qualification has arisen because of a *disagreement* with the directors or because of an *uncertainty* such as the non-availability of independent evidence to confirm a transaction or balance.

Qualifications highlight auditor concerns with information presented in financial statements and the directors will likely be required to defend their position in the face of questions from shareholders and other stakeholders.

Whether a qualification has impacted share price negatively? (A number of studies from around the world suggest there is little evidence of a share price effect when accounts with qualified audit reports are published.)

21 Information in the public domain

'It is much more convenient not to be a public company. As a private company you don't have to give information to the public...'

Marc Rich, Glencore plc

In a nutshell

Unlike sole traders and partners in partnerships, companies are limited liabilities. This means that the owners can only lose the money put into the business, and nothing else.

In return for the benefits of limited liability a company must disclose information about its activities including its management and ownership structure, its directors and shareholdings. It must also file its financial statements ('accounts'), although only the largest companies have to submit *statutory accounts annually,* disclosing extensive financial information about the company's affairs.

This information must be filed in the public domain and is available to view at Companies House (CH) in the UK. Companies must inform CH if there are changes to the information it holds and must file a **confirmation statement** annually that the information that CH holds is correct.

Directors are legally responsible for submitting information to CH within statutory filing deadlines.

Need to know

All companies (except dormant companies) must prepare financial statements, known also as 'statutory accounts' for shareholders and for tax authorities (HMRC in the UK).

The amount of financial information disclosed depends on the size of the company (see **Optional detail** section below). In general terms, the smaller the company, the less disclosure required.

PLCs and the largest companies are required to file *full* statutory accounts. Full accounts comprise a detailed profit and loss account, balance sheet, cash flow statement plus notes to the accounts.

Other companies can maintain a degree of confidentiality by filing *abridged* accounts (containing less financial disclosure). In the smallest companies, there is no requirement to file a profit and loss account.

Accounts sent to shareholders have to comply with all relevant accounting standards and Companies Act requirements (see **Chapter 19 Accounting and financial reporting standards** and **Chapter 20 External financial audit**).

Why and when is this important?

The preparation of accounts is the responsibility of directors. Accounts must be filed within statutory deadlines depending on the company:

- **Public limited companies:** Accounts must be filed within six months after the company's year end (known as the accounting reference date).
- **Private limited companies:** Accounts must be filed within nine months after the accounting reference date.

A director's residential address must be provided to Companies House. However, it will be placed on public record only if it is used as the company's registered office or director's service address.

It is important to note that CH has no restrictions on the way in which information can be used. Directors who therefore use their home address as their registered office may receive unsolicited mail and visits from creditors. Mortgage or insurance agreements may explicitly prevent or restrict the use of a home address for business purposes and lenders may routinely scrutinise publicly available information to confirm there has been no breach.

Not filing accounts or the confirmation statement is a criminal offence and can result in directors being fined personally in criminal proceedings. Note this is *in addition to* late filing penalties imposed against the company for filing accounts late.

Companies House can take steps to strike off a company from the public record where the accounts or confirmation statement are delivered late.

Nice to know

Filed information remains on public record, i.e. in the public domain indefinitely while the company is active.

Changes to information are shown under the company's filing history.

Directors' remuneration

Directors' remuneration is an area of interest in particular for public listed companies.

Disclosures depend on the size and nature of the company:

- Small unquoted companies do not have to disclose director remuneration unless the total of all remuneration paid to directors exceeds £200,000, in which case details of the highest paid director must be disclosed in the filed accounts. The identity of the highest paid director does not have to be disclosed.

- Listed companies must provide detailed disclosures relating to each director as required by Stock Exchange Listing Rules. In summary, to provide transparency, a single figure for *total* remuneration must be reported in the accounts for each director. This figure must show the total remuneration paid to each director howsoever it has been 'paid' (i.e. whether salary, bonus, long-term incentive or pension).

Optional detail

Size and disclosure requirements

Size limits as per June 2016 Companies House guidance:

Type of company and threshold	Dormant – a company with: No significant accounting transactions during the accounting period	Very small (Micro) company – defined by size thresholds:	Small company – defined by (higher) size thresholds	Publicly listed companies and other large companies
		▪ Turnover not more than £632,000 ▪ Balance sheet total not more than £316,000 ▪ Number of employees not more than 10	▪ Turnover not more than £6.5m ▪ Balance sheet total not more than £3.26m ▪ Number of employees not more than 50	
Filing disclosures	▪ No directors' report ▪ No profit and loss account ▪ Balance sheet ▪ Specific dormant balance sheet note disclosures	▪ No directors' report ▪ No profit and loss account ▪ Summary balance sheet ▪ Additional notes or disclosures not required	▪ Full accounts excluding directors' report and excluding profit and loss account ▪ Abridged* balance sheet option permitted ▪ * Abridged = certain disclosures combined	Full accounts comprising: ▪ Directors' report ▪ Profit and loss account ▪ Balance sheet ▪ Notes to the accounts
Audit requirements	Audit not required			Audit required (see **Chapter 20 External financial audit**)

Accounts sent to shareholders	Must also include directors' report	Full accounts required but *simplified* disclosures under the FRSSE (Financial Reporting Standard for Smaller Entities)	Full accounts required but *simplified* disclosures under the FRSSE (Financial Reporting Standard for Smaller Entities)	Full accounts required
Accounts sent to HMRC	No tax return required so no accounts required (HMRC write every five years to verify dormant status)	Same as version sent to shareholders		

Note: A 20 per cent uplift is applied on the above thresholds for turnover and balance sheet totals for groups (see **Chapter 16 Group accounting**).

Publicly available information at Companies House

Information available includes the following:

- Directors' details (see below) plus changes in directors (appointments and resignations)
- Company secretary details (if relevant)
- Registered office address
- Company status
- Company type
- Nature of business
- Filing history
- Details of persons with significant control (greater than 25% of shares held)
- Share capital (how many shares the company has in issue)
- Names of shareholders and shareholdings.

Directors – personal details held in the public domain

- Full name
- Date of birth (month and year only)

- Nationality
- Occupation
- Country of residence
- Correspondence address (residential or other).

Where to spot in company accounts

Key dates

Event	Where this information can be found	Greggs plc
Accounts approved by directors	See date of approval included on Balance Sheet	1 March 2016
Accounts filed at CH	Date accounts filed is recorded at CH website	15 June 2016
Accounts sent to shareholders		'Late March' – Greggs plc financial calendar

- The balance sheet shows the date when the accounts were approved and signed.
- Date accounts filed at Companies House is recorded at the CH website.
- Date accounts sent to shareholders – see 'financial calendar' included in most company accounts.

Directors' remuneration

Details included in the 'remuneration report' within the accounts.

Greggs plc, 2015 (extract from directors' remuneration report)

Remuneration payable for 2015 for each Executive Director (Audited)

The following table presents the remuneration payable for 2015 (showing the equivalent figures for 2014) for the Executive Directors:

	Salary £	Pension contribution (including salary in lieu) £	Taxable benefits £	Annual incentives (including profit share) £	Long-term incentives* £	Total remuneration £
Roger Whiteside						
2015	507,188	114,118	12,397	594,043	1,357,891	2,585,637
2014	495,300	111,442	12,381	619,125	–	1,238,248
Richard Hutton						
2015	289,736	37,233	13,659	244,334	493,628	1,078,590
2014	282,944	52,508	11,491	254,650	141,043	742,636
Raymond Reynolds						
2015	258,530	31,804	13,949	218,019	440,465	962,767
2014	252,472	31,060	12,433	227,225	125,858	649,048

Watch out for in practice

- Trading history.
- Changes in directors.
- Changes in share ownership.
- Change in address.
- Changes in capital structure.
- Changes in articles of association.
- Age of company.
- Pattern of previous filing dates (e.g. for listed companies, a delay may indicate the existence of significant issues preventing filing).

22 Corporate governance and whistleblowing

'The real mechanism for corporate governance is the active involvement of the owners.'

Louis Gerstner Jr, former CEO and chairman IBM

In a nutshell

Corporate governance refers to the system by which companies are managed (i.e. directed and controlled). 'Good' corporate governance systems prevent directors from making and taking decisions that benefit themselves to the detriment of shareholders and others.

Countries around the world have developed corporate governance regulations. In the UK, guidance is focused on directors (leadership, effectiveness and remuneration), board accountability (risks and going concern) and relations with shareholders ('stewardship'). Guidance also covers disclosure of information and potential conflicts of interest.

Whistleblowing is an important aspect of good corporate governance. *Whistleblowing* is the reporting of wrongdoing (fraud, illegality or unethical practice) in an organisation. A whistleblower bringing information to the attention of their employer or a relevant organisation is protected (in certain circumstances) under the Public Interest Disclosure Act 1998.

Need to know

Corporate governance

Corporate governance is a key issue whenever there is separation between a company's ownership and control.

In *public* companies (plcs) directors appointed to *run* a company are usually different to shareholders who *own* the company. This is an agency relationship in which shareholders, who typically have no involvement in the day to day running of the business, have to rely on directors ('agents') to use their expertise to run the company for the benefit of the shareholders. This agency relationship creates a risk that directors may take decisions that are in their own interests rather than the interests of shareholders.

In the UK, Corporate governance guidelines have been developed over many years and are mainly applicable to listed companies. They aim to ensure the interests of directors and shareholders are aligned.

The UK Corporate Governance Code (the Code) covers the requirements for listed companies.

The Code contains *principles* and *provisions* with listed companies required to report:

1   How they have applied the main *principles* of the Code.
2   Whether they have complied with the *provisions* of the Code. An explanation is required where they have not.

There is no requirement for private companies to follow the Code although they are encouraged to do so, particularly large private companies in the public eye such as BHS, the former UK fashion and homeware retailer which became insolvent in 2016. Private companies, even those that are majority or fully owned by directors, are strongly encouraged to comply with governance guidance because of the impact that insolvency can have on stakeholder groups (employees, customers, government, etc.).

Whistleblowing

The Code includes a requirement for boards to consider their whistleblowing procedures.

Whistleblowers are protected under law where a disclosure is made for the public interest. This protection is designed to encourage workers to speak out if they find malpractice in their organisation. The Public Interest Disclosure Act (PIDA) 1998 protects workers from detrimental treatment or victimisation from their employer when they blow the whistle on wrongdoing.

Why is this important?

The requirements of the Code have been shaped in response to past corporate failures. A statement of compliance by directors should give investors confidence that they are operating in the best interests of the shareholders.

Numerous company collapses have shaped the principles set out in the Code. High-profile UK corporate collapses included Maxwell Communications and Polly Peck in the early 1990s and Northern Rock and RBS during the financial crisis of the late 2000s. The more recent collapse of BHS has also in part been attributed to (poor) corporate governance in the organisation.

In practice

Compliance with the principles and provisions of the Code is not a legal requirement. Company directors are expected to *comply* with the recommendations or *explain* why they have decided not to. The Code is not a panacea for success nor is it a substitute for business strategy. Neither does non-compliance with one or more provisions indicate that the business will fail or suffer impropriety.

In fact, according to Grant Thornton, only 57 % of UK FTSE 350 companies were fully compliant with the Code in 2015. Thirty per cent of those not complying did not give a good explanation of why they had chosen not to comply.

Compliance with the Code is intended to give investors confidence and reassurance that the company and its directors are running the business in accordance with what might be considered 'best practice' guidance.

Nice to know

History and approach

The UK Code represents a consolidation of over a quarter of a century of developments and learning in corporate governance. Numerous committees have made recommendations covering how a company (the board) should be directed and managed, recommendations surrounding directors' compensation, strengthening financial reporting and audit, and dealings with shareholders (see **Optional detail** section below).

The UK Code is written as a set of principles, to recognise and reflect that every business is unique and a 'one size fits all' implementation of the Code would not work. Companies are expected to follow the Code or explain in their annual report those areas where they have decided not to do so. The UK Code requires a company to adhere to the 'spirit' rather than necessarily every letter of the Code. A principles-based approach enables greater flexibility to apply what is written to meet the requirements of a business and avoids the need to be overly prescriptive.

This 'comply versus explain' approach is different from the US approach which requires US listed companies to follow a rules-based approach (known as 'Sarbox' or 'Sarbanes–Oxley'). A rules-based approach instils the code into law, i.e. the rules are a legal requirement. While there is greater clarity, flexibility is lost as there is no choice to apply the rules in a way that best reflects the nature of the organisation (e.g. its size or stage of development).

Main board and committees

The UK Code requires a board of directors to be made up of 'executive' directors and 'non-executive' directors (NEDs). Executive directors are responsible for the day to day running of the board whereas non-executive directors have no day to day responsibility. Non-executive directors should be independent outsiders appointed to represent the interests of shareholders. Independence means the directors should have no financial or other interests in the business (except fees agreed for their work) and therefore do not stand to gain from decisions taken by the business. In effect the purpose of non-executive directors is to be the eyes and ears of shareholders in the boardroom. NEDs in effect exist to bridge the ownership versus control (agency) disconnect.

Companies run the business by holding 'main' board meetings attended by all directors (executive and non-executive). The main board is where key decisions are taken. All directors are collectively responsible for decisions and actions taken by the company.

The Code recommends the main board be supplemented by three committees. Each is given authority by the main board to focus on specific aspects of corporate governance. The main purpose of each committee is summarised below:

Committee	Main purpose	Composition
Nomination committee	Evaluate the balance of skills, experience, independence and knowledge on the board, lead the process for board appointments	Majority independent non-executive directors
Audit committee	Ensure the integrity of a company's financial statements	Minimum three independent non-executive directors. At least one director should have recent and relevant financial experience
Remuneration committee	Determine pay of executive directors	At least three independent non-executive directors

Note that the main board is not prevented from setting up other committees it may consider necessary. For example, many companies have an *executive* committee made up of the chief executive plus those who report directly to him/her.

Selected principles and provisions

Principle	Provision
	Chairman versus Chief Executive
Clear division of responsibilities between the running of the board and the running of the company's business. No one individual should have unfettered powers of decision-making.	Roles of chairman and chief executive should not be exercised by same individual.
	Executive versus Non-Executive Directors
The board and committees should have the appropriate balance of skills, experience, independence and knowledge to discharge their duties and responsibilities effectively.	At least half the board should comprise independent non-executive directors.

Principle	Provision
	Board appointments
There should be a formal, rigorous and transparent procedure for the appointment of new directors to the board.	There should be a nomination committee which should lead the process for board appointments. A majority of the nomination committee should be independent non-executive directors.
	Accounts
Board should present a fair, balanced and understandable assessment of the company's position and prospects.	In annual and half-yearly financial statements, the directors should state whether they considered it appropriate to adopt the going concern basis and identify material uncertainties to the company's ability to continue over a period of at least 12 months from the date of approval of the financial statements (see **Chapter 25 Insolvency and going concern risk**).
	Business risks
Board is responsible for determining the nature and extent of the principal risks it is willing to take in achieving its strategic objectives. The board should maintain sound risk management and internal control systems.	Directors confirm in the annual report that they have carried out a robust assessment of the principal risks facing the company, including those that would threaten its business model, future performance, solvency or liquidity. The directors should describe those risks and explain how they are being managed or mitigated.
	Audit committee and auditors
Board should establish formal transparent arrangements for considering how they should apply corporate reporting and risk management and internal control principles, and for maintaining appropriate relationship with auditors.	Audit committee (AC) should review arrangements by which staff may, in confidence, raise concerns about possible improprieties in matters of financial reporting/other. AC objective should be to ensure arrangements are in place for proportionate and independent investigation of matters and for appropriate follow-up action.

(*continued*)

Principle	Provision
	Remuneration
There should be a formal and transparent procedure for developing policy on executive remuneration and for fixing remuneration packages of individual directors. No director should be involved in deciding his or her own remuneration.	Board should establish remuneration committee of at least three independent non-executive directors. Remuneration committee should have responsibility for setting remuneration for all executive directors and the chairman.
	Shareholder engagement
The board should use general meetings to communicate with investors and encourage their participation.	The chairman should arrange for the chairmen of the audit, remuneration and nomination committees to be available to answer questions at the AGM and for all directors to attend.

Optional detail

Whistleblowing

Whistleblowers are not protected in all situations of disclosure. Workers are protected only if they make what are known as qualifying disclosures in the public interest. Qualifying disclosures are disclosures of information where a worker reasonably believes that one or more of the following matters has happened, is taking place, or is likely to happen in the future:

- a criminal offence;
- the breach of a legal obligation;
- a miscarriage of justice;
- a danger to the health and safety of any individual;
- damage to the environment;
- deliberate attempt to conceal any of the above.

A worker should make a disclosure to their employer first, or if they feel unable to follow the organisation's procedure the disclosure should be made to a relevant prescribed person. A prescribed person is a person or body included on the prescribed persons list (published by the Department for Business, Innovation and Skills) and includes, for example MPs, Ofsted (education services), Care Quality Commission (health and social care services), and the Information Commissioner (data protection issues).

Stewardship Code

According to the Office for National Statistics (ONS), only 12 % of FTSE shares are owned by individuals. Institutional shareholders such as pension funds, insurance companies, banks and investment trusts (many of which invest in shares on behalf of others) are more significant shareholders. Institutional investors have been criticised for being passive investors and not using their influence to look after the interests of their beneficiaries.

The Stewardship Code aims to encourage *institutional investors* (i.e. organisations that manage other people's money) to become more active in company matters. The Stewardship Code contains a set of principles and 'strongly encourages' institutional investors to disclose their level of compliance with the Code's principles.

Principles require institutional investors to:

- Monitor their investments.
- Have a clear policy on voting (and disclose their voting activity).
- Be willing to act collectively with other investors where appropriate.
- Establish clear guidelines on when and how they will escalate their activities as a method of protecting and enhancing shareholder value.
- Publicly disclose their policy on how they will discharge their stewardship responsibilities.
- Have a robust policy on managing conflicts of interest in relation to stewardship; this policy should be publicly disclosed.

UK Corporate Governance Code – history and development

Key committees in the development of the Code and their main purpose is summarised below:

Committee/Report	Purpose/Focus
Cadbury (1992)	Established the first Corporate Governance regime in the UK
Greenbury (1995)	Focus on directors' remuneration
Hampel (1998)	Review and consolidation (Combined Code)
Turnbull (1999)	Internal controls
Myners (2001)	Institutional investors
Higgs (2003)	Role and effectiveness of non-executive directors
Smith (2003)	Focus on auditors
Walker (2009)	Banking industry

Where to spot in company accounts

Look in the annual report for 'comply versus explain' disclosures in a section typically headed 'Governance'.

Extract of Greggs plc, 2015

The Company is subject to the UK Corporate Governance Code issued by the Financial Reporting Council. The edition of the Code issued in September 2014 applied throughout the 2015 financial year. This Governance report, together with information contained elsewhere within the Directors' report, describes how the relevant principles and provisions of the Governance Code were applied in 2015 and will be relevant to the Company for the 2016 financial year.

The Company was re-elected to the FTSE 350 index on 22 December 2014 and has remained a constituent of that index throughout 2015. The Company maintains a Premium listing on the London Stock Exchange.

The Board confirms that it was compliant with the Governance Code throughout the year, and all of the policies and terms of reference referred to in this report are available on the corporate website.

Watch out for in practice

Composition of the board and board committees.

Evidence of a risk report.

Non-compliance. Explanations given for not complying with the Code.

Monitoring websites such as the Pensions & Investment Research Consultants (PIRC) that give an independent perspective on how well a company is complying with the Code. PIRC make recommendations on how to vote at AGMs including whether to appoint/reappoint directors.

Assessing financial health

23 Profitability performance measures

> 'Profit is not the legitimate purpose of business. The legitimate purpose of business is to provide a product or service that people need and do it so well that it's profitable.'
>
> James Rouse, US real estate developer,
> civic activist and philanthropist

In a nutshell

Profit is often thought to be the main purpose of a business. However, even more important is the amount of profit relative to the investment required to generate that profit.

Therefore, return on investment, as opposed to profit alone, is a superior measure of commercial success.

To achieve long-run viability a business must ensure that its return on investment is greater than its cost of finance.

Need to know

Why is this important?

To achieve long-term success a business should regularly monitor its progress against profitability performance targets.

As profit generation requires investment, return on investment should be a primary financial performance measure for a business.

Three important profit-based performance measures are defined below:

1 Gross profit margin (GPM)

$$\text{Gross profit margin\%} = \frac{\text{Gross profit}}{\text{Revenue}} \times 100\,\%$$

Gross profit margin (GPM) measures the margin between price and direct costs.

If a business can increase its price or reduce its direct costs, then the GPM will increase.

GPM is different to 'absolute' gross profit. Although, selling more will increase gross profit in absolute terms, the gross margin may remain constant or fall depending on the rate that 'cost of sales' increases compared with sales.

2 Operating profit margin (OPM)

$$\text{Operating profit margin\%} = \frac{\text{Operating profit}}{\text{Revenue}} \times 100\,\%$$

Operating profit margin (OPM) measures the margin between price and all operating costs, both direct and indirect (overheads). It can be used to assess the ability of a business to control its costs.

If the OPM increases while the GPM remains the same, this means that the business is improving overhead control.

3 Return on investment (ROI)

$$\text{Return on investment\%} = \frac{\text{'Return'}}{\text{'Investment'}} \times 100\,\%$$

Return on investment (ROI) measures 'return' as a percentage of the 'investment' required to run the business which generated the 'return'.

- 'Return' is a relevant definition of profit, for example 'operating profit' or 'profit after tax'.
- 'Investment' is a relevant total taken from the balance sheet, for example 'net assets'.

See the **Optional detail** section below for more information on the definition of 'return' and 'investment'.

From an investment perspective this enables external stakeholders, such as shareholders to evaluate a business and benchmark it against other competing investments. For large and listed companies the ratio can be easily calculated from readily available public information and therefore ROI is a popular financial performance measure for analysts and investors.

For many businesses it makes sense to use the same financial performance measures internally, that are used to evaluate the business externally and therefore ROI is also a popular internal performance measure.

In practice

Maximising ROI

In practice businesses will use a combination of tactics to maximise their ROI such as:

- Increasing prices.
- Reducing direct costs.
- Controlling overheads.
- Lowering the cost of finance.
- Increasing activity (or volume) without proportionally increasing overheads.
- Minimising versus maximising investment.
- Changing the product, service or business mix.

Two of these practices are reviewed in more detail below.

Minimising versus maximising investment

Businesses can take a short-run or a long-run approach to maximising ROI.

On a short-term basis simply cutting back on investment, or letting it depreciate in value, will increase ROI. Consequently, businesses using this measure can sometimes inadvertently encourage short-term behaviour. ROI can be potentially manipulated through short-term decisions, which result in negative long-term consequences.

A more successful approach to maximising ROI is to focus on long-term returns. Actually making investments is the way to grow overall long-term profitability and thus ROI. For example, a business may invest in new retail outlets; plant and machinery; or research and development.

Changing the product, service or business mix

Adding new products, services or even acquiring new businesses, with higher ROIs will enable a business to boost its overall ROI.

The company Majestic Wine is a good example of both changing its business mix and minimising its future investment.

In 2015 Majestic Wine, a largely bricks-and-mortar wine retailer, acquired Naked Wines, an online wine retailer, for £70 million. Phil Wrigley, Majestic chairman, told the *Financial Times*: 'Their [Naked's] return on investment is about double the return on investment we get from opening new stores and we are going to slow down our store openings.' The acquisition price was contingent on return on investment targets set by Majestic.

Nice to know

Drivers of ROI

As a single ratio, ROI is simply a target. To be useful in managing a business, it should be divided into its component parts.

To analyse ROI's drivers, we can relate 'revenue' to both 'operating profit' and 'investment'. This creates the following two ratios:

1 Operating profit margin (OPM)

As covered earlier.

$$\text{Operating profit margin\%} = \frac{\text{Operating profit}}{\text{Revenue}} \times 100\%$$

2 Asset turnover (AT)

$$\text{Asset turnover (times)} = \frac{\text{Revenue}}{\text{Investment}}$$

AT looks at revenue in relation to investment. It measures utilisation of assets or activity. Although it is less well known than OPM, its contribution to ROI is as important as OPM. The following illustration uses 'operating profit' in the ROI formula. See the **Optional detail** section for other ways to calculate ROI.

To show the interrelationship altogether:

OPM	×	AT	=	ROI
$\dfrac{\text{Operating profit}}{\text{Revenue}}$	×	$\dfrac{\text{Revenue}}{\text{Investment}}$	=	$\dfrac{\text{Operating profit}}{\text{Investment}}$

Illustrative example

By using two contrasting examples we can see the interrelationship between the drivers of ROI and how there are different routes to improvement.

Assume that company A is a supermarket with low operating profit margins of say 3% and high asset turnover of say five times. This shows that a supermarket's route to success is through activity (or volume). Despite operating with low margins, supermarkets can be profitable and achieve a healthy ROI of say 15%. Increasing market share will increase revenue for any given investment. Note that attracting market share is often at the expense of operating margin (through lower prices) so, in reality, there is a trade-off here.

OPM	×	AT	=	ROI
3%	×	5	=	15%

Assume that company B is a heavy manufacturer with high profit margins of say 25% and a low asset turnover of say 0.6 times. A heavy manufacturer requires considerable investment in plant and machinery and therefore their route to success is through their profit margins. This enables company B to achieve a ROI of 15%, comparable to company A.

$$\begin{array}{ccccc} \text{OPM} & \times & \text{AT} & = & \text{ROI} \\ 25\% & \times & 0.6 & = & 15\% \end{array}$$

The examples of company A and company B show that in business it's not one size fits all and there are different ways to achieve a reasonable ROI. The examples also demonstrate the importance of understanding the drivers of ROI.

Optional detail

Although the concept of return on investment is widely used, there are many ways to calculate the ratio and different definitions of the numerator 'return' and the denominator 'investment'.

Possible definitions of 'return'	Possible definitions of 'investment'
Operating profit	Total (or gross) assets
PBIT (profit before interest and tax)	Capital employed (or TALCL*)
PBT (profit before tax)	Net assets
PAT (profit after tax)	Equity (or invested capital)

* Total assets less current liabilities.

As each of the above definitions could be used, it means there are a number of possible ways to calculate ROI. Common ROI formulae are:

Acronym	Full name	Description	Typical calculation
ROTA	Return on total assets	Calculates return relative to a company's entire asset base. Useful to compare the efficient use of assets by companies in asset intensive industries, irrespective of their financing and capital structure.	$\dfrac{\text{Operating profit or PBIT}}{\text{Total assets}}$
ROCE	Return on capital employed	As above except deducts current liabilities. The investment base is therefore fixed assets (see **Chapter 9 Tangible fixed assets and depreciation**) plus working capital (see **Chapter 24 Working capital and liquidity management**).	$\dfrac{\text{Operating profit or PBIT}}{\text{Capital employed}}$

Acronym	Full name	Description	Typical calculation
		Useful in assessing management performance and probably the most popular ROI measure.	
ROE	Return on equity	As above except deducts debt liabilities. Therefore, profit after deducting 'interest' is more relevant as the numerator.	$\dfrac{PAT}{Equity}$
		Calculates return relative to the amount invested by shareholders. Sometimes referred to as ROIC (return on invested capital).	
		Useful from a shareholders' perspective and for companies with similar capital structures.	
		ROE will usually be higher than ROTA and ROCE due to financial leverage (see **Chapter 30 Debt finance** and **Chapter 26 Long-term solvency performance measures**).	
RONA	Return on net assets	Alternative calculation to ROE, using the 'top half' of the balance sheet (see **Chapter 4 The balance sheet**) instead of the 'bottom half'.	$\dfrac{PAT}{Net\ assets}$

Example

Greggs use ROCE (return on capital employed) as their measure of ROI (see the **Where to spot in company accounts** section below). This is defined in their 2015 annual report as follows:

> [ROCE]alculated by dividing profit before tax before exceptional items by the average total assets less current liabilities for the year.

Using the Greggs, definition of ROCE, it is possible to derive the calculation used in Greggs 2015 annual report and its associated drivers (figures are stated in £'000):

PBT* margin	$\times$	AT	=	ROCE
$\dfrac{\text{PBT}}{\text{Revenue}}$	$\times$	$\dfrac{\text{Revenue}}{\text{TALCL}}$	=	$\dfrac{\text{PBT}}{\text{TALCL}}$
$\dfrac{73{,}028}{835{,}749}$	$\times$	$\dfrac{835{,}749}{277{,}336}$	=	$\dfrac{73{,}028}{277{,}336}$
9%	$\times$	3	=	27%

* Profit before tax before exceptional items.

Greggs 2015 annual report gives ROCE figures for the last 10 years. Over this period their average ROCE has been 25%.

Where to spot in company accounts

Some companies will display profitability ratios in their annual reports; however, the ratios are straightforward to calculate using figures from the P&L and balance sheet.

ROI is an important financial performance measure for Greggs. An extract from their 'Financial Review' included in their 2015 annual report is shown below:

We manage return on capital against predetermined targets and monitor performance through our Investment Board, where all capital expenditure is subject to rigorous appraisal before and after it is made. For investments in new shops and refurbishments we target an average cash return on invested capital of 25%, with a hurdle rate of 22.5%, over an average investment cycle of seven years. Other investments are appraised using discounted cash flow analysis.

The investment returns on our refurbishment expenditure in the year were good, with 2015 investments meeting our return hurdle and more mature refurbishments showing very strong returns, well above our target. The performance of new shops was excellent, with prior year openings maturing well and newer shops making a very strong start. In the year ahead we will increase the rate of openings further, as long as we continue to see strong investment returns.

We delivered an overall return on capital employed (ROCE) for 2015 of 26.8% (2014: 22.4% excluding exceptional items). The stronger ROCE reflects the improved operating performance in the year as well as good capital investment returns.

As an illustration of its importance, Greggs link their Directors' remuneration to long-term improvements in ROI. An extract from their 'Director's remuneration report' included in their 2015 annual report is shown below:

...our annual bonus provides a strong link to the operational delivery of the business strategy. The Performance Share Plan focuses the Executive Directors on the longer-term outputs of that strategy, by rewarding sustained improvements in earnings per share and long-term return on capital employed.

Watch out for in practice

- Although ROI is a good starting point to measure financial performance, don't look at it as a single measure. Look at ROI together with its drivers, profit margin and asset turnover.

- Subsequently, look at the drivers of both profit margin and asset turnover to further analyse financial performance.

  - For profit margin, look at each cost category as a percentage of revenue, for example employee costs as a percentage of turnover.

  - For asset turnover, look at each of the major asset categories (fixed assets, stocks and debtors) as a percentage of turnover.

- It is always useful to benchmark financial performance ratios against other companies in the same industry.

- Always check the definition of ROI being used. Check which 'profit' figure is being used and how 'investment' is made up.

- The value of 'investment' is dependent on a company's valuation of its assets, the age of its assets and its depreciation policies (see **Chapter 9 Tangible fixed assets and depreciation** and **Chapter 17 Revaluation**).

24 Working capital and liquidity management

In a nutshell

While the medium- to long-term goal of a business is to manage profitability, the short-term goal is to manage liquidity.

Liquidity is the ability to pay expenses and debts *as and when* they become due. Businesses must ensure they have sufficient liquidity in the form of cash by managing their 'working capital'.

Working capital is the difference between current assets (stock, debtors and cash) and current liabilities (creditors and bank overdrafts). Working capital management is the ability to make cash available when needed and to make the best use of surplus cash. Too little cash in the business could result in business insolvency, whereas too much cash tied up in stock, for example, is an indicator of inefficiency.

Ensuring the business has sufficient liquidity to continue operations is perhaps *the* overriding challenge even for the most profitable businesses. The inability to pay creditors is one of the most common reasons for business failure.

Effective working capital management helps a business to ensure profits tied up in stock and debtors are converted to cash (liquid resources) in time to meet current liabilities.

Need to know

A business which sells products typically needs to pay its creditors for stock before it generates sales and receives cash from customers. The timing of cash payments and receipts is therefore critical to working capital management.

Why is this important?

Effective working capital management requires every company to understand its *working capital* (or *cash conversion*) *cycle*. This cycle identifies the number of days it takes to convert current assets into cash. Comparing this to the time it takes to pay creditors enables a company to identify its 'working capital (or cash) requirement'.

The longer the working capital cycle of a business, the longer it is tying up cash, i.e. working 'capital'. A business with a long working capital cycle may find that it has run out of cash because it cannot generate cash from sales sufficiently quickly to pay its creditors.

Understanding the working capital cycle is the key to identifying whether a business is likely to suffer from cash flow difficulties.

Companies that invest heavily in stock and those that offer their customers extended payment periods are at heightened risk of cash flow difficulties that could result in insolvency (see **Chapter 25 Insolvency and going concern risk**).

Because working capital 'ties up' cash it is often seen as a *net investment* by a business.

Example – ABC Ltd

ABC Ltd is a reseller of branded paints to trade customers only. The company buys paint from specialist manufacturers on strict 30-day credit terms and offers identical (30-day) terms to trade customers although customers typically pay only after 35 days. The company has a full range of paints in stock, which are held for 22 days (on average) before sale.

At 31 December, ABC has a working capital requirement of £80,000 as follows:

	Days	£
Stock	22	£42,000
Debtors	35	£96,000
Working capital cycle	57	£138,000
Trade creditors, payroll, overheads	(30)	(£58,000)
Working capital requirement (days)	27	£80,000

Working capital (Liquidity) ratio: $\dfrac{\text{Current assets}}{\text{Current liabilities}}$ $\dfrac{£138,000}{£58,000} = 2.4$

ABC has a healthy liquidity ratio as it has more current assets than current liabilities.

Notwithstanding, ABC may not have enough cash to meet its liabilities *when* they fall due! Note that the time between stock purchase and cash receipt is 57 days (stock days + debtor days) whereas suppliers need to be paid on day 30. ABC has a gap of 27 days between when it is expected to pay its suppliers and receiving cash from its customers. ABC would need to finance this gap, i.e. find the cash to pay suppliers.

As it stands, unless ABC can borrow cash (e.g. via an overdraft) or has sufficient cash reserves it runs the risk of creditors taking action for recovery of debts that could result in insolvency (see **Chapter 25 Insolvency and going concern risk**).

When is this important?

Fast-growing (ambitious) companies are often at highest risk of insolvency because they typically reinvest surplus cash generated from sales into buying more stock in order to support further sales growth. They often risk suppliers going unpaid as they allow their working capital cycle to become too long. This is known as *overtrading*.

Managing the working capital cycle is (or should be) an operational priority in businesses to avoid the risk of cash shortages and insolvency.

Management of working capital

Techniques to manage/improve working capital include:

- Optimising stock holding. 'Just in time' (JIT) ordering ensures cash isn't tied up in stock (see **Chapter 11 Stock**). Supermarkets use JIT to avoid stock-outs while also minimising the physical space needed to hold stock.

- Faster debtor collection. Enforcing credit terms minimises risks of non-recovery. Early payment incentives coupled with strong credit control will improve timing of cash receipts. Businesses short of cash may decide to *factor* their debts. This involves selling debts for cash immediately to third parties (see **Chapter 12 Debtors and creditors**).

- Cash flow forecasting. This can minimise the cost of holding excessive cash balances as well as identify short-term funding gaps. A treasury function is typically responsible for this activity in large organisations (see **Chapter 1 Finance personnel and systems**).

In addition to freeing up cash (or minimising borrowing requirements) by shortening the working capital cycle well-managed businesses will also have in place alternative sources of short-term finance (see **Chapter 30 Debt finance**). An overdraft facility is an expensive but very common source of short-term finance although the benefits of having an overdraft have to be balanced carefully against the costs of borrowing and maintaining the facility.

Excessive working capital in a business may indicate management *inefficiency.* For example, holding a high multiple of current assets to current liabilities may indicate that management are unnecessarily tying up money in stock or not recovering debtors quickly enough. It might alternatively indicate that the company is offering excessively generous credit terms to its customers.

In practice

Some businesses delay payments to creditors as a tactic to fund working capital needs. Each day a creditor payment is delayed is a day that the creditor is financing the working capital of the business.

While legal, the morality of this practice is questionable (especially when *small* suppliers are financing larger companies). Large companies nowadays are encouraged to publish how long it takes to pay creditors and this is used by some companies to distinguish themselves from competitors by displaying their fair trading policy credentials.

There is no 'right' level of working capital. Each business is unique and will face its own challenges and opportunities including default by customers, cyclical sales patterns, etc. A business should aim to manage its working capital to ensure it is sufficient but not excessive for its operating needs. Sufficient in this sense implies having access to liquid resources that enable the business not only to meet identified short-term liability payments but also to deal with unexpected events, for example bad debts or customer refunds.

Nice to know

Net working capital

Net working capital is the *difference* between current assets and current liabilities.

A company with fewer current assets than current liabilities has negative working capital. This *could* indicate trouble but only if the business is unable to pay its debts when they are due. Conversely, the business model of cash based retailers such as Tesco is to operate with negative working capital because long creditor payment terms can be used to finance their working capital requirements. Tesco's most recent results show the company was operating with £5 billion of negative working capital at the year end.

Liquidity ratio

The adequacy of working capital is typically benchmarked using a working capital ratio, known as the 'liquidity ratio'.

The liquidity ratio is calculated as follows:

$$\frac{\text{Current assets}}{\text{Current liabilities}}$$

Where current assets equal current liabilities the ratio is 1.

Anything below 1 indicates a *negative* working capital, as current liabilities will exceed current assets for the working capital ratio to fall below 1.

A number above 1 indicates that a company has enough short-term assets to cover its short-term obligations although note the earlier comments around timing.

A number above 2 might be an indication of management inefficiency, i.e. that the company is not making good use of the excess working capital at its disposal.

Acid test ratio

An alternative measure of liquidity is the 'acid test' (or 'quick' ratio), which excludes stock. This ratio better highlights the company's ability to pay liabilities from *liquid* assets (stock will take time to sell and generate cash).

In the case of ABC Ltd, the ratio is still healthy as it is greater than one.

$$\frac{\text{Current assets less stock}}{\text{Current liabilities}} \quad \frac{£96,000}{£58,000} \quad = \quad 1.7$$

Working capital days

Working capital days' ratios are useful efficiency performance measures.

Using the earlier example of ABC Ltd as an illustration, the 'days' can be calculated as follows (assume that sales are £1m and cost of sales £700,000):

$$\text{Stock holding period} = \frac{\text{Stock}}{\text{Cost of sales}} \times 365$$

(see **Chapter 11 Stock**)

$$\text{Debtor collection period} = \frac{\text{Debtors}}{\text{Sales}} \times 365$$

ABC Ltd:

$$\frac{42,000}{700,000} \times 365$$
$$= 22 \text{ days}$$

$$\frac{96,000}{1,000,000} \times 365$$
$$= 35 \text{ days}$$

$$\text{Creditor collection period} = \frac{\text{Creditors}}{\text{Cost of sales}} \times 365 \qquad \boxed{\begin{array}{c} \dfrac{58,000}{700,000} \times 365 \\[2mm] = 30\,\text{days} \end{array}}$$

These ratios can be used to quickly calculate the working capital cycle and the associated funding gap which needs financing.

These ratios are a popular way to monitor short-term liquidity.

Optional detail

Investors and potential acquirers look closely at a company's working capital cycle because it gives an idea of management's effectiveness at managing balance sheet assets and generating cash flows. An acquirer will look to identify the need to inject additional working capital, e.g. to maintain a company's operations or to help fund expansion. For example, to expand ABC's business above requires cash not only to meet existing obligations but also additional sums to grow. More effective working capital management could reduce the working capital cycle, in turn reducing the cash needs of the business.

Some investors have been known to rule out companies in sectors that operate with negative working capital because they believe such businesses are not sustainable as they always require cash to maintain operations.

Where to spot in company accounts

Current assets are shown as stock, debtors and cash on the face of the balance sheet.

Current liabilities are totalled on the face of the balance sheet with details of each short-term liability disclosed in the notes.

Watch out for in practice

Companies showing significant year-on-year increases in stock holding but with no growth in sales. This could suggest difficulties in selling stock.

Companies with unusually low stock balances. Could indicate supply problems indicating missed revenue opportunities.

Growing debtor days. Late-paying customers tie up working capital. Could indicate recoverability problems.

Increasing creditor days. Could indicate increasing reliance on creditors to finance growth through suppliers or difficulties in repayment.

Excessive working capital.

Negative working capital.

Net working capital to sales. This represents the amount of pence in every pound required to finance working capital. As sales grow, working capital should usually grow in the same direction.

25 Insolvency and going concern risk

> 'Prudence is a rich ugly old maid, and her beau is Insolvency.'
>
> William Blake poet, painter, printmaker

In a nutshell

Companies that meet their debt obligations as they fall due are termed 'solvent'. *Insolvency* is a legal term used where a company is unable to repay the debts that it owes.

Going concern is an *accounting* concept used when preparing financial statements. It assumes that a company will continue to operate with no intention or need to stop trading.

Going concern and insolvency are interrelated because an insolvent company is not a going concern.

In the UK, the term insolvency should not be confused with bankruptcy. Bankruptcy is a term that applies to *individuals* whereas insolvency relates to *companies*.

This chapter focuses on companies, i.e. insolvency.

Need to know

Most businesses owe money at one time or another, whether through borrowing money from banks or taking advantage of short-term credit terms available when buying goods or services from suppliers. A well-managed company that can meet its liabilities when they fall due is a going concern. However, even the most respected of companies are at risk of failure if they do not have sufficient cash available when required to meet their financial obligations.

Why is this important?

Creditors are the most likely to suffer financial losses if a company has insufficient assets to pay its liabilities, as is the case in balance sheet insolvency (see **Nice to know** section below).

Insolvency affects other stakeholders. Employees will likely lose their jobs and may not receive redundancy payments. Shareholders may lose some or all of their monies invested.

Customers also may be affected. For example, Carcraft (a UK-based secondhand car retailer) was one of several high-profile insolvencies in 2015. Its customers were notified that any existing warranty, MOT, roadside assistance or servicing deals they had with the company would no longer be valid, leaving potentially thousands of customers out of pocket.

When is this important?

Directors have a legal obligation to ensure that the company does not continue to trade if it is insolvent.

Even where there is a *threat* of insolvency, the directors are required to consider their duty to protect the interests of creditors.

Warning signs

A company's directors have a legal duty to 'promote the success of the company'. This includes the need to maintain business solvency and take action when there is a risk of insolvency.

Warning indicators may give directors the time needed to secure alternative sources of cash (or change company strategy/the business model).

Directors can be remote from day-to-day business activity but are expected nevertheless to be alert to the risks of insolvency.

Early warning signs may include:

1 Overdue tax payments (PAYE, National Insurance, corporation tax, VAT (see **Chapter 8 Business tax**)).

2 Losses over a number of years.

3 Liquidity ratio falling to below 1 (see **Chapter 24 Working capital and liquidity management**).

4 Inability to borrow additional funds, e.g. because of poor relationships with lenders.

5 No alternative sources of finance.

6 Existing or new creditors placing the company on 'cash on demand' terms.

7 Frequent switching of suppliers (existing suppliers unwilling to continue supply until debts settled).

8 Creditors remaining unpaid outside contracted trading (see **Chapter 31 Management accounts**) terms.

9 Issuing post-dated cheques.

10 Not knowing the company's trading performance and financial position (timing/quality of financial information).

Directors should ideally be able to review up-to-date, timely financial information to understand how their company is trading (see **Chapter 31 Management accounts**). Detailed cash forecasts can provide the best early warning indicator of whether (and when) cash will be needed and identify the need to adapt or change strategy to survive over the long term.

In practice

Legal advisers will typically need to be engaged, to advise directors on actions that need to be taken as special rules exist to protect the interests of creditors.

Company insolvency is not always easily apparent and it can't always be predicted. The pace of business change can often take directors and their investors by surprise. A change in consumer behaviour (e.g. the move towards discounters in the UK supermarket sector) or the emergence of disruptive technologies (e.g. the impact of technology used by Netflix and iTunes on retailers such as HMV) can result in sudden, significant business challenges for established (typically high fixed cost) businesses.

A company's audited financial statements cannot be relied on to guarantee company solvency (see **Chapter 20 External and financial audit**). Company accounts include a going concern statement setting out the directors' judgements about the ability of the company to continue operating into the 'foreseeable future' (a period defined as being at least 12 months after the date the financial statements are signed by the directors). However, whilst may be correct at the time the accounts are signed, it provides no guarantee of longevity because companies report financial information annually. The pace of change in most companies means that a gap of 12 months between reporting is too long provide any meaningful insight into the changing trading position of a business. Additionally, for external stakeholders such as suppliers, reported financial information may not be available until nine months after the year end (see **Chapter 21 Information in the public domain**).

It is worth noting that the extent of disclosure varies significantly according to the type of company. While public listed companies (listed PLCs) disclose detailed information about a company's liquidity position and availability of finance, private limited companies often provide information that is of little help in assessing the solvency of a company. Creditors therefore typically turn to credit rating agencies before extending credit or require trade on a cash on delivery basis until a company has proven its credit worthiness (see **Chapter 21 Information in the public domain**).

Nice to know

There are two types of insolvency:

1 *Balance sheet insolvency* (known also as *technical* insolvency). This is the situation when the company's *total* liabilities exceed its *total* assets. A company typically set up initially with

net assets may make losses in one or more years. These losses deplete the asset base year on year until technical insolvency occurs. In this situation, any attempt to settle a creditor may prejudice repayment of other creditors because there are not enough assets to repay *all* creditors.

2 *Cash flow insolvency* (known also as *actual* insolvency) is the situation where a company has insufficient *cash* to repay its debts as they fall due. In cash flow insolvency the company may have sufficient assets but the problem is that it has insufficient liquid assets (i.e. cash) to meet its liabilities. A business expanding rapidly but not collecting cash from its customers quickly enough may find that it cannot meet supplier payments even though it is trading profitably.

It is possible for a company to be cash flow *insolvent* but balance sheet *solvent*.

In either of the above situations, the company may be placed into what is known as a *formal insolvency procedure*.

Optional detail

Insolvency procedures

In the UK any creditor owed more than £750, not paid for three weeks after the due payment date can instigate a 'winding up petition' to place the company into a 'formal insolvency procedure'. This could result in *winding up* the company.

An insolvent company can be managed in (one of) three ways depending on its likelihood of survival:

1 Corporate Voluntary Arrangement

2 Administration

3 Liquidation

1 Corporate Voluntary Arrangement (CVA)

- Where there is an intention to keep the business operating.

- Carried out under the supervision of an appointed Insolvency Practitioner.

- Directors continue to run and retain control of the business.
- Creditors agree to a reduced (or rescheduled) debt payment in return for a commitment by the company to restructure under a new business strategy.

The logic for creditors accepting a CVA is that by keeping the business going, there may be some hope of recovering the monies at risk.

2 Administration

- Alternative under which a qualified Insolvency Practitioner ('the Administrator') takes control and attempts to rescue the company in the interests of all creditors.
- Directors lose control of the business.
- If nothing can be done to rescue the company, the Administrator will wind up the company and distribute the assets.

3 Liquidation

Liquidation is the process designed to close down the company (cease trading) by converting all of the company's remaining assets into cash.

- Assets are broken up, sold off and distributed to creditors.
- Adopted if there is no realistic prospect of rescuing the business.

Going concern disclosure

In the UK, company directors are responsible for the preparation of the financial statements and for assessing the company's ability to continue operating as a going concern. Directors have to disclose whether it is appropriate to continue to adopt the going concern basis in preparing the annual report and accounts (see **Where to spot in company accounts** section below).

The going concern statement is reviewed and referenced by auditors in the audit report. Where they disagree with the disclosure or have concerns about the status of a company as a going concern, this can have implications for the audit report (see **Chapter 20 External financial audit**).

Viability statement disclosure

The UK Corporate Governance Code has introduced (from late 2014) a requirement for directors to include a viability statement in the annual report, to strengthen the focus of companies and investors on the longer term. Directors are required to look forward for more than a year when reporting to shareholders and explain the reasons why they consider the company will continue to be viable.

The viability statement is also subject to review by the auditor and reference is made to the viability statement in the audit report.

Where to spot in company accounts

Going concern disclosure is located in financial statements, typically in the 'basis of preparation' note (under accounting policies).

Where there are concerns about the ability of a company to continue as a going concern, the directors make sufficient disclosure to support the basis on which the accounts have been prepared.

The validity of the going concern and viability statement disclosures are reviewed and reported on by auditors (see **Chapter 20 External financial audit**).

Extracts from Greggs plc 2015 accounts

(b) Basis of preparation
Significant accounting policies note

Going concern
Directors have reviewed the Company's operational and investment plans for the next 12 months along with the principal risks and uncertainties that could affect these plans or threaten its liquidity. The key factors likely to affect future performance and the Company's exposure to risks are set out on pages 24 to 25 of the strategic report. In addition the financial review on pages 20 to 21 sets out the Company's net cash position and continued strong cash generation.

After making enquiries, the Directors have a reasonable expectation that the Company and the Group have adequate resources to continue in operational existence for the next 12 months. Accordingly, they continue to adopt the going concern basis in preparing the annual report and accounts.

Extract from audit report

> **5   We have nothing to report on the disclosures of principal risks**
>
> Based on the knowledge we acquired during our audit, we have nothing material to add or draw attention to in relation to:
>
> – the Directors' viability statement on page 25, concerning the principal risks, their management, and, based on that, the Directors' assessment and expectations of the Group's continuing in operation over the three years to 2018; or
>
> – the disclosures on page 76 concerning the use of the going concern basis of accounting.

Watch out for in practice

→ In addition to the warning signs above, be aware of signs of operational cash flow problems when working in the business. E.g. is the company:

→ Ignoring phone calls from its suppliers?

→ Using post-dated cheques?

→ Having to agree to staged repayment plans, to pay off outstanding debts?

→ Still able to pay staff wages? As an employee you would be the first to know!

→ Suffering from regular stock-outs? This may indicate supply replenishment problems (suppliers unwilling to offer credit terms).

→ Facing the prospect of bailiffs showing up and walking off with company assets?

→ Financial statements prepared on the alternative 'break up' basis. Fixed assets will be reclassified as short term and revalued down to a 'fire sale' (forced sale) valuation. Additional liabilities may need to be recognised, e.g. for breach of customer or supplier contracts plus liquidators' fees.

26 Long-term solvency performance measures

In a nutshell

Solvency is the ability of a business to pay its long-term debts. It is critical to risk management and long-term success.

Solvency performance measures give an indication of 'financial strength', i.e. the ability to withstand exposure to short-term operating setbacks and achieve long-term growth.

Solvency is the result of a business's ability to balance its risk and return by raising and maintaining the right type of cost-effective finance.

The key measures of solvency are gearing and interest cover.

Need to know

Why is this important?

Banks and other providers of debt place demands on a business in the form of regular interest payments and repayment of the outstanding balance.

While debt commits a business to future cash outflows, it is unlikely to be able to guarantee its future cash inflows with the same degree of certainty. This imbalance is a cause of financial risk. The more debt (or gearing) a company has, the greater its financial risk. See the **Nice to know** section below for more detail on financial risk.

Deciding upon an optimum level of gearing is a question of risk versus return. Debt can boost returns as it is usually a more cost-effective form of finance than equity (see **Chapter 29 Equity finance** and **Chapter 30 Debt finance**). If a business can lower its cost of finance, it can generate a higher return by undertaking more profitable projects and growing faster, which will ultimately increase the value of its business.

Gearing

Gearing (or 'debt to equity') measures a business's long-term financing structure. Its purpose is to compare a business's borrowings (debt) with its funding from shareholders (equity).

There are two common methods of calculating gearing:

$$\text{Method One: Debt to equity} = \frac{\text{Debt}}{\text{Equity}}$$

$$\text{Method Two: Debt to debt + equity} = \frac{\text{Debt}}{\text{Debt + equity}}$$

Both methods can be calculated as a traditional ratio or a percentage.

For example, a business with £100 million of debt and £200 million of equity would have a gearing of 0.5 times or 50% under method one. Under method two the same business would have a gearing of 0.33 times or 33%.

Method 2 (debt to debt + equity) is easier to understand as it gives a clear picture of a business's exposure to debt, in relation to its total funding and has a maximum of 100%, which is easier to interpret.

The higher the gearing, the riskier the business – in terms of dilution of earnings and sensitivity to changes in interest rates.

In practice

Management must determine an appropriate level of gearing based on the company's particular circumstances, the current economic climate and what is acceptable to shareholders.

As a rule of thumb, businesses with more predictable cash flows can absorb higher levels of debt than businesses in more volatile sectors, which should have lower levels of gearing.

In practice many businesses have gearing levels (debt to debt + equity) of much less than 100%.

Interest cover

Interest cover is a measure of the affordability of debt to the business. The more cover a business has, the more affordable its debt and the more 'headroom' it has to allow for volatility in earnings.

Interest cover is calculated as follows:

$$\text{Interest cover (times)} = \frac{\text{Profit before interest and tax}}{\text{Interest}}$$

This ratio indicates how many 'times' a business could theoretically afford to pay its interest charges.

The ability to service debt is a measure of risk to debt providers, shareholders and ultimately the business itself.

In practice

In practice a business should be able to cover its interest at least two or more times although this benchmark will vary across business types and industries.

The level of interest cover is affected by:

- the business's operating profit;
- the amount borrowed; and
- the rate of interest on debt.

The relationship between gearing and interest cover

For most businesses there is an inverse relationship between gearing and interest cover. Management will try and strike an appropriate balance between the two.

Low interest rates will make it easier for businesses to achieve a comfortable level of interest cover and hence lead to higher levels of gearing.

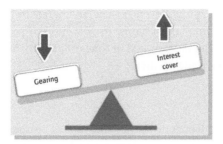

One of the causes of the 2007/8 financial crisis was an unprecedented prior period of low interest rates across the global economy. This encouraged companies, and banks in particular, to accept higher levels of gearing than normal, which left them severely exposed when parts of the financial system began to collapse.

However, the relationship between interest cover and gearing is not always simple, a highly profitable company may have a relatively high and comfortable interest cover, while maintaining a high level of gearing.

Nice to know

Leverage and financial risk

Directly related to gearing is the principle of leverage and financial risk.

Leverage is the utilisation of debt to obtain more finance than would otherwise be possible using equity finance alone. Businesses use leverage to multiply the returns possible from an investment on the assumption that the investment's returns are greater than the cost of borrowing.

Leverage is a cause of *financial risk* or volatility in profit. A high level of gearing usually equates to a high cost of interest. The higher the cost of interest in relation to pre-interest profits (a low interest cover), the higher the financial risk.

For businesses with high leverage, a small change in pre-interest profit will result in a large change in post-interest profits. Thus, these businesses can do very well in times of growth, but struggle, or even fail, when trade declines.

Example

Companies A and B operate in the same type of business and have identical PBITs (profits before interest and tax) of £100,000 p.a. Both companies have £500,000 of financing (equity plus debt). In fact, the only difference between the two companies is their gearing. Company A has 33% gearing and company B has 67% gearing. Both companies borrow at the same annual rate of interest, being 10%.

The following table considers the impact of a 20% rise in their PBITs on their PBTs (profits before tax).

	Company A (33% gearing)		Company B (67% gearing)	
	Current	20% increase in PBIT	Current	20% increase in PBIT
PBIT	100,000	120,000	100,000	120,000
Interest	(16,500)	(16,500)	(33,500)	(33,500)
PBT	83,500	103,500	66,500	86,500
		24% increase in PBT		30% increase in PBT

It is important to note that the same magnification would apply if profits declined.

The interest charge (which is the same irrespective of the volume of business) is calculated as follows:

- Company A: 33% × £500,000 × 10% = £16,500.
- Company B: 67% × £500,000 × 10% = £33,500.

The above example gives an illustration of both financial risk and leverage in practice.

A 20% change in PBIT leads to a 24% change in PBT for company A and a 30% change for company B.

As company B has higher fixed interest costs, its bottom line profits are more volatile. However, it can also experience higher percentage growth when profits increase.

To see the full picture, it is useful to consider ROE (return on equity – see **Chapter 23 Profitability performance measures** for further explanation). Although company A has higher 'absolute' profits than company B, it has used double the amount of equity to generate those profits.

Using the following definition of ROE, we can compare the results for both companies.

$$\text{ROE} = \frac{\text{PBT}}{\text{Equity}}$$

	Company A		Company B	
	Current	20% increase or decrease in PBIT	Current	20% increase or decrease in PBIT
PBT	83,500	103,500	66,500	86,500
Equity	335,000	335,000	165,000	165,000
ROE	25%	31%	40%	52%

The equity is calculated as follows:

- Company A: 67% × £500,000 = £335,000.
- Company B: 33% × £500,000 = £165,000.

Therefore, leverage enables Company B to always achieve higher returns on equity than Company A. In times of growth, leverage can act as a catalyst and significantly increase returns further still. However, the increased return comes with increased risk, especially to shareholders, and this is a trade-off which needs to be carefully considered by management.

Optional detail

Defining 'debt'?

To calculate gearing one needs to define 'debt'.

There are three main definitions used in practice:

1 long-term loans only;
2 long-term and short-term loans;
3 long-term loans plus current liabilities.

Definitions 1 and 2 include interest-bearing debt, for example bank loans. Therefore, these definitions are generally used by banks and other financial institutions, as they calculate gearing from their perspective.

However, from a business's perspective, amounts owed to suppliers can be just as relevant as debt due to banks and therefore a business may use definition 3 to calculate gearing. It will also depend on if the business wants to take a long-term or short- to medium-term view of gearing.

Overall, as long as there is a consistent benchmark, the definition of debt is mainly academic. As with other performance indicators it's the benchmark that counts.

Where to spot in company accounts

- Gearing can be derived solely from the balance sheet.
- Interest cover can be derived solely from the P&L account.
- In both cases it may be helpful to review the supporting notes for clarity.

Greggs is atypical in that they have no debt other than normal trading liabilities to creditors and obligations arising under commercial leases. In their 2015 annual report, the chairman, Ian Durant, said:

During 2015 the Board carried out a review of the appropriate capital structure of the Group, including consultation with some shareholders on different options for returning surplus capital. Given the leasehold nature of the shop portfolio the Board concluded that it is not currently appropriate to take on structural debt and intends to maintain a net cash position.

Watch out for in practice

Levels of fixed operating costs in the business (operating risk). Unless the business has a healthy interest cover, it is inadvisable to combine high operating risk (see **Chapter 33 Profit planning**) with high financial risk (gearing).

Year-on-year changes in gearing and interest cover.

Changes or announced planned changes to capital structure.

Redemption dates on debt.

The balance of short-term versus long-term debt.

Average effective interest rate (sometimes disclosed in the notes to accounts).

Levels of gearing and interest cover relative to other companies in the same industry.

27 Investor ratios

'As I've progressed in my career, I've come to appreciate – and really value – the other attributes that define a company's success beyond the P&L: great leadership, long-term financial strength, ethical business practices, evolving business strategies, sound governance, powerful brands, values-based decision-making...'

Ursula Burns, chairman and CEO, Xerox

In a nutshell

Investor ratios are reported daily in the financial press for listed companies. Ratios are calculated using publicly filed financial information and share price data.

Investor ratios can be used to assess investment opportunities as they help to make sense of data. Large amounts of information can be summarised to identify trends over time, comparisons between companies or against sector norms.

While they are considered an essential tool to assess investments, investor ratios should only ever form *part* of an investor's decision-making toolbox. Understanding the wider political, economic, social and technological influences on a business is also important. For example, the UK's vote to exit the European Union in 2016 created uncertainties and opportunities for many businesses that no review of ratios can explain.

Investor ratios focus primarily on profitability (returns) and security (risk). They enable:

1 Investors to assess the value and quality of investment opportunities.
2 Directors/managers to track the impact of company strategy on the key metrics that matter most to investors.

Need to know

Key investor ratios include the following:

1 Earnings per share
2 Price/Earnings ratio
3 Dividend cover
4 Dividend yield.

1 Earnings per share (EPS)

Calculated as:

$$\frac{\text{Net profit after preference dividends}}{\text{Average number of shares in issue}}$$

EPS is the profit generated *for each share* in issue. The ratio is reported as a number, e.g. an EPS of 10p means that each share has a profit allocation of 10p.

Advantage of EPS measure

Simple to calculate, yet a powerful way of showing how a company's profit is allocated among its shareholders.

It is a good measure to track growth in profits of a company over time. A Year-on-Year (or Period-on-Period) increase in the EPS figure indicates that profits per share are growing, i.e. the company is generating increasing returns for investors. Conversely, a falling EPS shows that the company's growth is slowing. Although past performance is never a guarantee of future performance, a company with a solid track record of EPS growth may be attractive to investors looking to get some degree of 'certainty' of future returns.

Disadvantage of EPS measure

The major limitation of EPS data is that it cannot be used to compare companies. This is because EPS ignores differences in capital structure between companies.

Example

Company A and Company B report identical net profits (after preference dividends) of £10,000. Each company also has 10,000 shares in issue. However:

▪ Company A issued shares at £1 nominal value (issued capital £10,000).

▪ Company B issued shares at 10p nominal capital (issued capital £1,000).

	Company A	Company B
EPS	£1	£1
	£10,000	£10,000
	10,000	10,000

Both companies report identical EPS of £1. However, company B has achieved this level of profit with (only) £1,000 of capital invested whereas company A has required £10,000 from investors. While the earnings per share are identical, the return on equity (see **Chapter 23 Profitability performance measures**) from company B is 10 times higher than company A. Put another way, a shareholder of company A invested £1 to earn £1. A shareholder of company B invested 10p to get a return of £1.

Other things being equal, company B would be the better investment but EPS does not capture the differences in capital structure.

2 Price/Earnings (P/E) ratio or PER

Calculated as:

$$\frac{\text{Market price } per\ share}{\text{Earnings } per\ share}$$

The ratio is reported as a number.

The Price/Earnings (P/E) ratio is the most widely published investor ratio. It shows the price (cost) of buying a share in comparison to the return generated. A company with a P/E of 20 means that £20 invested today generates an annual return of £1.

P/E data is calculated and published daily for listed companies based on the latest available price data and latest annual historic earnings data. P/E is most widely based on historic earnings data and is referred to more precisely as *trailing* P/E.

Current price data is available from the (relevant) stock market. Earnings data is based on historic published earnings annualised. For companies that report their results six monthly (UK) or quarterly (US), annualised earnings would be calculated as the sum of the latest two (half year) or four (quarter year) periods reported.

Advantage of P/E measure

The P/E ratio for a company is directly comparable to other companies in the same sector and can also be compared against itself over time or against sector averages.

P/E is used to establish whether a company is fairly valued relative to other companies in the sector or the sector in general. It can help identify whether a share is expensive or cheap relative to comparable companies.

- A high P/E (relative to other companies or the sector in general) might indicate a company is expected to outperform the sector or, more simply, that the shares are too expensive relative to the sector.
- A low P/E ratio relative to companies in the same industry might indicate that the company is undervalued, i.e. shares can be bought at a bargain price. Alternatively, the share price (and P/E) could be low as it reflects investor concerns about the company's ability to generate future profits.

A high P/E (relative to the sector) means that an investor will have to pay more for today's earnings than comparable investment opportunities, whereas a low P/E indicates that shares can be bought at relatively good value today.

Disadvantage of P/E measure

Interpreting what the number actually means. As explained above, a high or low P/E can have several possible explanations. In addition, while it is considered a good measure of *relative* value, the P/E doesn't tell a shareholder whether the shares are *correctly* valued. The price of any share is determined by many factors including a collective perception of risk and growth by investors. This does not necessarily mean that the collective perception is correct. P/E numbers are the result of many competing risks and opportunity considerations that could influence price. So using the P/E as a valuation tool in isolation is risky.

3 Dividend cover

Calculated as:

$$\frac{\text{Net profit (\textit{after} preference dividend)}}{\text{Annual dividend paid}}$$

Dividend cover is reported as a number, e.g. 5. This is the number of times earnings exceed (or are *covered* by) the dividend paid.

Advantage of dividend cover measure

Simple to calculate and easy to understand. It measures a company's *resilience* in paying dividends in the face of earnings volatility.

Example

	£
Net profit (after preference dividend)	100,000
Annual dividend paid	25,000
Dividend cover	4

Profits could fall by 75% (i.e. a decline of £75,000) before the company would be unable to pay a dividend out of current year profits.

Companies with high cover (typically a number above 4) are more resilient (or less risky) because they can better maintain dividend pay-out levels even when they suffer a significant decline in profits.

Disadvantage of dividend cover measure

Dividend payments are typically insensitive to earnings volatility in a year, i.e. the dividend cover ratio in any one year should not be interpreted in isolation. A company can continue to pay dividends for years even where it is making losses if it has built up reserves from earlier years.

While such a strategy cannot be used indefinitely, it is often used to maintain dividend levels especially where a company has a 'progressive' dividend policy. A progressive dividend policy is one in which the company aims to increase dividend per share year on year and is designed to attract investors seeking regular income (such as pension funds).

Note, however, that there is never any guarantee that dividends will be paid even when a company has the profits to do so. Dividends are paid at the discretion of directors. Equity shareholders have no legal *right* to receive dividends and cannot force the directors to pay them (see **Chapter 29 Equity finance**).

Unlike P/E ratios, which can be compared between companies, dividend cover can only be compared between companies that make dividend payments. A company that has a policy of not paying dividends cannot be compared to one that does.

4 Dividend yield

Calculated as:

$$\frac{\text{Annual dividend per share}}{\text{Market price per share}}$$

This ratio is reported as a percentage, e.g. 10%.

The dividend per share used to calculate dividend yield is the *net* dividend (in pence) declared by the company (i.e. with no allowance for tax credit).

Advantage of dividend yield measure

The ratio can be compared between investments to identify companies that are paying the highest dividend returns.

Disadvantage of dividend yield measure

Dividend yields, like P/E, are open to interpretation.

A high dividend yield *may* indicate a good investment opportunity, e.g. due to the share being undervalued. Alternatively, the share price may reflect expectations about (poor) future performance, i.e. that dividend payouts cannot be sustained.

Conversely, a low dividend yield relative to the sector may indicate that shares are overpriced. Alternatively, it may reflect a company decision to reinvest a higher proportion of earnings to generate higher returns over the long term.

There is no *right* level of dividend yield and changes in share price can make this measure volatile. A high dividend yield does not necessarily translate into a high dividend payout.

Investors looking for a steady dividend stream may find dividend cover a more useful measure than dividend yield.

In practice

Investor ratios provide investors with useful information on the profitability and security of investments and their alternatives. Comparing ratios can help investors distinguish between investing in a good company or a poorly performing company. However, ratios are open to interpretation and should not be reviewed in isolation.

Investor ratios can be subject to significant fluctuation, for example, as a result of share price volatility. Using published numbers from financial statements also limits the usefulness of ratios as historic data only provides trailing indicators rather than forward guidance.

Directors should consider the impact of their decisions on the ratios which are important to current and potential investors.

Nice to know

Price Earnings Growth (PEG) ratio

While the P/E ratio is the widest-used metric to compare companies, it is a metric based on historic earnings data (trailing P/E). In practice, Price Earnings Growth (PEG) is considered to provide a fuller picture of a share's valuation and attractiveness and may address some of the drawbacks of using the P/E in isolation.

PEG (or Future PEG) measures the relationship between P/E and a company's *expected* growth.

PEG requires an estimate of future earnings growth and is calculated as:

$$\frac{\text{Price/Earnings}}{\text{Future annual growth rate in EPS}}$$

A PEG of 1 is considered the base, i.e. that the shares are fairly valued. High P/E companies are generally expected to have higher growth rates.

A PEG ratio below 1 would generally be considered attractive because it indicates the company is undervalued as higher growth is expected in future years. A PEG ratio of 2 may indicate an overvaluation.

PEGs are often compared between companies to provide investment rankings.

Example

- Company A with a P/E ratio of 15 and expected to grow at 7.5 per cent would have a PEG of 2.
- Company B with a P/E of 15 and expected to grow at 20% would have a PEG of 0.75.

Considered in isolation, company A has a high P/E ratio and high PEG and looks expensive. Company B, while it has the same P/E, it has a lower PEG and therefore may be a better investment opportunity.

The main disadvantage of PEG is the necessity to *estimate* future earnings. This is often based on past earnings, which is an unreliable predictor of the future.

Optional detail

Price/Earnings and the dividend cover measure are based on historic earnings data. Investors really want to know about future earnings. This desire for *relevance* rather than *reliability* of data has led to the development of 'forward' P/E and dividend cover ratios. Forward ratios originated in the US and have been popular for a few decades.

Calculating a forward ratio for P/E uses *forecast* rather than *historic* earnings information. Forecast earnings are typically estimated by analysts and therefore will not be as reliable as audited (historic) earnings data.

Forward dividend yield can also be calculated and is based on estimated future dividends. These can be forecast with greater accuracy where companies have a published dividend policy.

Widely reported academic research has shown that the risk of using estimates is that they are more often than not overoptimistic and therefore wrong!

Basing decisions on forward ratios (rather than historic, audited information) may simply bring additional complexity and (some might say) even more uncertainty to already difficult investment decisions.

Where to spot in company accounts

Shares of privately owned corporations not traded have no readily available market value for the stock. Unlike listed companies, private companies are not required to report EPS numbers.

EPS for listed companies will be disclosed at the bottom of the profit and loss account with the calculation of EPS included in the notes to the accounts.

Extracts from Greggs plc

Consolidated income statement
for the 52 weeks ended 2 January 2016 (2014: 53 weeks ended 3 January 2015)

	Note	2015 Total £'000	2014 Excluding exceptional items (Restated) £'000	2014 Exceptional items (see Note 4) £'000	2014 Total (Restated) £'000
Revenue	1	835,749	806,096	–	806,096
Cost of sales		(305,116)	(304,786)	(5,932)	(310,718)
Gross profit		530,633	501,310	(5,932)	495,378
Distribution and selling costs		(412,426)	(403,003)	(282)	(403,285)
Administrative expenses		(45,094)	(40,223)	(2,302)	(42,525)
Operating profit		73,113	58,084	(8,516)	49,568
Finance (expense)/income	6	(85)	175	–	175
Profit before tax	3-6	73,028	58,259	(8,516)	49,743
Income tax	8	(15,428)	(13,997)	1,810	(12,187)
Profit for the financial year attributable to equity holders of the Parent		57,600	44,262	(6,706)	37,556
Basic earnings per share	9	57.3p	44.0p	(6.6p)	37.4p
Diluted earnings per share	9	55.8p	43.4p	(6.6p)	36.8p

Details of dividends paid are included in the notes to the accounts.

23. Capital and reserves 'extract'

Dividends

The following tables analyse dividends when paid and the year to which they relate:

	2015 Per share pence	2014 Per share pence
2013 final dividend	–	13.5p
2014 interim dividend	–	6.0p
2014 final dividend	16.0p	–
2015 interim dividend	7.4p	–
2015 special dividend	20.0p	–
	43.4p	19.5p

Watch out for in practice

→ When comparing ratios, it is important to consider the impact of differences in accounting policies, financing structures (debt versus equity) and different accounting year ends. No two businesses will be identical.

→ Investor ratios such as P/E make use of real-time (as well as historic) information so can be subject to extreme volatility. Trends over time and relative to the sector can be more informative.

→ Loss making companies will have negative (or zero) ratios for P/E. This makes interpretation more difficult. Again, trend data may be more informative as no one ratio can determine whether a company is an attractive investment.

→ Always read the 'small print' contained in financial statements. The notes to the published accounts highlight key risks that might seriously jeopardise future performance (e.g. product quality issues, over-reliance on customers or suppliers, lawsuits, corporate governance concerns, etc.) yet these are typically overlooked by the unsophisticated investor.

→ Never underestimate the importance of how the management team is perceived by investors. A departure/new appointment can have a dramatic effect on the ratios of a business.

28 Business valuation

'A year later, $19 billion for WhatsApp doesn't sound so crazy.'

Josh Constine, technology journalist and
editor-at-large for *TechCrunch*

In a nutshell

For a business the ultimate measure of success is its valuation, which is the amount a willing buyer is prepared to pay.

The stock market provides a platform for buyers and sellers to interact and set the price of shares. Public companies therefore have a real-time indication of their market value. For private businesses, however, no such market exists.

A number of methodologies exist to value a business, although in practice valuing a business is an art and is down to a number of factors, including negotiation. The aim of the various valuation techniques is to provide a range of prices for a buyer and seller in an open market.

Need to know

Why is this important?

Listed company directors are typically focused on maximising business value, reflected in the share price, while responding to dividend expectations of investors (see **Chapter 29 Equity finance**).

For a private entity, the sale or flotation of the business is an exit route for investors and building long-term value may be one of its main objectives. Even for companies which have no apparent intention of selling or floating, for example IKEA, building long-term value will correlate to long-term survival.

In addition, potential investors and business purchasers will need to assess valuations.

When is this important?

For a listed company its share price will be a continual focus for the directors and will influence many performance measures (see **Chapter 29 Equity finance** and **Chapter 27 Investor ratios**).

For a private business, valuations are typically required when:

- the owner wishes to sell or exit via a flotation;
- a purchaser wishes to buy the business;
- new shareholders are introduced, usually to raise further equity finance.

Techniques

There are two key methods of valuing a business:

1 Asset based.
2 Income based.

1 Asset based

Assets are the common-sense starting point for most valuations as they give the minimum valuation that a business should be willing to accept. Asset-based valuations are useful for asset-rich businesses, such as property holding and some manufacturing companies.

However, an asset-based valuation is not as simple as taking a number from the latest balance sheet (see **Chapter 4 The balance sheet**). The valuer will need to conduct an 'audit' (see **Chapter 20 External financial audit**) of the business to identify all its assets and liabilities and value them correctly. See the **Nice to know** section for further detail.

2 Income based

Income-based valuations often produce the highest valuations and give an indication of the maximum price an acquirer would wish to pay. If the company has a profitable trading history and is likely to continue as a going concern (see **Chapter 25 Insolvency and going concern risk**) an income-based valuation is usually preferable.

a *Multiples.* A simple approach to income-based valuations applies a multiplier to either revenue or ideally profit.

   ▪ Revenue multiples can be used for start-ups which may not yet be profitable or for businesses with volatile profits.

   ▪ Profit multiples are better than revenue multiples, as they account for costs as well as revenue. There is a high correlation between profit and value across an industry sector.

   In either case the revenue or profit figure used should be sustainable and not contain exceptional (one-off) items (see **Chapter 3 Profit and loss (P&L)**). This is often referred to as 'future maintainable earnings'.

   Multiples will vary between industries and economic cycles. For profit multiples, the quoted P/E ratio (see **Chapter 27 Investor ratios**) for the industry is a good starting point. For a private entity the P/E ratio quoted for its industry is typically discounted to reflect the fact that the business will be less marketable than a typically larger public listed company.

   BDO UK LLP publishes the quarterly PCPI (Private Company Price Index) which analyses the multiples typically used in valuing private companies. Historically, the larger the business, the larger the multiple.

b *Discounted cash flows.* Arguably the most sophisticated income-based valuation involves calculating the present value of future cash flows.

   This involves forecasting future cash flows based on various assumptions such as growth rate, margins, financing costs, tax rates and capital expenditure.

   Many companies use the concept of 'free cash flows', being operating cash flows less capital expenditure (see **Chapter 7 Opex and capex**).

   The future free cash flows are discounted back to present value using an appropriate cost of capital (see **Chapter 35 Investment appraisal**).

Estimating future cash flows, growth rates and the cost of capital is challenging. A small change in the assumptions can make a big difference to the valuation. In addition, past performance is not always a reliable predictor of future performance.

For an income-based valuation, due diligence (a comprehensive appraisal of the target business) will include an examination of income and expenditure (see **Chapter 3 Profit and loss (P&L)**), the target's cost structure (see **Profit planning**) and the reliability of estimates and forecast assumptions. Due diligence may also include an examination of accounting polices (see **Chapter 19 Accounting and financial reporting standards**) such as revenue recognition (see **Chapter 6 Revenue recognition**).

In practice

For a publicly listed company, maintaining a high share price is challenging, due to extrinsic factors largely beyond the control of directors, such as:

- competitors' actions or reactions;
- analysts' opinions;
- media stories and bid rumours;
- speculative behaviour;
- market sentiment, the economy and stock market bubbles.

For a private business, valuation is more of an art than a science because value is a matter of opinion. It is sometimes said that 'the value of a business is what it can be argued to be'.

Therefore, the best approach to valuation is to:

- Use a variety of valuation techniques and see if they are relatively close.
- Research the valuation of similar businesses which have recently been sold.
- Research the 'offer price' of similar businesses currently for sale.

The purpose of the various valuation techniques is to provide a range of values (rather than a precise figure) as the basis for negotiations between a buyer and seller. Like most successful negotiations, the skill in valuation is to find the common ground.

The final valuation will depend upon:

- Percentage of equity being valued (acquirers will pay a premium for the ability to influence/control strategic decisions).
- Strategic reasons for buying or selling and the willingness of the owners to sell.
- Quality and experience of management and their employees, including the organisational culture.
- Commercial potential of the target's products and services.
- Competitiveness of the target's marketplace.
- Number of competing buyers and sellers and their negotiation skills.
- If the transaction will be settled in cash or in shares.
- Macroeconomic and geopolitical factors.

Nice to know

Valuation premiums

In order to acquire another business, some businesses pay significant premiums above the values obtained by traditional valuation methods.

The technology sector has provided some interesting examples of premiums:

- In February 2014, Facebook Inc acquired WhatsApp Inc for USD $19.3 billion. At the time WhatsApp had circa USD $50 million turnover and employed just over 50 people. Facebook was clearly motivated by more than traditional financials. Potential user growth, user engagement, competitive and strategic factors played far more of a role in its valuation.
- In November 2006, Google acquired YouTube for USD $1.65 billion which bore little relation to YouTube's

financials at the time. Google saw the future potential of YouTube which at the time was one of the fastest-growing websites on the internet and is now (at the time of publication) one of most popular websites in the world.

- In July 2005, News Corporation acquired MySpace (at the time the largest social networking site in the world) for USD $580 million. However, they sold MySpace six years later in June 2011 for USD $35 million. MySpace lost users to Facebook and Twitter, which developed alternative user experiences.

See also **Chapter 10 Goodwill and other intangibles** for an example of the premium paid by AOL for Time Warner in 2001.

In deciding upon a valuation premium, acquirers will account for potential synergistic benefits. Examples of synergies are:

- Marketing – opportunities to cross-sell and build a bigger brand.
- Operations – economies of scale, purchasing power and elimination of duplicate costs.
- Financial – access to cheaper finance (see **Chapter 30 Debt finance**), lower cost of capital (see **Chapter 35 Investment appraisal**) and tax benefits (see **Chapter 8 Business tax**).
- Assets – access to unique resources, such as patents.
- Management – access to individuals, their reputation, experience and shared learnings.
- Risk-spreading – diversification into new markets and products/services.
- Competitive – to stop a rival obtaining the target.

However, the premium paid often far outweighs the synergistic benefits of an acquisition. Research by KPMG has shown that 70–80% of mergers and acquisitions fail to create shareholder value.[1] Some argue that excessive premiums are paid for acquisitions to meet investor's expectations of growth momentum, which cannot be achieved by organic growth alone.

---

1 'World Class Transactions: Insights into creating shareholder value through mergers and acquisitions', KPMG Transaction Services.

Asset-based valuations

Assets and liabilities will be revalued to reflect their current worth. Additional assets and liabilities may also be identified as part of any valuation process.

Balance sheet item	Valuation
Tangible fixed assets (see **Chapter 9 Tangible fixed assets and depreciation**)	▪ Property may need to be revalued if stated at purchase price. ▪ Other tangible assets will need to be valued as they will be stated at depreciated book value. ▪ Investments will need to be stated at market value.
Intangible fixed assets (see **Chapter 10 Goodwill and other intangibles**)	▪ Only intangible assets which have a market value, such as patents and trademarks should be included. This may require a specialist valuer. ▪ Other intangibles such as purchased goodwill should be excluded.
Stock (see **Chapter 11 Stock**)	▪ The age and saleability of stock will be evaluated.
Debtors (see **Chapter 12 Debtors and creditors**)	▪ The aged debtor listing will need to be closely reviewed together with the current bad debt provision.
Cash	▪ The exchange rate for cash held in other currencies will be retranslated at the point of the transaction.
Creditors (see **Chapter 12 Debtors and creditors**)	▪ Creditors to any group companies or related parties (see **Chapter 16 Group accounting**) should be checked for fair value. Any accruals (see **Chapter 13 Prepayments and accruals**) should be checked for accuracy.
Debt (see **Chapter 30 Debt finance**)	▪ Debt covenants and restrictions on the sale of certain assets should be checked. ▪ Debt may need to be repaid upon acquisition and there could be associated penalty clauses which would create additional liabilities.
Other liabilities	▪ Other liabilities would be accurately quantified including any closure/redundancy costs as a result of the potential acquisition (see **Chapter 14 Provisions and contingencies**). ▪ Contingent liabilities should be reassessed to see if provisions are required (see **Chapter 14 Provisions and contingencies**). ▪ Due diligence should aim to pick up any hidden liabilities such as an underfunded pension scheme and post balance sheet events.

Optional detail

Market to book ratio

The *market to book ratio* is one of a number of useful performance measures for a business (see **Chapter 23 Profitability performance measures**). It focuses on business valuation.

It is calculated as follows:

$$\frac{\text{Business Value}}{\text{Net Asset Value (NAV)}}$$

Providing a value can be obtained (which is naturally easier for a listed company), the ratio represents the markets perception of a business in terms of its profits, balance sheet strength and future prospects.

It compares shareholders' investment in a company with the value of the company. A value of less than one means that future profits are likely to be insufficient to justify the current level of investment in the company. A successful business should have a value greater than one and ideally two or more.

One of the exceptions to this rule, however, is property companies, which are usually valued at less than their NAV. One reason for this is the low liquidity of assets (i.e. property) owned by these companies.

Where to spot in company accounts

Acquisitions can be found in the balance sheet, under goodwill (see **Chapter 10 Goodwill and other intangibles**) and investments (see **Chapter 16 Group accounting**).

The annual report for a listed company will refer to its share price usually alongside other investor ratios (see **Chapter 27 Investor ratios**) and within the director's remuneration report (see **Chapter 22 Corporate governance and whistleblowing**).

Within Greggs 2015 annual report a performance graph for total shareholder return is provided as part of the directors' remuneration report. Total shareholder return is an investor ratio which measures combined returns from both dividends and capital growth.

Performance graph

The graph below shows a comparison of the total shareholder return for the Company's shares for each of the last seven financial years against the total shareholder return for the companies comprised in the FTSE Mid 250 index (excluding Investment Trusts) and the FTSE 350 (excluding Investment Trusts).

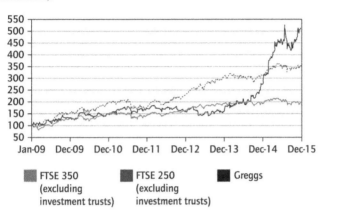

| FTSE 350 (excluding investment trusts) | FTSE 250 (excluding investment trusts) | Greggs |

Watch out for in practice

→ Trends in the share price against industry averages, as these should reflect information in the public domain, for example bid rumours.

→ Investor ratios (see **Chapter 27 Investor ratios**) and the market to book ratio.

→ Recent revaluations of assets, such as land and buildings, which may indicate preparation for a sale, or defence against a potential takeover.

→ Transactions which impact on asset values such as: changes to depreciation (see **Chapter 9 Tangible fixed assets and depreciation**); impairments (see **Chapter 9 Tangible fixed assets and depreciation**); provisions, for example bad debts (see **Chapter 14 Provisions and contingencies**); and related accounting policies (see **Chapter 19 Accounting and financial reporting standards**).

→ The value of goodwill (see **Chapter 10 Goodwill and other intangibles**) in the balance sheet and evidence of recent impairment testing.

→ Bid rumours and other media speculation which affect the share price of listed companies.

Sources of business finance

29 Equity finance

'If companies are able to raise equity from the market, then their problems for financing incomplete projects will come to end. Investment cycle in the capital market can kick-start with the money of savers and investors.'

Uday Kotak, executive vice chairman and managing director of Kotak Mahindra Bank

In a nutshell

Equity finance is money ('capital') raised by the sale of shares to investors (shareholders) who become owners with voting rights in the company, in return for their investment.

Equity is often a more expensive way to finance a business because shareholders require high rewards as compensation for risk. Shareholders suffer the highest risk because there is never a guarantee of return and no security is provided in return for the capital invested.

The *expectation* of growth in value of shares and/or the prospect of receiving a regular income (dividends) underpins the market for attracting equity finance.

Equity finance gives a right to influence the company as investors are shareholders. In practice, however, many investors do not exercise their rights (see **Chapter 22 Corporate governance and whistleblowing**).

Need to know

Equity carries no financial risk to a company because equity finance carries no obligation to pay a fixed return or to return capital. However, the key consideration is that the existing owner/ entrepreneur must give up some of their ownership rights. Equity investors are shareholders and therefore have a claim on the equity of a business.

Equity finance may be the *only* option for some companies. Since the impact of the credit crunch originating in 2007/2008, companies, in particular smaller entities, have been unable to access debt finance because banks have been unwilling or unable to lend.

Why is this important?

Deciding how to finance a company is a critical decision for most businesses. This decision should not be underestimated as it can determine a company's chances of survival or prosperity.

The choice between seeking debt or equity finance is not however straightforward.

Debt finance offers tax advantages as interest is a legitimate business expense and therefore tax deductible. However, debt *must* be serviced and repaid and therefore increases the financial risk of a company (see **Chapter 30 Debt finance**).

When is this important?

Most companies will require finance at various stages of their life cycle, i.e. from 'birth' to 'death'. The choice of finance available will differ at each stage of the cycle.

Incorporation and growth

In the early stages, a company will need to invest in product, people, process and marketing but is unlikely to generate the revenues and cash flows to meet debt repayments. The company may be unable to offer sufficient security, e.g. in the form of a charge over company assets that lenders typically require in return for debt finance. In early-stage growth companies therefore, equity financing is often the only realistic source of finance available. For entrepreneur-owned companies, giving up control or ownership becomes the key consideration because owners are unlikely to want to cede control. Whilst highly unappealing, this may be the only way to raise capital for a company that has no track record of profitability and little by way of asset security.

Start-up businesses are high risk. Early stage investors, often referred to as 'angel investors' (see **Nice to know** section below), are likely to demand a significant share in the business in return for capital invested, including a seat on the board as this ensures greater oversight over their investment.

Equity finance for the investor is a trade-off between the rights to future (uncertain) profits and cash flows in return for certain cash invested today.

Expansion and maturity

Once established, a successful business may have built up equity through retained profits. However, the company will likely require more finance to grow or to acquire to further expand. At this stage of the life cycle, a strong asset base with a track record of positive cash flows and profits should make it easier (and often cheaper) to attract equity finance and also make debt finance a realistic alternative. In addition, in the eyes of lenders, equity-financed companies are likely to be 'safer' companies precisely because they have no pre-existing debt finance commitments, i.e. they will have lower gearing than companies financed through debt (see **Chapter 26 Long-term solvency performance measures**).

Established companies may actively seek to take on debt at this stage of the cycle. Financial leverage (also known as 'trading on equity') can also be used as a strategy to increase shareholder returns and works well when assets increase in value although the reverse is equally true (see **Chapter 30 Debt finance** and **Chapter 26 Long-term solvency performance measures**).

Cessation ('death')

A company with debt finance has a higher risk of becoming insolvent because debt is a liability that must be serviced and repaid. If the company cannot repay, it may become insolvent. In this situation, holders of debt finance are repaid before shareholders. Where there are insufficient assets to cover liabilities, investors will lose their investment (see **Chapter 25 Insolvency and going concern risk**).

In practice

There is no *fixed* cost of raising equity or debt finance. Risk and marketability are key considerations. Listed PLCs for example can raise equity finance more cheaply than private companies because shares in listed companies can be bought and sold on a stock exchange. The lack of a 'market' for trading in a private company's shares restricts their liquidity. Listed companies are generally also perceived to be lower-risk investments because they are subject to greater scrutiny and required to publish more information (see **Chapter 21 Information in the public domain**).

A particular challenge for private companies seeking to raise equity finance is determining a fair price for a share in the business. New or existing shareholders may be unwilling to invest more because of disputes over the business valuation (see **Chapter 28 Business valuation**). Valuations may require independent professional advice which adds to cost and therefore is a barrier to raising equity finance.

Nice to know

Private companies – sources of equity finance

For non-listed businesses, the most common source of equity finance in reality is likely to be the owner/entrepreneur (or immediate family and friends).

For businesses with high growth potential, possible alternative sources of equity might include angel investors (also known as 'business angels'), crowdfunding or venture capital.

Angel investors (business angels)

Angel investors are wealthy individuals who invest their own capital in early stage companies in return for an equity stake in the business. A condition of any investment is typically a seat on the board as they expect to play an active role in the business. The owner may also be expected to invest capital as this is considered by some angels as a strong motivator to ensure the business succeeds.

Angel investors typically look to invest for periods of between three to eight years. Angels expect to invest in opportunities that enable them to at least double their investment.

One additional benefit of angel investors is that they are often a good source of free advice because they tend to be entrepreneurs or executives with considerable experience or extensive business contacts.

The challenge for a company seeking finance is finding an angel that 'fits' with the business and its ambitions. This search can take up valuable time that could be spent developing the business.

Equity crowdfunding

Equity crowdfunding is a more recent development (from around 2010). Like other types of equity finance, it involves offering shares in return for funding. One key difference however is that investors are sought through online platforms. Online platforms enable entrepreneurs to present their businesses through video pitches, literature, etc.

UK platforms are regulated by the Financial Conduct Authority allowing the public to invest money in return for an equity stake. 'Crowdcube' is one example of an online platform enabling investments from a minimum of £10.

Venture capital (VC)

Venture capital (VC) firms are typically set up as partnerships in which partners serve as managers of the firm. They invest monies raised from institutional investors (insurance companies, pension funds, etc), and wealthy individuals (including their own monies). They are typically well-known organisations, so are a more visible source of finance than angel investors. They will typically buy minority stakes in businesses and expect a seat on the board. VCs make money through selling at a higher price to another company or selling shares through the stock market ('IPO', see below).

Private equity

Private equity (PE) usually refers to organisations that raise funds to 'buy out' shareholders of existing companies rather than providing a source of new finance for companies. Depending on the nature of the deal, a PE firm will seek to buy (up to 100% of) the shares in an underperforming company.

Private equity firms such as The Carlyle Group, KKR, LDC, etc., typically invest to buy controlling stakes in established but underperforming 'large' companies. Unlike VCs, their aim is to manage a company better than existing management. Existing management teams are typically replaced by PE-appointed industry experts. The business will then be streamlined, e.g. by reducing the workforce and disposing of non-core assets.

High-profile examples of private equity investments include the acquisition of Boots plc (pharmacies) by KKR in 2007 and Learndirect (the UK's largest provider of apprenticeships and employment services) by LDC (Lloyds Development Capital) in 2011.

PE firms realise their investments through an IPO or trade sale, e.g. to a competitor.

Private equity firms are funded by institutional investors and high-worth individuals.

Public companies – other sources of equity finance

Initial public offering (IPO)

An *initial public offering (IPO)* is the first sale of shares to outside investors by a private company. The company issues shares in order to gain a listing on the stock market. Listed companies have an established share price but private companies have no historic price data. IPOs are therefore riskier (for investors) than public offerings as it is very difficult to determine the right price for its shares.

For listed companies, the most common routes to raising equity finance are:

Rights issue

Shares issued to *existing* shareholders typically at a discount and in proportion to shareholders' holding of existing shares. By taking up their rights, shareholders maintain their relative shareholding in the company. Rights issues are typically underwritten which means any shares not taken up by the shareholders are purchased by the underwriter (typically an investment bank) in return for a fee. The shares may then be sold ('placed') to institutional shareholders.

Public offering

Listed companies are more likely to raise capital through a *public offering* where their needs are significant and when their share price is high. An issue of shares to *new* shareholders can dilute *existing* shareholders' interests (see **Optional detail** section below).

Public offerings are regulated in the UK and have to be supported by a *prospectus*, which contains information to help investors make an informed decision about investing. The prospectus must include information about a company's activities and financial results, its directors and officers, what the money will be used for, as well as the risks of investing.

'Managing' the share price

(See also **Chapter 28 Business valuation.**)

A key advantage for listed (over non-listed) companies is their ability to access finance through the stock market. However, this creates additional challenges for management including the need to manage the share price to meet expectations and deliver against external performance measures (see **Chapter 27 Investor ratios**). Despite being profitable and having happy customers, directors may take risky decisions, such as major acquisitions, especially where organic growth becomes harder and harder to achieve (see **Chapter 22 Corporate governance and whistleblowing**). Some listed companies have returned to private (or private equity) ownership as it gives them the ability to take a longer-term view of the business, for example Michael Dell taking Dell computers private in 2013.

Optional detail

Pre-emption rights

A company seeking to raise finance from new shareholders first needs to disapply *pre-emption rights* of existing shareholders. These rights protect existing shareholders against dilution of their percentage shareholding in a company. If shareholders agree to disapply their rights then they accept dilution in exchange for bringing new finance (and shareholders) into the business.

The extent of shareholder 'dilution' depends on the price and volume of new shares issued.

Example

ABC plc issues 10 million shares at £10 each, a premium of £9 to their original issue price (nominal value of £1).

Before:	Equity Finance	Price	Shares issued	% holding
Original shareholders	£100m	£1	100m	100 %
New share issue	£100m	£10	10m	
			110m	
After:				
Existing shareholders			100m	91 %
New shareholders			10m	9 %
			110m	

New finance raised (£100m) is equivalent to the amount raised from original shareholders. However, the level of *dilution* is low because shares issued were at a significant premium to nominal value (see **Chapter 15 Capital and reserves**).

Dividends and dividend policy

Ordinary shares give the holder a right to ownership of the company. However, shareholders do not have an automatic right to dividends. Whether a dividend is paid typically disclose their dividend policy. For example, a company may have a 'progressive' dividend policy in which the dividend is expected to rise at least in line with increases in earnings per share (see **Extract from Greggs plc** below).

Companies that have a dividend policy are generally viewed positively by investors. There is a view that the share price of companies (that pay dividends) is also higher as a result although the relationship between dividends and the value of the share has been the subject of much debate among academics over many years (see also **Chapter 27 Investor ratios**).

Where to spot in company accounts

A company's sources of finance can be seen on the face of the balance sheet:

- Debt finance comprises long-term debt, included within non-current liabilities.
- Equity finance comprises share capital and share premium, under Equity (see **Chapter 15 Capital and reserves**).

Extract from Greggs plc, 2015

Dividend policy and capital structure

Our progressive dividend policy targets an ordinary dividend that is two times covered by earnings, with any further surplus capital being returned by way of special dividends.

In line with its progressive dividend policy the Board intends to recommend at the Annual General Meeting (AGM) a final dividend of 21.2p per share (2014: 16.0p), giving a total ordinary dividend for the year of 28.6p (2014: 22.0p), an increase of 30.0%.

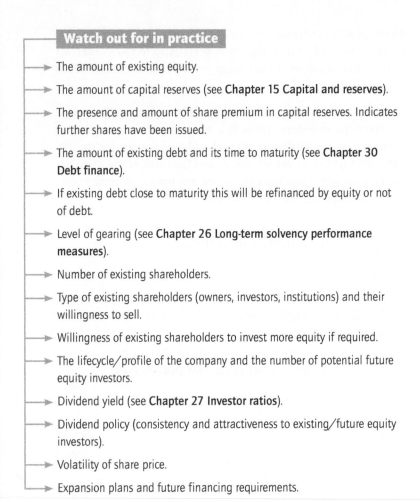

Watch out for in practice

- The amount of existing equity.
- The amount of capital reserves (see **Chapter 15 Capital and reserves**).
- The presence and amount of share premium in capital reserves. Indicates further shares have been issued.
- The amount of existing debt and its time to maturity (see **Chapter 30 Debt finance**).
- If existing debt close to maturity this will be refinanced by equity or not of debt.
- Level of gearing (see **Chapter 26 Long-term solvency performance measures**).
- Number of existing shareholders.
- Type of existing shareholders (owners, investors, institutions) and their willingness to sell.
- Willingness of existing shareholders to invest more equity if required.
- The lifecycle/profile of the company and the number of potential future equity investors.
- Dividend yield (see **Chapter 27 Investor ratios**).
- Dividend policy (consistency and attractiveness to existing/future equity investors).
- Volatility of share price.
- Expansion plans and future financing requirements.

30 Debt finance

'A small debt produces a debtor; a large one, an enemy.'

Publilius Syrus, former slave, writer

In a nutshell

Companies raise finance in one of two ways: debt or equity. Debt finance involves borrowing money that has to be repaid, plus interest.

Debt finance is money raised from debtholders (banks, finance houses, individuals, etc.). Debtholders lend money in return for repayment of the original amount borrowed (the principal) plus interest at an agreed rate and time in the future.

Debt finance is typically a cheaper form of finance for a company than equity. This is because:

Debt provides a contractual and certain return for debt holders, unlike equity which has no guarantee of return.

- Debt can be secured against assets of the company mitigating the risk of loss.
- Debts are ranked higher on insolvency providing greater protection to debtholders (see **Chapter 25 Insolvency and going concern risk**).
- Debt finance provides tax advantages to the company because interest is a tax deductible expense.

However, highly indebted (geared) businesses have a higher financial risk of default (see **Chapter 26 Long-term solvency performance measures**).

Need to know

Why is this important?

Deciding how to finance a company is a critical decision for most businesses and can affect a company's chances of survival or prosperity.

Debt finance is more attractive than equity finance (see **Chapter 29 Equity finance**) for a number of reasons including:

Retaining ownership and control	Debtholders have no automatic right to get involved in the business. A business that borrows money enters a commercial relationship that ends when the amounts borrowed are repaid. Unlike equity finance, control and ownership remain with the owners throughout. From an existing ownership and management perspective, this is highly attractive as it avoids interference in the running of business.
Tax advantages	Interest is a deductible expense for tax purposes. In the UK (which had a corporation tax rate of 20 % in 2016), this means that for every £100 interest paid, the company incurs an £80 expense.
Certainty	From a practical cash flow perspective, budgeting and financial planning should be more certain as the company will know how much interest and principal has to be paid and when.
Cost	Debt finance is generally cheaper than equity because loans may be secured against the assets of the business. In a situation of insolvency, lenders rank higher than shareholders in the 'pecking order' for repayment and are therefore more likely to recover some or all of the amounts invested as companies are required to maintain capital reserves to protect creditors' interests (see **Chapter 15 Capital and reserves**).

Businesses often raise debt finance to reduce the overall cost of capital for the company. Project viability improves as cost of capital falls. Lowering the cost of capital can therefore improve profitability as more projects with positive values are taken on (see **Chapter 35 Investment appraisal**).

Debt finance has its drawbacks, however. Debt increases the financial risk (see **Chapter 26 Long-term solvency performance measures**) of a business because it commits the company to paying interest and (repaying) the amounts borrowed. Where debts are secured against a company's assets, a failure to pay interest (default) could result in the company having to sell secured assets which will reduce operating capability or could threaten a company's survival (see **Chapter 25 Insolvency and going concern risk**).

In practice

While debt is cheaper than equity, it may not be an option for every business.

New or small companies may be unable to secure debt finance either because the business does not generate sufficient cash to pay interest or because the business does not have sufficient assets to offer as security. Equity finance could by default be the only option (see **Chapter 29 Equity finance**).

Companies generating revenue and cash are more easily able to raise debt finance and many choose debt over equity in order to finance their growth because this reduces their overall cost of capital (see **Chapter 35 Investment appraisal**).

A company's cost structure can also influence its choice of finance. Companies operating with high fixed costs for example should seek to avoid debt finance as a small decline in revenue can have a significant adverse effect on profits, increasing the risk of interest payment default (see **Chapter 33 Profit planning**).

There is no optimum mix of debt and equity finance. Most businesses have a mixture of both. A debt–equity mix enables a company to benefit from advantages while limiting the drawbacks, i.e. gaining tax advantages available while keeping the financial commitments to an acceptable level.

In practice the mix of debt and equity should be considered as part of a company's financing strategy (see **Chapter 26 Long-term solvency performance measures**). From a financial risk perspective, companies that want to minimise financial risk will seek greater equity finance. From a commercial viewpoint, the debt–equity mix will depend on the company's ability to raise debt finance. Lenders will look at credit ratings, cash flow forecasts, business plans, etc. when deciding whether to lend.

Relatively low interest rates during the 21st century have made debt finance a more attractive form of finance for business. Paradoxically although interest rates have remained low (and negative in some countries) this has not translated into a growth in debt financing because smaller companies in particular have found it difficult to borrow.

Nice to know

Cost of borrowing

Finance costs (interest rates) charged depend on the level of risk or creditworthiness of the company. A company is charged higher rates where there is a bigger risk of default to reflect higher compensation for the borrower in return for taking the higher risk.

Covenants

Debt finance typically comes with 'strings attached'. A company is required to adhere to *covenants*. These are financial performance limits or targets that must be met (or not breached). For example, *interest cover* thresholds and *gearing ratio* limits exist to prevent a company from taking on more debt and therefore offer protection to existing lenders (see **Chapter 26 Long-term solvency performance measures**).

Asset-based lending (see **Types of finance** section below) involves borrowing money in return for security over the company's assets, typically debtors. In the event of default the lender is able to recover their money through the collection (or sale) of the asset(s) secured.

Types of debt finance

- *Fixed term loans*: Money is borrowed from banks or other financial institutions. Loans have a fixed term (e.g. five years) requiring repayment of the principal at the end of the term. Interest payments are made monthly or annually until the principal has been fully repaid.
- *Bonds*: Larger entities can issue debt securities, known as bonds or debentures, to finance the business. A bond is a debt

liability that typically requires the company to pay regular (for example annual or six monthly) interest payments to investors and to pay back the principal when the bond matures. The advantage of bonds is that they can be bought and sold by bondholders although, like shares, their price may fluctuate because of factors such as demand and supply, analysts' opinions, state of the economy, etc.

- *Convertible bonds*: These bonds give holders the additional right to convert debt to equity (shares) in a company. If the company performs well the lender will convert bonds to shares at a pre-determined rate and benefit from any share price increase of the company. If the bondholder chooses not to convert, the company still has to pay interest on the bond and repay the principal when the term of the bond expires.

- *Crowd lending or peer-to-peer (P2P) lending*: P2P lending involves online lending directly to small and medium-sized businesses. Crowd lending uses online platforms similar to crowdfunding (see **Chapter 29 Equity finance**). Because all activity is internet based, lenders operate with lower overheads, enabling borrowers to obtain funds more cheaply than might otherwise be available. Funding Circle is one example of a marketplace business lender and was the first online platform in the UK.

- *Asset-based finance*: Businesses, especially smaller companies, can be significantly affected when customers delay in paying amounts due. Asset-based finance can help a business to unlock working capital to focus on generating growth in sales (see **Chapter 24 Working capital and liquidity management**). Asset-based finance is a source of debt finance for smaller businesses that are unable to access debt finance through more traditional routes, e.g. banks.

An example of asset-based finance is invoice finance (IF) which involves factoring organisations (known as 'factors') that provide upfront cash against the value of specific unpaid invoices in a company's ledger. The factors make their money by retaining a percentage of the debt as fees.

Optional detail

Secured versus unsecured debt

Debt finance is typically 'secured' on one or more assets, giving debtholders security over their lending. The legal mechanism by which this is achieved is known as a 'charge'.

A *fixed charge* is created on *specific* assets. A mortgage is the most common example of a fixed legal charge on specific property (land and/or buildings).

Fixed charges secure debt lending against particular assets. Where a company fails to meet its debt obligations a charge legally limits what the company can do with the assets charged. While fixed charges do not give lenders any ownership rights over the assets, they give the right to dispose of the asset in a situation of default to recover amounts owed. In the UK, fixed charges are registered at Companies House (and in the case of land and buildings registered also at the Land Registry).

A floating charge is 'unsecured', i.e. it is not secured against particular assets. Lenders may resort to seeking a floating charge where a company does not have fixed assets, typically freehold land and buildings, or where its assets have already been secured with existing debt finance.

A floating charge can crystallise into a fixed charge if a company falls into financial difficulty. This typically happens when a receiver is appointed (see **Chapter 25 Insolvency and going concern risk**).

Floating charges provide less security to a lender than fixed charges and therefore loans secured with a floating charge normally have a higher rate of interest. The exact status of a floating charge in a winding up remains contentious legally, as the rights of lenders continue to be shaped by case law.

Credit ratings and the cost of borrowing

A company's credit rating can have a significant impact on the price of its debt securities, typically bonds. Companies (and even countries) carry credit ratings from organisations such as Moody's and Standard & Poor's. For a company wanting to raise debt finance through issuing bonds, the effect of a poor rating or rating downgrade can reduce the issue price of the bond, thus increasing the interest rate (yield) on the bond to the buyer.

On 27 June 2016, Standard & Poor's downgraded the UK's credit rating from the highest (AAA) credit rating to AA, making it more expensive for the UK to borrow. The downgrade followed the country's Brexit vote which, according to Standard & Poor's, could lead to 'a deterioration of the UK's economic performance, including its large financial services sector'.

Where to spot in company accounts

Debt is a *liability* of the company. Debt finance is *long-term* debt and is included within non-current liabilities. Greggs plc does not have debt finance. A note included in the company's financial review statement explains why.

Extract from Greggs 2015 financial review

In 2015 the Board reviewed the capital structure of the Group and its distribution policy, taking into account the views of shareholders and advisers. The Board continues to be mindful of the leverage inherent in the Group's predominantly leasehold shop estate (which will in due course appear as part of the balance sheet in line with new accounting requirements) and of working capital requirements. As a result we have concluded that it is not currently appropriate to take on structural debt and we will aim to maintain a year-end net cash position of around £40 million to allow for seasonality in our working capital cycle.

Watch out for in practice

→ 'Fine print' in debt agreements. Lenders charge severe penalties for late or missed payments. Missing payments can lead to repossession of assets or cancellation of loan facilities.

→ Debt covenants in debt agreements. Breaches can lead to loan cancellation, repossession of property or penalties.

Credit history. A failure to make payments on time adversely affects credit ratings and reduces the ability to obtain financing in future.

→ Personal guarantees. Lenders often require guarantees from owners, particularly in smaller businesses where the company has insufficient assets available as security. While a company may be a 'separate legal entity', personal guarantees blur that distinction.

→ Off balance sheet debt (e.g. see reference to leasehold shops in the extract above).

→ Year-on-year growth/change in debt financing.

→ Gearing levels (see **Chapter 26 Long-term solvency performance measures**).

→ Interest cover (see **Chapter 26 Long-term solvency performance measures**).

→ Security of debt (e.g. unsecured/secured).

→ Maturity dates for existing debt.

part

seven

Financial management

31 Management accounts

'Two accountants are in a car. The financial accountant looks out the back window and records its journey. The management accountant is in the driving seat, plans where the car is going and aligns its direction.'

Popular accounting allegory

In a nutshell

Management accounts are best understood by contrasting them with financial accounts.

The purpose of financial accounts is to report the historic financial results of a company to shareholders as well as other internal and external stakeholders (such as employees and creditors).

The purpose of management accounts is to help internal stakeholders, such as company directors, run a business efficiently and effectively.

Management accounts use past and present information, both financial and non-financial, to help a company make informed decisions about its future.

Need to know

Management accounts are often produced by management accountants in a 'pack', sometimes referred to as the 'monthly management pack' or 'management accounts pack', hereafter MAP.

Why is this important?

The success of a business is directly related to the quality of its decisions. In order to make quality decisions, businesses need access to timely, accurate, reliable, relevant and insightful information. The key source of information for a board of directors is the MAP.

The role of finance is changing in many organisations. Management accountants, in particular, can provide a value added service through 'finance business partnering'.

When is this important?

Frequency

Whereas financial accounts are produced annually (although listed companies, for example, will also release 'interim' or six-monthly accounts), MAPs are produced far more frequently.

MAPs are typically produced monthly, although some companies may produce them more often, for example on a weekly, or even daily basis. Although technology has enabled more companies to move closer to the ideal of real-time information, monthly MAPs are still common and will include other relevant management information (see the **Nice to know** section below) to be discussed at monthly board meetings. In addition, there is a difference between real-time data (which may just be numbers) and MAPs (which also include analysis and require professional judgement).

Time lag

For a large company, financial accounts can take weeks, if not months to produce. This is mainly due to ensuring that all transactions are included, various required disclosures are made (see **Chapter 19 Accounting and financial reporting standards**) and audits are undertaken (see **Chapter 19 External financial audit**). In addition, it could be up to nine months after the year end before the accounts are released into the public domain.

As MAPs are used to run a business and make critical decisions it is essential that they are produced promptly. A well organised accounting and finance function can produce MAPs within a few days following the month end. Timely information not only enables quicker decisions to be made but also enables issues and opportunities to be identified earlier.

In practice

Requirement

Unlike financial accounts, which are a requirement under company law, there is no requirement to produce MAPs. While full MAPs will be common in large companies, they are less likely to be produced in many SMEs (small and medium sized enterprises). A factor in the success and growth of SMEs into large companies is likely to be the quality of its MAPs.

Format

While financial accounts are standardised through comprehensive accounting regulation (see **Chapter 19 Accounting and financial reporting standards**), there are no accounting standards for MAPs. Indeed, one of their key advantages is that they can be tailored to business needs. There are, however, some established conventions (see the **Nice to know** section below) and many MAPs follow the format of the primary financial statements.

Scope

Financial accounts summarise a whole business, even where there are many different products and/or services sold in different markets.

MAPs can include whatever detail is required, about the whole business, divisions, departments, individual products, services, markets or customers.

Accuracy

Financial accounts need to be 'true and fair' and free from 'material' misstatements (see **Chapter 20 External financial audit**). Figures are often produced in £'000 or £m depending on the size of the company.

As management accounts are used to make critical business decisions, they will usually need to be more accurate than financial accounts, depending upon the decision being made.

The ideal MAP

The ideal MAP should be tailored and relevant to each company's needs. It should be produced on a timely basis and contain the right quantity of quality information, presented clearly and cost effectively.

Nice to know

Contents of a typical MAP

According to CIMA (Chartered Institute of Management Accountants) the ideal MAP should be between 10 and 20 pages and contain the following:

- Executive summary identifying all key issues with a synopsis of KPIs (key performance indicators).
- Action plan specifying corrective actions and contingencies with best and worst case scenarios.
- P&L account showing period and cumulative positions with updated projections. Variances against budget should be highlighted with major variances explained. Trend analysis should be shown graphically.
- Projected profit recalculated on the basis of actual performance and action plans.
- Profiled cash flow summarising actual and projected receipts, payments and balances on a regular basis to year end.
- Analysis of progress of major capital schemes showing percentage completion, current and projected expenditure, completion cost and timescale.
- Balance sheet showing working capital position in tabular form or using performance indicators, e.g. debtor and creditor days.

CIMA also emphasises that the MAP should be easy to assimilate and contain graphs, charts, colour-coding, clear headings and selective highlighting. CIMA suggests that supplementary information should be provided as an appendix only if it is vital to the board's understanding of the report.

Other useful contents for a MAP include:

- Commentary. To add value, the MAP should 'make the numbers talk' and provide a 'story' of what has happened and its impact on projections.
- The order book and other 'lead' versus 'lag' indicators of performance.
- Non-financial information. Kaplan and Norton's 'Balanced Scorecard' suggests balancing financial information with the following additional perspectives:
  - Customer – for example new, repeat and lost customers
  - Internal business processes – for example productivity and efficiency measures
  - Learning and growth – for example new product development and training.

As indicated in the **Need to know** section above, MAPs are not one size fits all, and their size, complexity and contents will differ from organisation to organisation, depending on the size of the company and the requirements of its users.

Extract of typical headings in a MAP

A MAP will typically contain detailed financial statements on a month-by-month and year-to-date (cumulative) basis.

Benchmarks are useful to management in assessing performance and 'actual' results will usually be compared to budget, forecast (see **Chapter 34 Budgeting and forecasting**) as well as prior year.

Example

Last month's marketing expenditure						
£'000				Comparison		
Actual	Budget	3QF	Prior Yr	Act v Bug	Act v Fcst	Act v P Yr
100	95	102	90	(5) (5 %)	2 2 %	(10) (11 %)

(continued)

Year to date (YTD) marketing expenditure						
£'000				Comparison		
Actual	Budget	3QF	Prior Yr	Act v Bug	Act v Fcst	Act v P Yr
1,000	1,050	980	1,100	50 5 %	(20) 2 %	100 11 %

Full year (FY) marketing expenditure						
£'000				Comparison		
Act + Fcst	Budget	3QF	Prior Yr	FY v Bug	FY v Fcst	FY v P Yr
1,150	1,200	1,250	1,200	50 4 %	100 8 %	50 4 %

Optional detail

Reconciliation between financial and management accounts

Financial and management accounts must ultimately reconcile. This is an essential control in business, especially when the information comes from different sources and MAPs are being used to make critical business decisions.

Enterprise resource planning (ERP) and spreadsheets

ERP is a system of integrated IT applications used to manage a business and automate many back office functions, including accounting, supply chain, operations, manufacturing and human resources. ERP has made the production of MAPs much quicker and more efficient.

Alongside the growth in ERP, technological developments such as CRM (customer relationship management), cloud computing and social media have increased the amount of data available for businesses to analyse. This has led to the emergence of new management accounting practices, such as:

- *business intelligence*: the interpretation of raw data to explain performance;

- *business analytics*: insights into performance from a continuous, iterative and methodical exploration of data; and
- *big data*: computational analysis of very large data sets to reveal patterns, trends, and associations, such as customer behaviour and interactions.

Spreadsheets still play a central role in the majority management accounting departments. While ERP systems are established in many large organisations, they are less common in SMEs which tend to rely mostly on spreadsheets to produce MAPs. Most accounting systems are designed for processing transactions such as invoices and payments and therefore MAPs are produced by importing data from these systems and 'crunching' the numbers in a spreadsheet.

Where to spot in company accounts

The MAP is an internal document and will not be published.

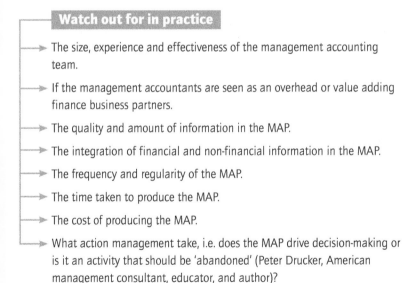

Watch out for in practice

- The size, experience and effectiveness of the management accounting team.
- If the management accountants are seen as an overhead or value adding finance business partners.
- The quality and amount of information in the MAP.
- The integration of financial and non-financial information in the MAP.
- The frequency and regularity of the MAP.
- The time taken to produce the MAP.
- The cost of producing the MAP.
- What action management take, i.e. does the MAP drive decision-making or is it an activity that should be 'abandoned' (Peter Drucker, American management consultant, educator, and author)?

32 Profitable pricing

> 'Pricing is the third business skill. (The first being the ability to create value and produce goods or services. The second being the ability to sell products or services.)'
>
> Ernst-Jan Bouter, pricing professional and author

In a nutshell

Increasing price is one of the most effective ways to grow profit.
£1 extra on the 'top line' is £1 extra on the 'bottom line'.

Given the competitive environment facing the majority of businesses, pricing decisions are too important to leave to operational departments using traditional cost based approaches. Pricing has strategic importance.

Competition and customer pressure often result in the temptation to offer discounts; however, this can have a detrimental effect on profit. By focusing on customer 'value' instead, businesses can successfully increase prices and profitability.

Need to know

Why is this important?

There are a number of ways a business can increase profit. These include:

- Efficiency – through productivity of the workforce and reducing overheads.
- Attracting new customers.
- Retaining existing customers and encouraging repeat business.
- Increasing the frequency of customer transactions.

- Increasing the average value of each transaction by selling more to each customer.
- Increasing the average value of each transaction through higher prices.

Although all the above actions are beneficial, higher prices generally have the biggest impact, by far, on profit. In addition, compared to the other actions, pricing takes the least time, effort and cost to change. For many businesses, the increase in profit as a result of higher prices can more than compensate for any lost business.

Many businesses, however, have an unfounded fear of raising prices. Increasing competition in most industries keeps businesses from putting up prices.

It is important that businesses understand the impact of price on the 'bottom line' and how to price profitably while giving customers the value they desire.

In practice

Except for low-value generic goods, customers are not as price sensitive as believed. 'Value for money' is usually more important than price. A higher price is usually acceptable in return for higher benefits and conversely a lower price for lower benefits. It's a trade-off.

Additionally, a purchase is often much more than a 'value for money' decision. Customers consider many conscious and subconscious factors when making an important purchase. Rarely do they simply go for the cheapest option.

Many businesses ignore this when setting their own prices and don't emphasise the value differentiators between themselves and their competitors. For example:

- Quality of service including after sales service and support.
- Other products and services offered (perhaps through 'bundles').
- Guarantees offered.
- Efficiency of account management.
- The degree of personalisation offered.

- The reliability of their product or service.
- Their reputation and brand.

How to set prices

1 *Cover costs.* A business should calculate its minimum acceptable price by identifying all the direct costs associated with a product or service and adding their minimum acceptable 'premium' to cover indirect costs and profit (see the **Nice to know** section below). Covering costs will ensure that the business does not make a loss. This is however only the starting point as it does not consider the customer's perception of value (see below).

2 *Watch competitors.* It is important to benchmark competitors' prices of similar products and services, not to undercut their prices, but to consider positioning. Undercutting competitors' prices is a risky game which can only be played by those with scale and volume.

   Price sends a message of what a company stands for in the eyes of its customers (and potential customers), relative to its competitors. Customers will consider relative benefits against relative prices.

3 *Price according to value.* A customer-centric approach to pricing focuses on what customers are willing to pay, based on the value they receive from a product or service.

   A business should try to understand its customer's perception of value. Undertaking research, such as focus groups can be helpful. For bespoke products or services this is best done through dialogue to understand what is important and what is non-value adding for each customer (see price customisation in the **Optional detail** section below). These conversations should be used to raise the customer's appreciation of all the features and benefits they will receive and to balance their value scales.

4 *Regularly review prices.* Over time, costs may change, new competitors may enter the market and old ones leave. Just as importantly a customer's perception of value can change over time. Prices should be as dynamic as possible and the topic of 'value' should be a regular conversation with customers.

Note: Every industry and market is different. Each business may be in a different position. One size does not fit all with pricing. Not every approach will be appropriate nor can be used.

Nice to know

Offering discounts

The presence of high street and online discounters in the retail world has influenced the rest of the business world and many purchasers are now conditioned into automatically requesting discounts. Many people, especially in sales, have an inbuilt desire to please others and avoid conflict. Consequently, it is common for businesses to offer discounts. Unfortunately, the potential increase in sales is rarely compensated by an increase in profit, in fact, mostly the opposite.

Example

ABC Ltd sells product X for £100. The direct costs of X are £75 and ABC sells 1,000 units of X per month.

The table below calculates the following:

1. The impact of a 10% discount assuming no change in sales volume.
2. The sales volume required to maintain the same level of profit with a 10% discount.

	Before discount	1. After discount (no change in volume)	2. After discount (volume to maintain profit)
Price/unit	£100	£90	£90
Cost/unit	(£75)	(£75)	(£75)
Profit/unit	£25	£15	£15
Sales volume	1,000	1,000	1,667
Gross profit	£25,000	£15,000	£25,000*
		40% reduction in profit	67%* increase in sales volume

Note: * rounded

Therefore, given a 25 % gross margin:

▪ a 10% discount would lead to a 40% reduction in gross profit (assuming no change in sales volume); or

▪ sales volume would need to increase by 67% to maintain the same level of profit.

The cost of discounts is magnified with lower margins. For example, if product X had a 20% gross profit margin instead, a 10% discount would cause a 50% reduction in profit (assuming no change in sales volume); or would require a 100 % increase in sales volume (to maintain gross profit).

Margins and mark-ups

Despite the benefits of value based pricing, many businesses still set prices by adding a 'premium' to costs in order to cover overheads and profit. There are two ways to calculate the premium:

1 A *margin*.

2 A *mark-up*.

1 Margin

Margin is profit as a percentage of the 'sales price' (see also '**gross profit margin**' in **Chapter 23 Profitability performance measures**). It's often used by managers as it enables them to calculate the profit from each sale. It is calculated as follows:

$$\frac{\text{Gross profit}}{\text{Sales price}} \times 100\,\% = \text{Margin}\,\%$$

2 Mark-up

Mark-up is profit as a percentage of 'direct costs' (for example, stock (see **Chapter 11 Stock**)). It's often used when setting prices as it is easier to use in practice than the margin. The mark-up is simply added to direct costs, rather than working backwards as required by the margin. Using a mark-up is often referred to as 'cost plus' pricing.

$$\frac{\text{Gross profit}}{\text{Direct costs}} \times 100\,\% = \text{Mark-up}\,\%$$

Example

ABC Ltd sells product Y. The direct costs of each Y are £1,000. If ABC uses a 30 % mark-up it will price each Y for £1,300. This also represents a 23 % margin as illustrated below:

$$\frac{£300}{£1,300} \times 100\% = 23\% \text{ margin}$$

$$\frac{£300}{£1,000} \times 100\% = 30\% \text{ mark-up}$$

The margin will always be less than the mark-up.

It is important to understand the difference between these methods. In practice, confusion between these terms may lead to under-pricing, for example, if managers use margins and price setters use mark-ups.

Optional detail

Price customisation

Technology has enabled *price customisation* (a.k.a. 'dynamic pricing' or 'demand yield' pricing or price discrimination), i.e. setting different prices for different customers based on their relative perceptions of value.

For example, airline prices change according to the availability of seats, seasonal demand, the actual time of the flight, the number of days before departure and competitor pricing. It is possible for prices to change several times in one day.

A investigation in *The Wall Street Journal* published on 24 December 2012 reported that 'Websites vary prices, deals based on users' information'. An extract follows:

> The *Journal* identified several companies, including Staples, Discover Financial Services, Rosetta Stone Inc. and Home Depot Inc., that were consistently adjusting prices and displaying different product offers based on a range of characteristics that could be discovered

about the user. Office Depot, for example, told the *Journal* that it uses 'customers' browsing history and geolocation' to vary the offers and products it displays to a visitor to its site.

Ethical pricing

Price customisation is effectively price discrimination; however, there is nothing illegal about offering different prices to different customers. As *The Wall Street Journal* noted in its above article: 'Nobody is surprised if, say, a gallon of gas is cheaper at the same chain, one town over.'

Despite being legal, a business needs to be careful that its pricing is and is seen to be ethical. A company's prices should be as clear and as transparent as possible to avoid misleading customers.

Profitable pricing can be perfectly ethical in a competitive market where customers have choice. However, pricing can be contentious in monopoly situations if the monopolist uses its market power to set high prices and earn excessive profits. For example, Turing Pharmaceuticals and its former CEO Martin Shkreli, received widespread criticism for raising the price of the drug 'Daraprim' by over 5,000% in 2015.

Price skimming

'Price skimming' is a strategy used for new products or services which are highly desirable, differentiated from the competition and usually high quality, for example the latest smart phone or accessory. This is evidenced by a high initial price, which is gradually lowered over time. Early adopters who are keen to buy the product or experience the service are willing to pay a relatively high price. As the price is lowered more people are attracted (or 'skimmed') towards making a purchase at each price point. This pricing strategy enables the supplier to maximise revenue and often recoup high initial costs, such as research and marketing.

Where to spot in company accounts

While an annual report may refer to 'competitive pricing' in its annual report, its actual prices are unlikely to appear in a company's accounts.

Watch out for in practice

➤ How does the business set its prices? For example, does it use 'cost plus'; competitive based; and/or customer-centric prices?

➤ Does the business compete on price alone or does it make an effort to demonstrate value for money and other value differentiators?

➤ Does the business regularly offer discounts? Does it have a discount policy?

➤ How often are prices changed?

➤ Who has responsibility for setting prices within the organisation?

➤ Are price matching guarantees offered, for example John Lewis uses the slogan 'Never knowingly undersold'.

➤ Is there evidence of anti-competitive or anti-consumer behaviour? In 2015, the UK Competition and Markets Authority (CMA) launched an investigation following a 'super-complaint' from the consumer group Which? about 'misleading and opaque' pricing by supermarkets. In April 2016 the CMA reported that 'supermarkets generally take compliance seriously, but there were some promotional practices that could mislead shoppers'.[1]

---

1 www.gov.uk/government/news/groceries-promotions-to-be-clearer-for-shoppers

33 Profit planning

In a nutshell

Businesses undertake 'profit planning' to calculate forecast profits for different
products and services.

Profit planning requires an understanding of variable and fixed costs as well
as the concept of 'contribution'.

By using simple ratios businesses can calculate target profits and their
sensitivity to the breakeven sales revenue.

Need to know

This chapter will cover the following three elements of profit
planning:

1 Cost classification.

2 The concept of contribution.

3 The contribution percentage of sales ratio.

1 Cost classification

The first step in profit planning is to classify operating costs into
'variable' and 'fixed' categories.

Variable costs

Costs which are 'variable' will change as a result of changes in business activity. For example:

- For a company which sells products, the cost of stock sold will change in proportion to the quantity sold.
- For a business which provides services and uses contractors, such as a firm of builders, the 'labour' cost of contractors will vary with the volume of building undertaken.
- Sales commissions are an example of variable costs as they are usually directly correlated to sales revenue.

Fixed costs

Costs which are 'fixed' are the opposite, i.e. they do not change when 'activity' (the volume of goods or services) changes. For example:

- Head office rent will usually remain the same, even if revenue increases or decreases.
- Other examples of fixed costs are insurance, marketing and salaried employees.

Fixed costs can, however, change over time.

2 The concept of contribution

Consider the example of XYZ Ltd, which sells two products X and Y and makes £250,000 overall profit.

	Product X	Product Y	Total
	£'000	£'000	£'000
Sales revenue	700	300	1,000
Variable costs	(200)	(150)	(350)
Fixed costs	(200)	(200)	(400)
Profit/(loss)	300	(50)	250

On first read, one may suggest that XYZ Ltd should stop selling product Y as it is showing a loss of £50,000 and instead focus solely on product X which makes a profit of £300,000.

The challenge is that in many businesses fixed costs are often centrally allocated on an arbitrary basis to departments (such as product Y).

If the total fixed costs of £400,000 relate to costs of running a warehouse, which has been allocated to each product equally, the costs would be unavoidable (i.e. they would still exist with or without product Y). Discontinuing product Y will mean that product X alone must absorb all the fixed costs of £400,000. This would in effect reduce overall profit from £250,000 to £100,000 as follows:

	Product X
	£'000
Sales revenue	700
Variable costs	(200)
All fixed costs	(400)
	100

Instead, a company should calculate *contribution* when making profit planning decisions:

Contribution = sales revenue less variable costs

Therefore, XYZ Ltd should consider contribution at the product level and profit at the company level as follows:

	Product X	Product Y	Total
	£'000	£'000	£'000
Sales revenue	700	300	1,000
Variable costs	(200)	(150)	(350)
Contribution	500	150	650
Fixed costs			(400)
Profit			250

This analysis shows that despite initially appearing to make a loss after allocated fixed costs, product Y still makes a positive contribution of £150,000 towards fixed costs and profit. Therefore, product Y should not be discontinued. As long as product Y has less than £150,000 of avoidable fixed costs it will make a positive contribution.

3 The contribution percentage of sales ratio

The contribution percentage of sales (CPS) ratio, alternatively known as the profit to volume ratio, is very useful in profit planning.

CPS can be illustrated using the example of XYZ Ltd:

	£'000
Total contribution	650
Total sales	1,000
CPS (contribution/sales)	65 %

The CPS ratio can be used to calculate the following:

a The sales revenue required to break even.

b The sales revenue required to achieve a target profit.

a The sales revenue required to break even

This is calculated as follows:

$$\text{Breakeven sales revenue} = \frac{\text{Fixed costs}}{\text{CPS}}$$

For XYZ Ltd:

Fixed costs	£400,000
CPS	65 %
Breakeven sales revenue (rounded)	£615,000

The calculation below demonstrates that XYZ Ltd will break even with a sales revenue of £615,000, assuming products X and Y continue to be sold in the same mix (70/30).

	Product X	Product Y	Total
	£'000	£'000	£'000
Sales revenue	431	184	615
Variable costs*	(123)	(92)	(215)
Contribution	308	92	400
Fixed costs			(400)
Profit			0

Note: * Variable costs vary directly with sales revenue.

Margin of safety

An additional benefit of calculating breakeven levels of sales, is that a business can measure its *margin of safety*. This answers the question 'by how much would sales have to fall before a product (or service) makes a loss?' The margin of safety can be expressed as either an absolute amount or as a percentage.

For XYZ Ltd:

	£'000
Original sales revenue	1,000
Breakeven sales revenue	615
Margin of safety	385
Margin of safety %	38.5 %

This means that sales revenue can fall by £385,000 or 38.5% before the company makes a loss, assuming that products continue to be sold in the same mix.

b   The sales revenue required to achieve a target profit

The techniques above can be developed further to help drive business performance through budget planning and target setting.

This is calculated as follows:

$$\text{Sales revenue to achieve a target profit} = \frac{\text{Fixed costs + target profit}}{\text{CPS}}$$

This can be illustrated for XYZ Ltd as a whole with the assumption that the company wishes to increase its profit by 20 % from £250,000 to £300,000.

$$\text{Sales revenue to achieve a target profit} = \frac{£400,000 + £300,000}{65\%} = £1,077,000^{[1]}$$

---

[1] Numbers have been rounded to the nearest £100,000 in the above calculation.

As proof of the above:

	£000
Sales revenue	1,077
Variable costs[2]	(377)
Contribution	700
Fixed costs	(400)
Profit	300

2 Variable costs will vary directly with sales revenue.

This means that a 7.7 % increase in sales revenue is required to achieve a 20% increase in profits.

Why is this important?

Profit planning enables a business to forecast the impact of changes in sales revenue on profit. It enables a business to calculate its margin of safety before the breakeven point is reached.

This is useful for both existing and new products or services.

Additionally, the CPS ratio can be used to determine which are the most profitable products and services in a company's portfolio. It can then divert resources to the highest earning products and services or alternatively attempt to make the lowest earning more profitable.

When is this important?

Profit planning is important when budgeting and forecasting (see **Chapter 34 Budgeting and forecasting**) and planning for new products and services.

In practice

Businesses should attempt to influence their breakeven points through a combination of the following activities. The activities will need to be balanced as they are interconnected.

Activity	Impact	Risk
Increase prices.	This will increase contribution and the CPS ratio, which will lower the volume of sales required to break even.	This is challenging to achieve without offering more value and increasing variable costs.
Reduce variable costs by sourcing better value supplies and labour.	Same impact as increasing prices.	If this reduces quality, it may impact on the sales volume.
Increase the quantity sold by increasing market share or entering new markets.	This will not impact on the CPS ratio and will instead increase total contribution, which will increase profit.	This may be challenging to achieve without increasing overheads.
Reduce fixed costs by controlling overheads.	This will increase the margin of safety as a lower sales revenue will be required to break even.	If this reduces quality and service, it may impact on the sales volume.

Businesses should be aware of the limitations of contribution and the CPS ratio:

- If the mix of products/services sold changes (for example XYZ Ltd was to sell more of product X than product Y) the overall CPS ratio would also change.

- If fixed costs change with 'activity' the breakeven point will change. Some fixed costs will change in the medium to long term. For example, if a business grows significantly and a larger head office is required, its rent would become what is known as a 'stepped' fixed cost.

- Not all relationships are linear. For example, businesses may offer volume discounts to certain customers reducing price and therefore the CPS ratio. Similarly, businesses may receive volume discounts from their suppliers and variable costs per unit may fall at higher levels of output, increasing the CPS ratio.

- The calculation of breakeven sales revenue for individual products and services should include only 'avoidable' fixed costs specific to each product – however, in practice these may be hard to identify accurately.

Nice to know

Operating risk

Operating risk (or operating gearing) looks at the percentage of variable and fixed costs in a business. The higher the percentage of fixed costs to profit, the higher the operating risk.

For businesses with a high percentage of fixed costs, a small change in sales volume will result in a large change in operating profits. Thus, these businesses can do very well in times of growth, but struggle, or even fail, when trade declines.

Note that a similar relationship can be ascertained by comparing contribution to profit.

Example

Companies A and B operate in the same type of business and have identical revenues of £200,000 p.a. The difference between the two companies is their operating cost structure:

- Company A's operating costs are 20% fixed and 80% variable.
- Company B's operating costs are 80% fixed and 20% variable.

The following table considers the impact of a 25% rise in sales revenue.

	Company A (20% operating gearing)		Company B (80% operating gearing)	
	Current	25% increase in revenue	Current	25% increase in revenue
Sales revenue	200,000	250,000	200,000	250,000
Variable costs	(80,000)	(100,000)	(20,000)	(25,000)
Fixed costs	(20,000)	(20,000)	(80,000)	(80,000)
Operating profit	100,000	130,000	100,000	145,000
		30% increase in operating profit		45% increase in operating profit

A 25% change in revenue leads to a 30% change in operating profit for company A and a 45% change for company B.

As company B has a higher percentage of fixed costs, its operating profits are more volatile. However, it can also experience a higher percentage growth when profits increase.

Note that although company B has a higher operating risk than company A, it has a higher 'contribution margin' and therefore has more flexibility with pricing (see **Chapter 32 Profitable pricing**).

It is also important to note that the same magnification would apply if revenue declined.

Optional detail

Mixed costs

Some costs are also 'mixed' in that they include an element of both fixed and variable costs. For example, a phone bill is made up of a fixed rental charge plus a variable charge for calls made. To calculate 'contribution' *mixed costs* will need to be split into their fixed and variable parts.

CVP analysis

Accountants sometimes refer to profit planning with calculations of contribution as *CVP (cost-volume-profit) analysis.*

Contribution per unit

This chapter has looked at total contribution. CVP analysis can also be undertaken on a unit basis, looking at sales price per unit, variable cost per unit and therefore contribution per unit. Although more complicated, this has the added benefit of being able to calculate a breakeven sales quantity (units sold) in addition to the breakeven sales revenue demonstrated in this chapter.

Where to spot in company accounts

Profit planning is an internal process and therefore does not feature in company accounts.

Watch out for in practice

→ Does profit planning using the concept of contribution take place?

→ Is there an opportunity to increase profits?

→ Is the organisation operating close to its breakeven point?

→ Are variable and fixed costs by product and service identifiable?

→ Are prices and variable costs linear over the standard range of activity?

→ Levels of fixed operating costs in the business (operating risk). Unless the business has a healthy interest cover (see **Chapter 26 Long-term solvency performance measures**), it is inadvisable to combine high operating risk with high financial risk (gearing).

34 Budgeting and forecasting

In a nutshell

A *budget* is a financial and operational business plan. It is used to implement an organisation's objectives by setting financial targets.

A *forecast* is an estimation of an organisation's financial performance for specific periods in the future, for example the final quarter of the year.

Budgets are usually set annually in advance of a financial year, whereas forecasts are typically prepared more frequently and a number of times during a financial year.

Management accounts (see **Chapter 31 Management accounts**) will usually include a report of actual performance compared to budget and a forecast of the predicted activity level and results. The budget is used to benchmark past performance, whereas the forecast is used to predict future performance.

Need to know

The format of the budget

The main budget (known as the master budget) follows the format of the primary financial statements. For example:

- A budgeted profit and loss account, supported by:
  - sales and production/purchasing budgets, detailed by individual products and/or services as well as by geographical area

- expenditure budget, including salaries and other overheads.
- A budgeted balance sheet, supported by:
  - capital expenditure budget
  - working capital budget.
- A cash flow budget, comprising:
  - operational cash flows, including receipts from customers and payments to suppliers, employees, tax authorities and bank interest
  - investing activities, including payments to acquire new assets and receipts from the sale of old assets and other investments
  - financing activities, including dividend payments, repayments of debt and inflows from further borrowing.

The board of directors will focus on the big picture, i.e. the bottom line profit and other KPIs (key performance indicators) such as return on capital employed (see **Chapter 23 Profitability performance measures**).

Why is this important?

Budgets and forecasts are important for the following reasons:

Planning

Even though actual results are often different from budgets, the process of planning is an important business discipline. Successful businesses set themselves clear objectives as part of their strategic planning. Setting and managing a budget is helpful in trying to meet those objectives.

Identification and utilisation of scarce resources

The process of budgeting helps to identify scarce resources and other constraints that need to be carefully managed. For example, companies do not have unlimited cash reserves. The budget process will help allocate cash to those departments which can generate the most value.

Communication and coordination

All the areas of an organisation must fit and work together to drive the business in the right direction.

A budget gives a sense of the big picture. It is an effective way to communicate objectives to every area of a business and to make sure that everyone works towards the same goal.

Organisational control

Budgets provide a basis for authorising expenditure and delegating financial responsibility to 'budget holders'.

Most budget holders are 'cost centres', which means they are responsible for managing and controlling their costs. Other responsibility centres are:

- Revenue centres – for example, a sales team.
- Profit centres – for example, a retail outlet responsible for both sales and purchases.
- Investment centres – for example, regional offices of multinationals responsible for managing profits as well as some balance sheet items, such as working capital (see **Chapter 24 Working capital and liquidity management**).

Budget holders can be motivated by setting realistic but challenging targets. However, if the budget is too challenging this can sometimes have the reverse effect.

Performance measurement and evaluation

Budgets are a useful benchmark against which to measure and evaluate performance. Monitoring actual performance against budget is also an effective method of organisational control. It helps to ensure that income, expenditure and cash flows are managed and is good corporate governance (see **Chapter 22 Corporate governance and whistleblowing**).

Management can take corrective action against underperformance against budget ('negative variances') to steer the organisation back on track. Alternatively, performance improvements ('positive variances') can be encouraged, where desirable.

In practice most businesses will use the principle of 'management by exception', concentrating on variances above a certain percentage or amount.

Budgeting problems

It is also important to be aware of the drawbacks of the budgeting and forecasting process.

Time and money

The budget-setting process can take several months in some organisations and involves a large number of finance and non-finance personnel. The budget-setting and monitoring process can be a large cost for a business.

Out of date

Ironically, despite budgets taking a long time to create, they are often out of date a few months into the new financial year as events unfold. Budgeting is usually an annual event and budget cycles do not always coincide with cycles in the business environment.

Research by Develin & Partners on corporate budgeting found that the average time to produce a budget is 3.7 months. At the same time half of organisations find that, on average, after four months their budget is out of date and for practical management purposes ignored.[1]

A constraint

In some organisations the budget can act as a constraint, in that once it is set, management do not allow any movement away from budget. Some argue that this restricts creativity and causes businesses to miss out on opportunities which were not foreseen when the budget was set. In addition, it is argued that an undue emphasis on the budget results in an overly internal focus.

---

1 www.develin.co.uk and www.pcsconsulting.com/index.php/resources/papers/27-repaireorreplace

Budgetary slack and padding

Budget holders may be motivated to underestimate revenue and overestimate costs when setting budgets, to ensure they exceed their budget and receive a positive evaluation. This motivation may be enhanced when rewards such as bonuses are received for meeting or exceeding budgets.

If a significant percentage of budget holders build in budgetary slack this can potentially lead to inaccurate planning and potentially wasted resources.

When is this important?

In most organisations the budget-setting process takes place annually, several months before the year end. The process is usually a combination of 'top-down' guidance with 'bottom-up' input involving budget holders from every area of the business and centrally coordinated by the finance department.

During the financial year budget holders will receive regular reports, usually monthly, of their progress against their budget.

Forecasting on the other hand is more of a 'top-down' process undertaken by the finance department with input from selected budget holders. Forecasts usually take place either monthly or quarterly.

In practice

- Businesses should be aware of the drawbacks of budgeting and make efforts to avoid them where possible, for example by using additional systems of performance evaluation which include non-financial measures.
- Budgets should clearly identify those elements which are under the control of the budget holder and those which are not, for example centrally allocated overheads.
- Businesses should consider the time and resources required to build and monitor budgets and ensure that the benefits of budgeting exceeds its cost.

Nice to know

Alternative methods of budgeting

Incremental

An *incremental* approach is where *budgets* are based on the previous year's budget plus or minus a set percentage.

The advantage of this approach is that it is quick and involves less effort. It is the most common form of budgeting in organisations. The drawback is that any inefficiencies, padding or slack are carried forward.

Zero-based

The opposite of incremental budgeting is *zero-based budgeting*. This approach calculates the budget from a 'zero base', i.e. starting from scratch.

The advantage is that any inherited efficiencies can be eliminated and the budget is more accurate. The drawback is the time, resources and hence cost required to set the budget in this way.

In practice, an effective compromise is to zero base the budget every few years or alternatively to zero base different parts of the budget on a rotational basis each year, with the drawback that this can lead to inconsistency across the organisation.

Rolling

An alternative to a 'fixed' (or 'periodic') budget is a *rolling* (or 'continuous') *budget*, which re-budgets on a regular basis, usually monthly or quarterly. Each period the budget is updated, i.e. 'rolled forward'.

The advantage is that new information is incorporated as events unfold and the budget is more up to date. Additionally, as budget holders are aware that the budget will be updated they may be less likely to build in 'contingencies for unplanned events'. The drawback is the time required each period to update the budget. However, supporters of rolling budgets argue that as budgeting takes place more regularly the time is simply spread over the year and doesn't require as much 'up front' time.

Cisco Systems, Electrolux and General Electric are examples of companies who use rolling budgets in practice.

Rolling budgets are most effective when the budget period is continually extended for at least 12 months ahead as this reduces the 'shrinking visibility' problem of most fixed annual budgets. Some organisations opt for a compromise and use annual budgets together with rolling re-forecasts, continually extended at least 12 months ahead.

Research by SAP BusinessObjects in association with CIMA (Chartered Institute of Management Accountants) reported Reset in standard text that 53 % of UK companies wanted to re-forecast more frequently.[2]

Optional detail

The use of spreadsheets for budgeting

Many accounting systems have budgeting capability – however, in practice spreadsheets remain a well-used and popular budgeting tool.

Microsoft has previously reported that 40 % of SMEs use Excel to prepare their accounts, forecasting and budgeting.

The accounting software firm 'Sage' has previously claimed to have lost market share to Excel.

While spreadsheets are invaluable and flexible tools, it is important to be aware of their risks when budgeting and forecasting.

Professor Ray Panko of the University of Hawaii is one of the world's leading experts on spreadsheet errors. In association with EuSpRIG (European Spreadsheet Risks Interest Group) Professor Panko notes that his research has found 'ample evidence demonstrating that spreadsheet errors are common and nontrivial.'[3]

---

2 www.cimaglobal.com/Documents/ImportedDocuments/The_Reforecasting_Survey.pdf

3 www.eusprig.org/quotes.htm

For example, the London 2012 organising committee (LOCOG) reported that a spreadsheet error led to four synchronised swimming sessions being oversold by 10,000 tickets.[4]

In another example, the US town of Framingham had to request $600,000 in unexpected state aid, after a spreadsheet error led it to believe it had $1.5 million more funds in its 2012 operating budget than it actually did.[4]

Beyond budgeting

Operating since 1998, the Beyond Budgeting Round Table (BBRT), an independent research collaborative, has proposed that budgeting, as it is currently practised by most organisations (a traditional command and control management model), should be abandoned.

The BBRT has attracted over 60 organisations from all over the world, including American Express, Charles Schwab, MasterCard International, Thomson, Unilever and the World Bank.

BBRT assert that their members have 'broken free from the shackles of budgeting and its culture of gaming and misinformation'. They suggest that planning is undertaken on a continuous, participative basis and only high-level forecasts are needed.

BBRT suggest that performance evaluation should be based on relative performance indicators which take account of the conditions, including long-term external benchmarks, under which the business is operating.[5]

Where to spot in company accounts

Budgets do not feature in company accounts.

Public company announcements may include forecasts of their year-end results and sometimes future outlook.

---

4 www.eusprig.org/horror-stories.htm

5 http://bbrt.org

Watch out for in practice

Does the budget setting process coincide with the strategic planning process? An ideal budget should follow an organisation's objectives and be linked to its strategy.

Is the budget setting process 'top-down', 'bottom-up' or a combination of both? There are disadvantages of both extremes. Realistic budgets will involve a degree of iteration between the top and bottom of an organisation.

Budget holders incorporating 'padding' or 'slack' during the budget setting process.

An escalation of expenditure by budget holders towards the year end. This could be evidence of a 'use it or lose it' mentality which can result in carried forward inefficiencies in incremental budgets.

Does management take corrective action upon finding variances from budget? If variances are not followed up there is a risk that they are deemed 'acceptable'.

35 Investment appraisal

In a nutshell

Capital investment, i.e. money, is required for most business opportunities, for example purchasing a new long-term asset, developing a new product, entering a new market or acquiring another entity. An organisation will need to invest cash today in expectation of future returns.

There should be a process to evaluate opportunities to see if their benefit is greater than their cost and also which projects should receive priority where capital is limited. This process is known as 'investment appraisal'.

The main benefits from an investment are its future net cash inflows. Its two main costs are the amount of the actual investment (capital outflows) and the cost of financing the investment over the long term (the *cost of capital*). The non-financial benefits and costs of an investment as well as its risk are also relevant considerations.

Ideally a range of financial appraisal methods should be used to assess an investment.

Need to know

There are several ways to appraise investments:

1   Payback period
2   Annual yield
3   Measures which use discounted cash flows.

Example

ABC Ltd has two competing investments: A and B which both require £250,000 of initial investment and generate positive returns totalling £500,000 over the following five years.

	Investment A	Investment B
	£'000	£'000
Initial investment	(250)	(250)
Year 1	100	50
Year 2	100	75
Year 3	100	100
Year 4	100	125
Year 5	100	150

The only difference between the investments is the timing of the returns within the five years. Investment A has constant returns of £100,000 per year, whereas investment B has escalating returns.

1 Payback period

The simplest form of 'investment appraisal' is the *payback period* (PBP). It measures the time required to pay back an investment.

In the above example of ABC Ltd, investment A 'pays back' during year three – i.e. by year three, project A has generated £300,000 (£100,000 in each year). However, it takes project B until year four to pay back the cost of investment (£50 + £75 + £100 + £125).

The PBP provides a measure of risk. The longer the PBP, the higher the risk. Therefore, according to the PBP method, investment B appears riskier than investment A.

As well as using PBP to compare competing investments, some organisations set a target PBP for all investments.

By itself the PBP is an incomplete method of investment appraisal. It does not give any indication of 'return' and it also does not consider the total life of an investment. For example, if investment B was able to generate an additional year of returns of say, £175,000 in year six, it would now generate total returns of £675,000 versus the £500,000 from investment A. Nevertheless, PBP would still choose investment A over investment B as its sole criteria is the speed of payback.

PBP is therefore best used alongside the other methods of investment appraisal.

2 Annual yield (also known as ARR/annual rate of return)

While there are a number of ways to calculate the annual yield, the simplest method is to divide the annual returns (net inflows) by the amount of the investment (capital outflows).

$$\text{Annual yield \%} = \frac{\text{net annual inflow}}{\text{capital outflows}} \times 100$$

For investments A and B, the annual yield can be calculated as follows:

	Investment A	Investment B
Year 1	40 %	20 %
Year 2	40 %	30 %
Year 3	40 %	40 %
Year 4	40 %	50 %
Year 5	40 %	60 %
Average	40 %	40 %

Investment A's annual yield is 40% each year, whereas investment B's yield increases from 20% to 60% in line with the growth in its annual returns. Both investments have an average yield of 40% over their life. Investments A and B are therefore challenging to compare using the annual yield.

The annual yield calculation is synonymous with other internal performance measures such as return on investment (see **Chapter 23 Profitability performance measures**). This method of investment appraisal is therefore useful as it benchmarks potential investments against a company's performance measures.

However, the annual yield by itself it is not an effective method of investment appraisal, mainly because it does not consider the timing of investment returns.

3 Discounted cash flows

The most effective methods of investment appraisal account for the time value of money by discounting all future net cash inflows (and further capital outflows, if any) back to their equivalent present value (PV). The objective is to compare all cash flows from an investment on a like-for-like basis.

Accounting for the time value of money is important because there is an 'opportunity cost' of money (capital) being tied up in an investment. This 'opportunity cost' will depend upon the following factors, which can be unique to each business and its economic environment:

- interest paid if money is borrowed;
- returns to shareholders if the investment is equity financed;
- interest received on surplus funds if available;
- the risk of the investment not performing as expected;
- the risk of missing out on alternative opportunities;
- inflation.

There are two ways to appraise investments using discounted cash flows (*DCFs*):

a Net Present Value (NPV) – which focuses on values.

b Internal Rate of Return (IRR) – which focuses on returns.

a NPV:

PV of future returns (inflows)	X
PV of the investment (capital outflow)	(X)
NPV	X

The *NPV* represents the value or contribution of an investment for a business.

- If the NPV is positive, the investment is potentially worthwhile.
- If the NPV is negative, the investment is likely to make a loss.

See also 'non-financial considerations' under the **In practice** section below.

b IRR:

The *IRR* represents the 'rate of return' of an investment. IRR uses DCFs to calculate a percentage return on investment.

For investments A and B, the NPV and IRR are:

	Investment A	Investment B
NPV	£129,079	£111,084
IRR	29 %	23 %

Investment A has a higher NPV and IRR than investment B and therefore should be ranked higher. The reason that A is ranked higher is simply because its cash returns arise earlier than investment B.

The calculation of NPV assumes a 10% opportunity cost of capital (see the **Nice to know** section below).

See also the **Optional detail** section below for a discussion of when NPV and IRR have different outcomes.

Why is this important?

Businesses face many competing investment opportunities. As capital is limited a business must rank and choose between these opportunities.

A prioritisation system is required to make the most profitable investment decisions. Ultimately there is a correlation between the success of a company and the success of its investments.

A financial cost versus benefit analysis using the above methods is an essential part of the decision-making process.

When is this important?

The timing of an investment can be critical to its success. Making an investment before competitors or waiting until the market is opportune can affect an investment's outcome.

In practice

Any investment decision should focus not just on the returns but also on the risks.

PBP provides a partial assessment of risk – however, it is important to consider other risk factors when making an investment, such as:

- Will the product actually sell and be positively received by customers?
- Will competitors launch similar or better products?
- Will suppliers be able to deliver the required materials on time and at the right quality?
- How reliable is the forecast? For example, will the opportunity still be profitable if the sales price is 10% lower?
- If the investment fails, will there be a negative impact on the company's brand?
- If the investment fails, will there be unforeseen costs, such as redundancy payments?

The non-financial considerations on an investment, especially those involving customers and competitors can be just as important when making an investment decision. Many organisations require investment opportunities to be presented within a formal business plan which includes the non-financial and strategic benefits and costs.

Nice to know

Cost of capital

The cost of capital or the cost of financing an investment over the long term refers to the discount rate used in NPV and IRR calculations. It is one of the main costs of making an investment.

To utilise DCF methods of investment appraisal, an organisation needs to know its cost of capital.

- The cost of capital is used to 'discount' future cash flows to their PV, so an NPV can be calculated.
- The cost of capital is required to benchmark the IRR.
  If an investment's IRR is greater than an organisation's cost

of capital, then the investment is potentially worthwhile. If it is less, then the investment is likely to make a loss.

The cost of capital is essentially a weighted average of the cost of all a company's sources of finance, made up of equity finance (see **Chapter 29 Equity finance**) and debt finance (see **Chapter 30 Debt finance**).

Even if a company has raised finance specifically for an investment, it should still use its weighted average cost of capital. All investments should be treated as if they are financed out of a 'pool' of company finance.

In practice some organisations will use a risk adjusted cost of capital to appraise non-core investments. This effectively provides an additional hurdle rate which investments must pass in order to be viable.

Optional detail

NPV versus IRR

Many organisations will calculate both the NPV and IRR of an investment. In practice, however, there are some organisations that place more reliance on the IRR as it gives a percentage outcome. This is easier to relate to and can be more conceptually benchmarked against other 'returns'.

For the majority of investments, the NPV and IRR will provide the same assessment of an investment:

- a positive NPV usually means that the IRR is greater than the cost of capital; and
- a negative NPV usually means that the IRR is less than the cost of capital.

However, from a purely mathematical perspective NPV is a superior measure. If it provides a different outcome to IRR, then NPV should be used instead. NPV and IRR may differ when:

- There are different sized competing investments.
- An investment requires tranches of capital outflows during its life.

Where to spot in company accounts

The annual report for a listed company may include details of investment opportunities the business has undertaken or is planning to undertake.

A company may include its basis for making investment decisions for example, its hurdle rate, but it is unlikely to disclose details as this is sensitive information.

Watch out for in practice

→ Is there a formal process for assessing investment opportunities?

→ Do investment opportunities need to be presented within a business plan which incorporates non-financial and strategic considerations?

→ Are a number of alternative financial assessment methods used including payback, the annual yield, NPV and IRR?

→ Is there an assessment of risk as well as the return from potential investments?

→ Is the cost of capital regularly assessed?

→ Does the business accept or reject the majority of projects? This may indicate its attitude to risk aversion or a too high/low hurdle rate.

What did you think of this book?

We're really keen to hear from you about this book, so that we can make our publishing even better.

Please log on to the following website and leave us your feedback.

It will only take a few minutes and your thoughts are invaluable to us.

www.pearsoned.co.uk/bookfeedback

Appendix: Greggs 2015 Financial Accounts and supporting notes

The following accounts are extracted with permission from Greggs Annual Report and Accounts 2015. They represent pages 70 to 99 of the original document. Please see https://corporate.greggs.co.uk/sites/default/files/GREGGS_23781_AR_2015_web.pdf for the full original.

Consolidated income statement

for the 52 weeks ended 2 January 2016 (2014: 53 weeks ended 3 January 2015)

	Note	2015 Total £'000	2014 Excluding exceptional items (Restated) £'000	2014 Exceptional items (see Note 4) £'000	2014 Total (Restated) £'000
Revenue	1	835,749	806,096	–	806,096
Cost of sales		(305,116)	(304,786)	(5,932)	(310,718)
Gross profit		530,633	501,310	(5,932)	495,378
Distribution and selling costs		(412,426)	(403,003)	(282)	(403,285)
Administrative expenses		(45,094)	(40,223)	(2,302)	(42,525)
Operating profit		73,113	58,084	(8,516)	49,568
Finance (expense)/income	6	(85)	175	–	175
Profit before tax	3-6	73,028	58,259	(8,516)	49,743
Income tax	8	(15,428)	(13,997)	1,810	(12,187)
Profit for the financial year attributable to equity holders of the Parent		57,600	44,262	(6,706)	37,556
Basic earnings per share	9	57.3p	44.0p	(6.6p)	37.4p
Diluted earnings per share	9	55.8p	43.4p	(6.6p)	36.8p

Consolidated statement of comprehensive income

for the 52 weeks ended 2 January 2016 (2014: 53 weeks ended 3 January 2015)

	Note	2015 £'000	2014 £'000
Profit for the financial year		57,600	37,556
Other comprehensive income			
Items that will not be recycled to profit and loss:			
Re-measurements on defined benefit pension plans	21	4,915	(8,575)
Tax on re-measurements on defined benefit pension plans	8	(885)	1,715
Other comprehensive income for the financial year, net of income tax		4,030	(6,860)
Total comprehensive income for the financial year		61,630	30,696

Balance sheets
at 2 January 2016 (2014: 3 January 2015)

	Note	Group 2015 £'000	Group 2014 £'000	Parent Company 2015 £'000	Parent Company 2014 £'000
ASSETS					
Non-current assets					
Intangible assets	10	10,248	04,721	10,248	4,721
Property, plant and equipment	11	284,163	262,719	284,756	263,312
Investments	12	-	-	4,987	4,987
Deferred tax asset	13	3,830	-	4,305	-
		298,241	267,440	304,296	273,020
Current assets					
Inventories	14	15,444	15,290	15,444	15,290
Trade and other receivables	15	27,647	26,091	27,647	26,091
Assets held for sale	16	-	6,500	-	6,500
Cash and cash equivalents	17	42,915	43,615	42,915	43,615
Other investments	12	-	10,000	-	10,000
		86,006	101,496	86,006	101,496
Total assets		384,247	368,936	390,302	374,516
LIABILITIES					
Current liabilities					
Trade and other payables	18	(92,780)	(89,954)	(100,587)	(97,761)
Current tax liability	19	(9,580)	(8,056)	(9,580)	(8,056)
Provisions	22	(3,675)	(4,109)	(3,675)	(4,109)
		(106,035)	(102,119)	(113,842)	(109,926)
Non-current liabilities					
Other payables	20	(6,071)	(6,555)	(6,071)	(6,555)
Defined benefit pension liability	21	(3,910)	(8,518)	(3,910)	(8,518)
Deferred tax liability	13	-	(2,539)	-	(2,012)
Long-term provisions	22	(1,957)	(2,502)	(1,957)	(2,502)
		(11,938)	(20,114)	(11,938)	(19,587)
Total liabilities		(117,973)	(122,233)	(125,780)	(129,513)
Net assets		266,274	246,703	264,522	245,003
EQUITY					
Capital and reserves					
Issued capital	23	2,023	2,023	2,023	2,023
Share premium account		13,533	13,533	13,533	13,533
Capital redemption reserve	23	416	416	416	416
Retained earnings		250,302	230,731	248,550	229,031
Total equity attributable to equity holders of the Parent		266,274	246,703	264,522	245,003

The accounts on **pages (70 to 99)** were approved by the Board of Directors on 1 March 2016 and were signed on its behalf by:

Roger Whiteside
Richard Hutton

Company Registered Number 502851

Statements of changes in equity

for the 52 weeks ended 2 January 2016 (2014: 53 weeks ended 3 January 2015)

Group
53 weeks ended 3 January 2015

	Note	Issued capital £'000	Share premium £'000	Capital redemption reserve £'000	Retained earnings £'000	Total £'000
				Attributable to equity holders of the Company		
Balance at 29 December 2013		2,023	13,533	416	220,205	236,177
Total comprehensive income for the year						
Profit for the financial year		–	–	–	37,556	37,556
Other comprehensive income		–	–	–	(6,860)	(6,860)
Total comprehensive income for the year		–	–	–	30,696	30,696
Transactions with owners, recorded directly in equity						
Sale of own shares		–	–	–	5,257	5,257
Purchase of own shares		–	–	–	(7,873)	(7,873)
Share-based payment transactions	21	–	–	–	529	529
Dividends to equity holders	23	–	–	–	(19,570)	(19,570)
Tax items taken directly to reserves	8	–	–	–	1,487	1,487
Total transactions with owners		–	–	–	(20,170)	(20,170)
Balance at 3 January 2015		2,023	13,533	416	230,731	246,703

52 weeks ended 2 January 2016

	Note	Issued capital £'000	Share premium £'000	Capital redemption reserve £'000	Retained earnings £'000	Total £'000
				Attributable to equity holders of the Company		
Balance at 4 January 2015		2,023	13,533	416	230,731	246,703
Total comprehensive income for the year						
Profit for the financial year		–	–	–	57,600	57,600
Other comprehensive income		–	–	–	4,030	4,030
Total comprehensive income for the year		–	–	–	61,630	61,630
Transactions with owners, recorded directly in equity						
Sale of own shares		–	–	–	3,876	3,876
Purchase of own shares		–	–	–	(11,125)	(11,125)
Share-based payment transactions	21	–	–	–	3,662	3,662
Dividends to equity holders	23	–	–	–	(43,714)	(43,714)
Tax items taken directly to reserves	8	–	–	–	5,242	5,242
Total transactions with owners		–	–	–	(42,059)	(42,059)
Balance at 2 January 2016		2,023	13,533	416	250,302	266,274

Parent Company
53 weeks ended 3 January 2015

	Note	Issued capital £'000	Share premium £'000	Capital redemption reserve £'000	Retained earnings £'000	Total £'000
				Attributable to equity holders of the Company		
Balance at 29 December 2013		2,023	13,533	416	218,505	234,477
Total comprehensive income for the year						
Profit for the financial year	7	–	–	–	37,556	37,556
Other comprehensive income		–	–	–	(6,860)	(6,860)
Total comprehensive income for the year		–	–	–	30,696	30,696
Transactions with owners, recorded directly in equity						
Sale of own shares		–	–	–	5,257	5,257
Purchase of own shares		–	–	–	(7,873)	(7,873)
Share-based payment transactions	21	–	–	–	529	529
Dividends to equity holders	23	–	–	–	(19,570)	(19,570)
Tax items taken directly to reserves	8	–	–	–	1,487	1,487
Total transactions with owners		–	–	–	(20,170)	(20,170)
Balance at 3 January 2015		2,023	13,533	416	229,031	245,003

52 weeks ended 2 January 2016

	Note	Issued capital £'000	Share premium £'000	Capital redemption reserve £'000	Retained earnings £'000	Total £'000
				Attributable to equity holders of the Company		
Balance at 4 January 2015		2,023	13,533	416	229,031	245,003
Total comprehensive income for the year						
Profit for the financial year	7	–	–	–	57,548	57,548
Other comprehensive income		–	–	–	4,030	4,030
Total comprehensive income for the year		–	–	–	61,578	61,578
Transactions with owners, recorded directly in equity						
Sale of own shares		–	–	–	3,876	3,876
Purchase of own shares		–	–	–	(11,125)	(11,125)
Share-based payment transactions	21	–	–	–	3,662	3,662
Dividends to equity holders	23	–	–	–	(43,714)	(43,714)
Tax items taken directly to reserves	8	–	–	–	5,242	5,242
Total transactions with owners		–	–	–	(42,059)	(42,059)
Balance at 2 January 2016		2,023	13,533	416	248,550	264,522

Statements of cashflows

for the 52 weeks ended 2 January 2016 (2014: 53 weeks ended 3 January 2015)

	Note	Group 2015 £'000	Group 2014 £'000	Parent Company 2015 £'000	Parent Company 2014 £'000
Operating activities					
Cash generated from operations (see below)		119,637	108,552	119,637	108,552
Income tax paid		(15,916)	(11,462)	(15,916)	(11,462)
Net cash inflow from operating activities		103,721	97,090	103,721	97,090
Investing activities					
Acquisition of property, plant and equipment		(65,785)	(44,456)	(65,785)	(44,456)
Acquisition of intangible assets		(5,981)	(3,809)	(5,981)	(3,809)
Proceeds from sale of property, plant and equipment		8,086	2,231	8,086	2,231
Interest received	6	222	173	222	173
Redemption/(acquisition) of other investments	12	10,000	(7,000)	10,000	(7,000)
Net cash outflow from investing activities		(53,458)	(52,861)	(53,458)	(52,861)
Financing activities					
Sale of own shares		3,876	5,257	3,876	5,257
Purchase of own shares		(11,125)	(7,873)	(11,125)	(7,873)
Dividends paid	23	(43,714)	(19,570)	(43,714)	(19,570)
Net cash outflow from financing activities		(50,963)	(22,186)	(50,963)	(22,186)
Net (decrease)/increase in cash and cash equivalents		(700)	22,043	(700)	22,043
Cash and cash equivalents at the start of the year	17	43,615	21,572	43,615	21,572
Cash and cash equivalents at the end of the year	17	42,915	43,615	42,915	43,615

Cash flow statement - cash generated from operations

	Note	2015 £'000	2014 £'000	2015 £'000	2014 £'000
Profit for the financial year		57,600	37,556	57,548	37,556
Amortisation	10	454	100	454	100
Depreciation	11	39,687	37,463	39,687	37,463
Impairment	11	66	414	66	414
Loss on sale of property, plant and equipment		2,952	3,576	2,952	3,576
Release of government grants		(484)	(473)	(484)	(473)
Share-based payment expenses	21	3,662	529	3,662	529
Finance expense/(income)	6	85	(175)	85	(175)
Income tax expense	8	15,428	12,187	15,480	12,187
(Increase)/decrease in inventories		(154)	115	(154)	115
Increase in receivables		(1,555)	(1,079)	(1,555)	(1,079)
Increase in payables		2,875	17,089	2,875	17,089
(Decrease)/increase in provisions		(979)	1,250	(979)	1,250
Cash from operating activities		119,637	108,552	119,637	108,552

Notes to the consolidated accounts
Significant accounting policies

Greggs plc ('the Company') is a company incorporated and domiciled in the UK. The Group accounts consolidate those of the Company and its subsidiaries (together referred to as 'the Group'). The results of the associate are not consolidated on the grounds of materiality. The Parent Company accounts present information about the Company as a separate entity and not about its Group.

The accounts were authorised for issue by the Directors on 1 March 2016.

(a) Statement of compliance

Both the Parent Company accounts and the Group accounts have been prepared and approved by the Directors in accordance with International Financial Reporting Standards as adopted by the EU ('adopted IFRSs'), IFRIC interpretations and the Companies Act 2006 applicable to companies reporting under IFRS. On publishing the Parent Company accounts here together with the Group accounts, the Company is taking advantage of the exemption in s408 of the Companies Act 2006 not to present its individual income statement and related notes that form a part of these approved accounts.

(b) Basis of preparation

The accounts are presented in pounds sterling, rounded to the nearest thousand, and are prepared on the historical cost basis except the defined benefit pension asset/liability, which is recognised as plan assets less the present value of the defined benefit obligation.

The Group's business activities, together with the factors likely to affect its future development, performance and position are set out in the Directors' report and strategic report on pages 01 to 65. The financial position of the Group, its cash flows and liquidity position are described in the Financial Review on pages 20 to 21. In addition, Note 2 to the accounts inclues: the Group's objectives; policies and processes for managing its capital; its financial risk management objectives, details of its financial instruments and hedging activities; and its exposures to credit risk and liquidity risk.

The Group chose not to restate business combinations prior to the IFRS transition date (1 January 2004), as no significant acquisitions had taken place during the previous ten years. The Group's policy up to and including 1997 was to eliminate goodwill arising upon acquisitions against reserves. Under IFRS 1 and IFRS 3, such goodwill remains eliminated against reserves.

The accounting policies set out below have been applied consistently throughout the Group and to all years presented in these consolidated accounts and are unchanged from previous years with the exception of the adoption of the following relevant standards, amendments and interpretations:

– Defined Benefit Plans: Employee Contributions – Amendments to IAS 19
– Annual Improvements to IFRSs – 2010–2012 Cycle
– Annual Improvements to IFRSs – 2011–2013 Cycle

The adoption of the above has not had a significant impact on the Group's profit for the year or equity. The other standards and interpretations that are applicable for the first time in the Group's accounts for the year have no effect on these accounts.

Restatement of comparatives

During the current year the Group has continued to expand its franchise operations. Certain of these arrangements include up-front payments from franchisees receivable in respect of the capital fit-out of the franchise operators' shops. Due to these up-front payments becoming material in the year, the Directors have reconsidered the application of IAS 18 to these specific transactions. They have now determined that the Group is acting as a principal in these transactions whilst previously these had been presented as if they were acting as agents. The prior-year figures have been restated for this change in presentation. For the 53 weeks ended 3 January 2015 both turnover and cost of sales have increased by £2,135,000. There is no impact on profit, balance sheet or cash flows for this change in presentation.

In addition, a review of income statement categorisations was carried out which identified two re-categorisations. Firstly it was determined that it was more appropriate for all wage costs associated with bakery and distribution centre despatch activities to be included in distribution and selling costs, rather than some being included in cost of sales. The net impact of this for the 53 weeks ended 3 January 2015 has been a decrease in cost of sales and a corresponding increase in distribution and selling costs of £7,294,000. Secondly, early settlement discounts should have been included in administrative costs rather than cost of sales. The net impact for the 53 weeks ended 3 January 2015 has been an increase in cost of sales and a decrease in administrative costs of £80,000. There is no impact on profit, balance sheet or cash flows arising from these changes in categorisation.

Going concern

Directors have reviewed the Company's operational and investment plans for the next 12 months along with the principal risks and uncertainties that could affect these plans or threaten its liquidity. The key factors likely to affect future performance and the Company's exposure to risks are set out on pages 24 to 25 of the strategic report. In addition the financial review on pages 20 to 21 sets out the Company's net cash position and continued strong cash generation.

After making enquiries, the Directors have a reasonable expectation that the Company and the Group have adequate resources to continue in operational existence for the next 12 months. Accordingly, they continue to adopt the going concern basis in preparing the annual report and accounts.

Key estimates and judgements

The preparation of financial information in conformity with adopted IFRSs requires management to make judgements, estimates and assumptions that affect the application of policies and reported amounts of assets and liabilities, income and expenses. The estimates and underlying assumptions are reviewed on an ongoing basis. Revisions to accounting estimates are recognised in the year in which the estimate is revised if the revision affects only that year, or in the year of revision and future years if the revision affects both current and future years.

Provisions

Provisions have been estimated for onerous leases and dilapidations. These provisions represent the best estimate of the liability at the balance sheet date, the actual liability being dependent on future events such as trading conditions at a particular shop or the ability of the Group to exit from the lease commitment. Expectations will be revised each period until the actual liability arises, with any difference accounted for in the period in which the revision is made.

Impairment of property, plant and equipment

Property, plant and equipment is reviewed for impairment if events or changes in circumstances indicate that the carrying value may not be recoverable. For example, bakery equipment may be impaired if it is no longer in use and/or shop fittings may be impaired if sales in that shop fall. When a review for impairment is conducted the recoverable amount is estimated based on value-in-use calculations which include management's estimates of future cash flows generated by the assets and an appropriate discount rate. Consideration is also given to whether the impairment assessments made in prior years remain appropriate based on the latest expectations in respect of value-in-use and recoverable value. Where it is concluded that the impairment has reduced a reversal of the impairment is recorded. The sensitivities for growth rate, discount rate and lease term have been considered and are deemed not significant. For instance, a two per cent change in the growth rate would result in a £43,000 change in the impairment charge.

Post retirement benefits

The determination of the defined benefit obligation of the Group's defined benefit pension scheme depends on the selection of certain assumptions including the discount rate, inflation rate and mortality rates. Differences arising from actual experience or future changes in assumptions will be reflected in future years. The key assumptions made for 2015 are given in Note 21.

(c) Basis of consolidation

The consolidated accounts include the results of Greggs plc and its subsidiary undertakings for the 52 weeks ended 2 January 2016. The comparative period is the 53 weeks ended 3 January 2015.

(i) Subsidiaries

Subsidiaries are entities controlled by the Company. The Company controls an entity when it is exposed to, or has rights to, variable returns from its involvement with the entity and has the ability to affect those returns through its power over the entity. The accounts of subsidiaries are included in the consolidated accounts from the date on which control commences until the date on which control ceases.

(ii) Associates

Associates are those entities in which the Group has significant influence, but not control, over the financial and operating policies. Significant influence is presumed to exist when the Group holds between 20 and 50 percent of the voting power of another entity. At the year end the Group has one associate which has not been consolidated on grounds of materiality (see Note 12).

(iii) Transactions eliminated on consolidation

Intragroup balances, and any unrealised gains and losses or income and expenses arising from intragroup transactions, are eliminated in preparing the consolidated accounts.

(d) Exceptional items

Exceptional items are defined as items of income and expenditure which are material and unusual in nature and which are considered to be of such significance that they require separate disclosure on the face of the income statement. Any future movements on items previously classified as exceptional will also be classified as exceptional.

(e) Foreign currency

Transactions in foreign currencies are translated at the foreign exchange rate ruling at the date of the transaction. Monetary assets and liabilities denominated in foreign currencies at the balance sheet date are translated at the foreign exchange rate ruling at that date. Non-monetary assets and liabilities that are measured in terms of historical cost in a foreign currency are translated using the exchange rate at the date of the transaction. Foreign exchange differences arising on translation are recognised in the income statement.

(f) Intangible assets

The Group's only intangible assets relate to software and the costs of its implementation which is measured at cost less accumulated amortisation and accumulated impairment losses.

Subsequent expenditure is capitalised only when it increases the future economic benefits embodied in the specific asset to which it relates. All other expenditure is recognised in the income statement as incurred.

Amortisation is recognised in the income statement on a straight-line basis over the estimated useful lives of intangible assets from the date that they are available for use. The estimated useful lives for the current and comparative periods are five years.

Assets in the course of development are re-categorised and amortisation commences when the assets are available for use.

(g) Property, plant and equipment

(i) Owned assets
Items of property, plant and equipment are stated at cost or deemed cost less accumulated depreciation (see below) and impairment losses (see accounting policy (k)). The cost of self-constructed assets includes the cost of materials, direct labour and an appropriate proportion of production overheads.

(ii) Subsequent costs
The cost of replacing a component of an item of property, plant and equipment is recognised in the carrying amount of the item if it is probable that the future economic benefits embodied within the component will flow to the Group, and its costs can be measured reliably. The carrying value of the replaced component is derecognised. The costs of the day-to-day servicing of property, plant and equipment are recognised in the income statement as incurred.

(iii) Depreciation
Depreciation is provided so as to write off the cost (less residual value) of each item of property, plant and equipment during its expected useful life using the straight-line method over the following periods:

Freehold and long leasehold buildings	40 years
Short leasehold properties	10 years or length of lease if shorter
Plant, machinery, equipment, vehicles, fixtures and fittings	3 to 10 years

Freehold land is not depreciated.

Depreciation methods, useful lives and residual values (if not insignificant) are reassessed annually.

(iv) Assets in the course of construction
These assets are re-categorised and depreciation commences when the assets are available for use.

(h) Investments

Non-current investments comprise investments in subsidiaries and associates which are carried at cost less impairment.

Current investments comprise fixed-term fixed-rate bank deposits where the term is greater than three months.

(i) Inventories

Inventories are stated at the lower of cost and net realisable value. Net realisable value is the estimated selling price in the ordinary course of business, less the estimated costs of completion and selling expenses. The cost of inventories includes expenditure incurred in acquiring the inventories and direct production labour costs.

(j) Cash and cash equivalents

Cash and cash equivalents comprises cash balances and call deposits with an original maturity of three months or less. Bank overdrafts that are repayable on demand and form an integral part of the Group's cash management are included as a component of cash and cash equivalents for the purpose of the statement of cash flows.

(k) Impairment

The carrying amounts of the Group and Company's assets, other than inventories and deferred tax assets, are reviewed at each balance sheet date to determine whether there is any indication of impairment. If any such indication exists, the asset's recoverable amount is estimated. Impairment reviews are carried out on an individual shop basis unless there are a number of shops in the same location, in which case the impairment review is based on the location.

An impairment loss is recognised whenever the carrying amount of an asset exceeds its recoverable amount. Impairment losses are recognised in the income statement. Impairment losses recognised in prior years are assessed at each reporting date and reversed if there has been a change in the estimates used to determine the recoverable amount. An impairment loss is reversed only to the extent that the asset's carrying amount does not exceed the carrying amount that would have been determined, net of depreciation, if no impairment loss had been recognised.

(l) Non-current assets held for sale

Non-current assets that are expected to be recovered primarily through sale rather than through continuing use are classified as held for sale. Immediately before classification as held for sale, the assets are re-measured in accordance with the Group and Company's accounting policies. Thereafter generally the assets are measured at the lower of their carrying amount and fair value less cost to sell. Once classified as held for sale assets are no longer depreciated or amortised.

(m) Share capital

(i) Re-purchase of share capital
When share capital recognised as equity is re-purchased, the amount of the consideration paid, including directly attributable costs, is recognised as a deduction from equity. Re-purchased shares that are held in the employee share ownership plan are classified as treasury shares and are presented as a deduction from total equity.

(ii) Dividends
Dividends are recognised as a liability when the Company has an obligation to pay and the dividend is no longer at the Company's discretion.

(n) Employee share ownership plan

The Group and Parent Company accounts include the assets and related liabilities of the Greggs Employee Benefit Trust ('EBT'). In both the Group and Parent Company accounts the shares held by the EBT are stated at cost and deducted from total equity.

(o) Employee benefits

(i) Short-term employee benefits
Short-term employee benefits are expensed as the related service is provided. A liability is recognised for the amount expected to be paid if the Group has a present legal or constructive obligation to pay this amount as a result of past service provided by the employee and the obligation can be measured reliably.

(ii) Defined contribution plans
Obligations for contributions to defined contribution pension plans are recognised as an expense in the income statement when they are due.

(iii) Defined benefit plans
The Company's net obligation in respect of defined benefit pension plans is calculated by estimating the amount of future benefit that employees have earned in return for their service in the current and prior periods; that benefit is discounted to determine its present value, and the fair value of any plan assets (at bid price) is deducted. The Company determines the net interest on the net defined benefit asset/liability for the period by applying the discount rate used to measure the defined benefit obligation at the beginning of the annual period to the net defined benefit asset/liability.

The discount rate is the yield at the reporting date on bonds that have a credit rating of at least AA, that have maturity dates approximating to the terms of the Company's obligations and that are denominated in the currency in which the benefits are expected to be paid.

Re-measurements arising from defined benefit plans comprise actuarial gains and losses and the return on plan assets (excluding interest). The Company recognises them immediately in other comprehensive income and all other expenses related to defined benefit plans in employee benefit expenses in the income statement.

When the benefits of a plan are changed, or when a plan is curtailed, the portion of the changed benefit related to past service by employees, or the gain or loss on curtailment, is recognised immediately in profit or loss when the plan amendment or curtailment occurs.

The calculation of the defined benefit obligation is performed by a qualified actuary using the projected unit credit method. When the calculation results in a benefit to the Company, the recognised asset is limited to the present value of benefits available in the form of any future refunds from the plan or reductions in future contributions and takes into account the adverse effect of any minimum funding requirements.

(iv) Share-based payment transactions

The share option programme allows Group employees to acquire shares of the Company. The fair value of share options granted is recognised as an employee expense with a corresponding increase in equity. The fair value is measured at grant date, using an appropriate model, taking into account the terms and conditions upon which the share options were granted, and is spread over the period during which the employees become unconditionally entitled to the options. The amount recognised as an expense is adjusted to reflect the actual number of share options that vest except where forfeiture is only due to share prices not achieving the threshold for vesting.

(v) Termination benefits

Termination benefits are expensed at the earlier of the date at which the Group can no longer withdraw the offer of these benefits and the date at which the Group recognises costs for a restructuring. If benefits are not expected to be settled wholly within 12 months of the reporting date they are discounted.

(p) Provisions

A provision is recognised if, as a result of a past event, the Group has a present legal or constructive obligation that can be estimated reliably, and it is probable that an outflow of economic benefits will be required to settle the obligation. Provisions are determined by discounting the expected future cash flows at a pre-tax rate that reflects current market assessments of the time value of money and the risks specific to the liability.

(i) Restructuring

A provision for restructuring is recognised when the Group has approved a detailed and formal restructuring plan, and the restructuring either has commenced or has been announced publicly. Future operating costs are not provided for.

(ii) Onerous leases

Provisions for onerous leases are recognised when the Group believes that the unavoidable costs of meeting the lease obligations exceed the economic benefits expected to be received under the lease. Before a provision is established the Group recognises any impairment loss on the associated assets.

(iii) Dilapidations

Provisions for dilapidations are recognised on a lease-by-lease basis and are based on the Group's best estimate of the likely committed cash outflow.

(q) Revenue

(i) Retail sales

Revenue from the sale of goods is recognised as income on receipt of cash or card payment. Revenue is measured net of discounts, promotions and value added taxation.

(ii) Franchise sales

Franchise sales are recognised when goods are dispatched to franchisees. Any additional franchise fee income relating to franchise sales is recognised on an accruals basis in accordance with the substance of the relevant agreement. Capital fit-out costs are recharged to the franchisee and recognised when they are completed.

(iii) Wholesale sales

Wholesale sales are recognised when goods are dispatched to customers.

(iv) Loyalty programme/gift cards

Amounts received for gift cards or as part of the loyalty programme are deferred. They are recognised as revenue when the Group has fulfilled its obligation to supply products under the terms of the programme or when it is no longer probable that these amounts will be redeemed. No adjustment is made to revenue to reflect the fair value of the free items provided under the loyalty scheme as these would be immaterial to the accounts. The costs of these free items are expensed as the products are provided to the customer.

(r) Government grants

Government grants are recognised in the balance sheet initially as deferred income when there is a reasonable assurance that they will be received and that the Group will comply with the conditions attaching to them. Grants that compensate the Group for expenses incurred are recognised in the income statement on a systematic basis in the same periods in which the expenses are incurred. Grants that compensate the Group for the cost of an asset are recognised in the income statement over the useful life of the asset.

(s) Operating lease payments

Payments under operating leases are recognised in the income statement on a straight-line basis over the term of the lease. Lease incentives received are recognised in the income statement as an integral part of the total lease expense over the term of the lease.

(t) Finance income and expense

Interest income or expense is recognised using the effective interest method.

(u) Income tax

Income tax comprises current and deferred tax. Income tax is recognised in the income statement except to the extent that it relates to items recognised directly in equity, in which case it is recognised in equity.

Current tax is the expected tax payable on the taxable income for the year, using tax rates enacted or substantively enacted at the balance sheet date, and any adjustment to tax payable in respect of previous years.

Deferred tax is recognised using the balance sheet liability method, providing for temporary differences between the carrying amounts of assets and liabilities for financial reporting purposes and the amounts used for taxation purposes. The amount of deferred tax recognised is based on the expected manner of realisation or settlement of the carrying amounts of assets and liabilities, using tax rates that are expected to apply when the temporary differences reverse, based on rates enacted or substantively enacted at the balance sheet date.

Deferred tax is not recognised for the following temporary differences: the initial recognition of assets or liabilities in a transaction that is not a business combination and that affects neither accounting nor taxable profit, and differences relating to investments in subsidiaries to the extent that it is probable that they will not reverse in the foreseeable future.

A deferred tax asset is recognised only to the extent that it is probable that future taxable profits will be available against which the asset can be utilised. Deferred tax assets are reviewed at each reporting date and are reduced to the extent that it is no longer probable that the related deferred tax benefit will be realised.

(v) Research and development

The Company continuously strives to improve its products and processes through technical and other innovation. Such expenditure is typically expensed to the income statement as the related intellectual property is not capable of being formalised and does not always have distinguishable research and development phases.

(w) IFRSs available for early adoption not yet applied

The following standards and amendments to standards which will be relevant to the Group were available for early adoption but have not been applied in these accounts:

- Clarification of Acceptable Methods of Depreciation and Amortisation – Amendments to IAS 16 and IAS 38 for accounting periods commencing on or after 1 January 2016.
- Equity Method in Separate Financial Statements – Amendments to IAS 27 for accounting periods commencing on or after 1 January 2016.
- Annual Improvements to IFRSs – 2012–2014 Cycle for accounting periods commencing on or after 1 January 2016.
- Disclosure Initiative – Amendments to IAS 1 for accounting periods commencing on or after 1 January 2016.

These standards and amendments will be adopted as they become effective and none of them is expected to have a significant impact on the accounts.

1 Segmental analysis

The Board is considered to be the 'chief operating decision maker' of the Group in the context of the IFRS 8 definition. In addition to its retail activities, the Group generates revenues from franchise and wholesale. However, these elements of the business are not sufficiently significant to be 'Reportable Segments' in the context of IFRS 8.

Products and services – the Group sells a consistent range of fresh bakery goods, sandwiches and drinks in its shops. The Group also provides frozen bakery products to its wholesale customers.

Major customers – the majority of sales are made to the general public on a cash basis. A small proportion of sales are made on credit to certain organisations, including wholesale customers, but these are immaterial in a Group context.

Geographical areas – all results arise in the UK.

The Board has carefully considered the requirements of IFRS 8 and concluded that, as there is only one reportable segment whose revenue, profits, assets and liabilities are measured and reported on a consistent basis with the Group accounts no additional numerical disclosures are necessary.

2 Financial risk management

Credit risk

Credit risk is the risk of financial loss to the Group if a customer or counterparty to a financial instrument fails to meet its contractual obligations.

Retail sales represent a large proportion of the Group's sales and present no credit risk as they are made for cash or card payments. The Group does offer credit terms on sales to its wholesale and franchise customers. In such cases the Group operates effective credit control procedures in order to minimise exposure to overdue debts.

Counterparty risk is also considered low. All of the Group's surplus cash is held with highly-rated banks, in line with Group policy.

Liquidity risk

Liquidity risk is the risk that the Group will not be able to meet its financial obligations as they fall due.

The Group operates with net current liabilities and is therefore reliant on the continued strong performance of the retail portfolio to meet its short-term liabilities. This is a well-established and proven business model. Any increase in short-term liquidity risk can be mitigated by reducing capital expenditure. The model has been tested in various scenarios for the Group's viability statement which is included in the strategic report on page 25. The Group had significant cash resources at the year end.

Market risk

Market risk is the risk that changes in market prices, such as foreign exchange rates, interest rates and equity prices will affect the Group's income or the value of its holdings of financial instruments.

Market risk is not significant and therefore sensitivity analysis would not be meaningful.

Currency risk

The Group has no regular transactions in foreign currency although there are occasional purchases, mainly of capital items, denominated in foreign currency. Whilst certain costs such as electricity and wheat can be influenced by movements in the US dollar, actual contracts are priced in sterling. In respect of those key costs which are volatile, such as electricity and flour, the price may be fixed for a period of time in line with Group policy. All such contracts are for the Group's own expected usage.

Interest rate risk

The Group has low exposure to interest rate risk. Interest only arises on its bank deposits and overdrafts and the defined benefit pension scheme liability. Net financial expense in the year was £85,000 (2014: income of £175,000).

Equity price risk

The Group has no equity investments other than its subsidiaries and associate. As disclosed in Note 21 the Group's defined benefit pension scheme has investments in equity-related funds.

Capital management

The Board defines capital as the equity of the Group. The Group has remained net cash positive with funding requirements met by cash generated from retail operations. The Board considers that it is not currently appropriate to take on structural debt given the inherent leverage of the leasehold shop estate and working capital requirements. The Board's policy on dividend levels is to pursue a progressive dividend policy that pays due regard to the growth of earnings per share over the medium term, the cash-generative nature of the business and the continuing determination to deliver value to shareholders. The Board would expect to return any material level of surplus capital to shareholders, likely by way of a special dividend.

The Board reserves the option to purchase its own shares in the market dependent on market prices and surplus cash levels. The trustees of the Greggs Employment Benefit Trust also purchase shares for future satisfaction of employee share options.

Financial instruments
Group and Parent Company
All of the Group's surplus cash is invested as cash placed on deposit or fixed-term deposits.

The Group's treasury policy has as its principal objective the achievement of the maximum rate of return on cash balances whilst maintaining an acceptable level of risk. Other than mentioned below there are no financial instruments, derivatives or commodity contracts used.

Financial assets and liabilities
The Group's main financial assets comprise cash and cash equivalents and fixed-term deposits. Other financial assets include trade receivables arising from the Group's activities.

Other than trade and other payables, the Group had no financial liabilities within the scope of IAS 39 as at 2 January 2016 (2014: £nil).

Fair values
The fair value of the Group's financial assets and liabilities is not materially different from their carrying values. Financial assets and liabilities comprise principally of trade receivables and trade payables and the only interest-bearing balances are the bank deposits and borrowings which attract interest at variable rates.

Interest rate, credit and foreign currency risk
The Group has not entered into any hedging transactions during the year and considers interest rate, credit and foreign currency risks not to be significant.

3 Profit before tax

Profit before tax is stated after charging/(crediting):

	2015 £'000	2014 £'000
Amortisation of intangible assets	454	100
Depreciation on owned property, plant and equipment	39,687	37,463
Impairment of owned property, plant and equipment	66	414
Loss on disposal of fixed assets	2,952	3,576
Release of government grants	(484)	(473)
Payments under operating leases - property rents	46,173	48,451
Research and development expenditure	320	465
Auditor's remuneration:		
Audit of these accounts	140	140
Audit of pension schemes' accounts	7	7
Other services - tax compliance	21	21
Other services - tax advisory	12	25
All other services	12	5

Amounts paid to the Company's auditor in respect of services to the Company, other than the audit of the Company's accounts, have not been disclosed as the information is required instead to be presented on a consolidated basis.

4 Exceptional items

	2015 £'000	2014 £'000
Cost of sales		
Closure of in-store bakeries – redundancy and disruption costs	–	3,190
– loss on disposal of assets	–	664
– dilapidations	–	2,078
	–	5,932
Distribution and selling		
Shop asset impairment reversal	–	(149)
Onerous leases	–	431
	–	282
Administrative expenses		
Restructuring of support functions	–	2,302
Total exceptional items	–	8,516

The judgements made in calculating the provisions which arose as prior year exceptional items have been revisited. No additional amounts have been charged or reversed in the current year in respect of these. There remains some uncertainty in relation to these provisions which will be re-assessed in future periods, with any movements being classified as exceptional.

Closure of in-store bakeries
The charge arose from the decision to consolidate the Company's in-store bakeries into its regional bakery network and comprised of redundancy costs, disruption costs arising on the transfer of production from stores to regional bakeries, asset write-offs and the costs of making good the shops (dilapidations) as bakery equipment is removed.

Shop impairment and onerous leases
The charges arose from the decision to focus on reshaping the Group's existing estate through closure and resite of shops and withdrawal from the Greggs moment brand.

Restructuring of support functions
The charge related to the redundancy costs incurred in respect of restructuring within the support functions.

5 Personnel expenses

The average number of persons employed by the Group (including Directors) during the year was as follows:

	2015 Number	2014 Number
Management	713	698
Administration	454	386
Production	3,029	3,143
Shop	15,651	15,136
	19,847	19,363

The aggregate costs of these persons were as follows:

	Note	2015 £'000	2014 £'000
Wages and salaries		280,559	281,336
Compulsory social security contributions		19,485	19,578
Pension costs – defined contribution plans	21	10,302	9,901
Equity-settled transactions	21	3,662	529
		314,008	311,344

In addition to wages and salaries, the total amount accrued under the Group's employee profit sharing scheme is contained within the main cost categories as follows:

	2015 £'000	2014 £'000
Cost of sales	2,107	1,657
Distribution and selling costs	5,025	3,952
Administrative expenses	974	765
	8,106	6,374

For the purposes of IAS 24 'Related Party Disclosures' key management personnel comprises the Directors and their remuneration was as follows:

	2015 £'000	2014 £'000
Salaries and fees	1,388	1,343
Taxable benefits	40	36
Annual bonus (including profit share)	1,056	1,101
Post-retirement benefits	183	195
Share-based payments	1,394	304
	4,061	2,979

The aggregate amount of gains made on exercise of share options by the Directors was £1,195,000 (2014: £1,000). The number of Directors in the defined contribution pension scheme and in the defined benefit pension scheme was two (2014: two).

6 Finance (expense)/income

	Note	2015 £'000	2014 £'000
Interest income on cash balances		198	183
Foreign exchange gain/(loss)		24	(10)
Net interest related to defined benefit obligation	21	(307)	2
		(85)	175

7 Profit attributable to Greggs plc

Of the Group profit for the year, £57,548,000 (2014: £37,556,000) is dealt with in the accounts of the Parent Company. The Company has taken advantage of the exemption permitted by section 408 of the Companies Act 2006 from presenting its own income statement.

8 Income tax expense

Recognised in the income statement

	Total 2015 £'000	Excluding exceptional items 2014 £'000	Exceptional items 2014 £'000	Total 2014 £'000
Current tax				
Current year	17,970	15,776	(1,534)	14,242
Adjustment for prior years	(530)	(229)	–	(229)
	17,440	15,547	(1,534)	14,013
Deferred tax				
Origination and reversal of temporary differences	(1,038)	(1,471)	(276)	(1,747)
Reduction in tax rate	(254)	–	–	–
Adjustment for prior years	(720)	(79)	–	(79)
	(2,012)	(1,550)	(276)	(1,826)
Total income tax expense in income statement	15,428	13,997	(1,810)	12,187

Reconciliation of effective tax rate

	2015	2015 £'000	2014	2014 £'000
Profit before tax		73,028		49,743
Income tax using the domestic corporation tax rate	20.25%	14,788	21.5%	10,695
Non-deductible expenses	0.95%	698	1.0%	521
Non-qualifying depreciation	1.7%	1,263	2.5%	1,245
Loss on disposal of non-qualifying assets	0.1%	53	0.1%	34
Impact of reduction in deferred tax rate	(0.2%)	(124)	–	–
Adjustment for prior years	(1.7%)	(1,250)	(0.6%)	(308)
Total income tax expense in income statement	21.1%	15,428	24.5%	12,187

Reconciliation of effective tax rate (underlying excluding exceptional items)

	2015	2015 £'000	2014	2014 £'000
Profit before tax		73,028		58,259
Income tax using the domestic corporation tax rate	20.25%	14,788	21.5%	12,526
Non-deductible expenses	0.95%	698	0.8%	500
Non-qualifying depreciation	1.7%	1,263	2.1%	1,245
Loss on disposal of non-qualifying assets	0.1%	53	0.1%	34
Impact of reduction in deferred tax rate	(0.2%)	(124)	–	–
Adjustment for prior years	(1.7%)	(1,250)	(0.5%)	(308)
Total income tax expense in income statement	21.1%	15,428	24.0%	13,997

On 26 October 2015 reductions in the rate of corporation tax from 20 per cent to 19 per cent with effect from 1 April 2017 and from 19 per cent to 18 per cent with effect from 1 April 2020 were substantively enacted. Any timing differences which reverse before 1 April 2017 will be charged/credited at 20 per cent, any timing differences which reverse between 1 April 2017 and 1 April 2020 will do so at 19 per cent and any timing differences which exist at 1 April 2020 will reverse at 18 per cent.

Tax recognised in other comprehensive income or directly in equity

	2015 Current tax £'000	2015 Deferred tax £'000	2015 Total £'000	2014 Total £'000
Debit/(credit):				
Relating to equity-settled transactions	–	(5,242)	(5,242)	(1,487)
Relating to defined benefit plans – re-measurement gains/(losses)	–	885	885	(1,715)
	–	(4,357)	(4,357)	(3,202)

The deferred tax credit in the year relating to equity-settled transactions is in respect of share-based payments and arises primarily as a result of the increased share price in the year and the stage of maturity of existing schemes.

9 Earnings per share

Basic earnings per share

Basic earnings per share for the 52 weeks ended 2 January 2016 is calculated by dividing profit attributable to ordinary shareholders by the weighted average number of ordinary shares outstanding during the 52 weeks ended 2 January 2016 as calculated below.

Diluted earnings per share

Diluted earnings per share for the 52 weeks ended 2 January 2016 is calculated by dividing profit attributable to ordinary shareholders by the weighted average number of ordinary shares, adjusted for the effects of all dilutive potential ordinary shares (which comprise share options granted to employees) outstanding during the 52 weeks ended 2 January 2016 as calculated below.

Profit attributable to ordinary shareholders

	Total 2015 £'000	Excluding exceptional items 2014 £'000	Exceptional items 2014 £'000	Total 2014 £'000
Profit for the financial year attributable to equity holders of the Parent	57,600	44,262	(6,706)	37,556
Basic earnings per share	57.3p	44.0p	(6.6p)	37.4p
Diluted earnings per share	55.8p	43.4p	(6.6p)	36.8p

Weighted average number of ordinary shares

	2015 Number	2014 Number
Issued ordinary shares at start of year	101,155,901	101,155,901
Effect of own shares held	(551,314)	(638,815)
Weighted average number of ordinary shares during the year	100,604,587	100,517,086
Effect of share options on issue	2,616,364	1,517,722
Weighted average number of ordinary shares (diluted) during the year	103,220,951	102,034,808

10 Intangible assets

Group and Parent Company

	Software £'000	Assets under development £'000	Total £'000
Cost			
Balance at 29 December 2013	1,715	–	1,715
Additions	817	2,992	3,809
Balance at 3 January 2015	2,532	2,992	5,524
Balance at 4 January 2015	2,532	2,992	5,524
Additions	–	5,981	5,981
Balance at 2 January 2016	2,532	8,973	11,505
Amortisation			
Balance at 29 December 2013	703	–	703
Amortisation charge for the year	100	–	100
Balance at 3 January 2015	803	–	803
Balance at 4 January 2015	803	–	803
Amortisation charge for the year	454	–	454
Balance at 2 January 2016	1,257	–	1,257
Carrying amounts			
At 29 December 2013	1,012	–	1,012
At 3 January 2015	1,729	2,992	4,721
At 4 January 2015	1,729	2,992	4,721
At 2 January 2016	1,275	8,973	10,248

Assets under development relate to software projects arising from the investment in new systems platforms.

11 Property, plant and equipment

Group

	Note	Land and buildings £'000	Plant and equipment £'000	Fixtures and fittings £'000	Assets under construction £'000	Total £'000
Cost						
Balance at 29 December 2013		135,031	120,152	249,194	–	504,377
Additions		429	10,121	34,278	278	45,106
Disposals		(612)	(6,654)	(32,748)	–	(40,014)
Transfer to assets held for sale		(6,885)	–	–	–	(6,885)
Balance at 3 January 2015		127,963	123,619	250,724	278	502,584
Balance at 4 January 2015		127,963	123,619	250,724	278	502,584
Additions		70	9,265	45,510	10,890	65,735
Disposals		(1,034)	(3,120)	(28,527)	–	(32,681)
Balance at 2 January 2016		126,999	129,764	267,707	11,168	535,638
Depreciation						
Balance at 29 December 2013		31,936	74,701	129,943	–	236,580
Depreciation charge for the year		2,838	10,529	24,096	–	37,463
Ordinary impairment charge for the year		–	–	974	–	974
Ordinary impairment release for the year		–	–	(411)	–	(411)
Exceptional impairment release for the year	4	–	–	(149)	–	(149)
Disposals		(297)	(5,468)	(28,442)	–	(34,207)
Transfer to assets held for sale		(385)	–	–	–	(385)
Balance at 3 January 2015		34,092	79,762	126,011	–	239,865
Balance at 4 January 2015		34,092	79,762	126,011	–	239,865
Depreciation charge for the year		2,772	10,544	26,371	–	39,687
Impairment charge for the year		–	133	537	–	670
Impairment release for the year		–	–	(604)	–	(604)
Disposals		(845)	(2,789)	(24,509)	–	(28,143)
Balance at 2 January 2016		36,019	87,650	127,806	–	251,475
Carrying amounts						
At 29 December 2013		103,095	45,451	119,251	–	267,797
At 3 January 2015		93,871	43,857	124,713	278	262,719
At 4 January 2015		93,871	43,857	124,713	278	262,719
At 2 January 2016		90,980	42,114	139,901	11,168	284,163

Assets are reviewed for impairment on a regular basis and provision made where necessary. For shop assets a discounted cashflow is calculated for each shop using historic cashflows including attributable overheads, a zero per cent growth rate, the Group's cost of capital of ten per cent and an appropriate assumption regarding the remaining lease term. The net book value of the relevant assets attributable to the shop is impaired to the extent that the net present value of the cashflows is lower than the net book value. Supply chain assets are impaired to their estimated net realisable value.

Included within disposals for the prior year were fixtures and fittings with a net book value of £849,000 which related to the closure of the in-store bakeries. The loss on disposal of these assets was £664,000 and formed part of the exceptional charge detailed in Note 4.

Parent Company

	Note	Land and buildings £'000	Plant and equipment £'000	Fixtures and fittings £'000	Assets under construction £'000	Total £'000
Cost						
Balance at 29 December 2013		135,541	120,685	249,682	–	505,908
Additions		429	10,121	34,278	278	45,106
Disposals		(612)	(6,654)	(32,748)	–	(40,014)
Transfer to assets held for sale		(6,885)	–	–	–	(6,885)
Balance at 3 January 2015		128,473	124,152	251,212	278	504,115
Balance at 4 January 2015		128,473	124,152	251,212	278	504,115
Additions		70	9,265	45,510	10,890	65,735
Disposals		(1,034)	(3,120)	(28,527)	–	(32,681)
Balance at 2 January 2016		127,509	130,297	268,195	11,168	537,169
Depreciation						
Balance at 29 December 2013		32,213	74,971	130,334	–	237,518
Depreciation charge for the year		2,838	10,529	24,096	–	37,463
Ordinary impairment charge for the year		–	–	974	–	974
Ordinary impairment release for the year		–	–	(411)	–	(411)
Exceptional impairment release for the year	4	–	–	(149)	–	(149)
Disposals		(297)	(5,468)	(28,442)	–	(34,207)
Transfer to assets held for sale		(385)	–	–	–	(385)
Balance at 3 January 2015		34,369	80,032	126,402	–	240,803
Balance at 4 January 2015		34,369	80,032	126,402	–	240,803
Depreciation charge for the year		2,772	10,544	26,371	–	39,687
Impairment charge for the year		–	133	537	–	670
Impairment release for the year		–	–	(604)	–	(604)
Disposals		(845)	(2,789)	(24,509)	–	(28,143)
Balance at 2 January 2016		36,296	87,920	128,197	–	252,413
Carrying amounts						
At 29 December 2013		103,328	45,714	119,348	–	268,390
At 3 January 2015		94,104	44,120	124,810	278	263,312
At 4 January 2015		94,104	44,120	124,810	278	263,312
At 2 January 2016		91,213	42,377	139,998	11,168	284,756

Land and buildings

The carrying amount of land and buildings comprises:

	Group		Parent Company	
	2015 £'000	2014 £'000	2015 £'000	2014 £'000
Freehold property	90,780	93,808	91,013	94,041
Long leasehold property	3	1	3	1
Short leasehold property	197	62	197	62
	90,980	93,871	91,213	94,104

12 Investments

Non-current investments
Parent Company

	Shares in subsidiary undertakings £'000
Cost	
Balance at 29 December 2013, 3 January 2015 and 2 January 2016	5,828
Impairment	
Balance at 29 December 2013, 3 January 2015 and 2 January 2016	841
Carrying amount	
Balance at 29 December 2013, 3 January 2015, 4 January 2015 and 2 January 2016	4,987

The undertakings in which the Company's interest at the year end is more than 20 per cent are as follows:

	Principal activity	Country of incorporation	Proportion of voting rights and shares held
Charles Bragg (Bakers) Limited	Non-trading	England and Wales	100%
Greggs (Leasing) Limited	Dormant	England and Wales	100%
Thurston Parfitt Limited	Non-trading	England and Wales	100%
Greggs Properties Limited	Property holding	England and Wales	100%
Olivers (U.K.) Limited	Dormant	Scotland	100%
Olivers (U.K.) Development Limited*	Non-trading	Scotland	100%
Birketts Holdings Limited	Dormant	England and Wales	100%
J.R. Birkett and Sons Limited*	Non-trading	England and Wales	100%
Greggs Trustees Limited	Trustees	England and Wales	100%
Solstice Zone A Management Company Limited	Non-trading	England and Wales	28%

* Held indirectly.

Solstice Zone A Management Company Limited was not consolidated on the grounds of materiality.

The Company's subsidiary undertakings listed above were all entitled to exemption, under subsections (1) and (2) of section 480 of Companies Act 2006 relating to dormant companies, from the requirement to have their accounts audited.

Current investments

	Group and Parent Company	
	2015 £'000	2014 £'000
Fixed-term deposit	–	10,000

This represents cash placed on deposit that had a maturity of between three and six months at the date of inception. The fair value of the deposit is the same as its book value.

13 Deferred tax assets and liabilities

Group

Deferred tax assets and liabilities are attributable to the following:

	Assets		Liabilities		Net	
	2015 £'000	2014 £'000	2015 £'000	2014 £'000	2015 £'000	2014 £'000
Property, plant and equipment	–	–	(5,080)	(7,054)	(5,080)	(7,054)
Employee benefits	8,878	4,034	–	–	8,878	4,034
Short-term temporary differences	32	481	–	–	32	481
Tax assets/(liabilities)	8,910	4,515	(5,080)	(7,054)	3,830	(2,539)

The movements in temporary differences during the year ended 3 January 2015 were as follows:

	Balance at 29 December 2013 £'000	Recognised in income £'000	Recognised in equity £'000	Balance at 3 January 2015 £'000
Property, plant and equipment	(8,608)	1,554	–	(7,054)
Employee benefits	809	82	3,143	4,034
Short-term temporary differences	291	190	–	481
	(7,508)	1,826	3,143	(2,539)

The movements in temporary differences during the year ended 2 January 2016 were as follows:

	Balance at 4 January 2015 £'000	Recognised in income £'000	Recognised in equity £'000	Balance at 2 January 2016 £'000
Property, plant and equipment	(7,054)	1,974	–	(5,080)
Employee benefits	4,034	487	4,357	8,878
Short-term temporary differences	481	(449)	–	32
	(2,539)	2,012	4,357	3,830

Parent Company

Deferred tax assets and liabilities are attributable to the following:

	Assets		Liabilities		Net	
	2015 £'000	2014 £'000	2015 £'000	2014 £'000	2015 £'000	2014 £'000
Property, plant and equipment	–	–	(4,605)	(6,527)	(4,605)	(6,527)
Employee benefits	8,878	4,034	–	–	8,878	4,034
Short-term temporary differences	32	481	–	–	32	481
Tax assets/(liabilities)	8,910	4,515	(4,605)	(6,527)	4,305	(2,012)

The movements in temporary differences during the year ended 3 January 2015 were as follows:

	Balance at 29 December 2013 £'000	Recognised in income £'000	Recognised in equity £'000	Balance at 3 January 2015 £'000
Property, plant and equipment	(8,081)	1,554	–	(6,527)
Employee benefits	809	82	3,143	4,034
Short-term temporary differences	291	190	–	481
	(6,981)	1,826	3,143	(2,012)

The movements in temporary differences during the year ended 2 January 2016 were as follows:

	Balance at 4 January 2015 £'000	Recognised in income £'000	Recognised in equity £'000	Balance at 2 January 2016 £'000
Property, plant and equipment	(6,527)	1,922	–	(4,605)
Employee benefits	4,034	487	4,357	8,878
Short-term temporary differences	481	(449)	–	32
	(2,012)	1,960	4,357	4,305

The deferred tax asset, which principally arises in respect of employee benefits is expected to reverse within 12 months. As the Company anticipates having sufficient taxable profits to utilise these deductions it is considered appropriate to recognise the deferred tax asset.

14 Inventories

	Group and Parent Company	
	2015 £'000	2014 £'000
Raw materials and consumables	12,213	11,833
Work in progress	3,231	3,457
	15,444	15,290

15 Trade and other receivables

	Group and Parent Company	
	2015 £'000	2014 £'000
Trade receivables	9,496	7,311
Other receivables	4,513	6,512
Prepayments	13,638	12,268
	27,647	26,091

At 2 January 2016 trade receivables are shown net of an allowance for bad debts of £31,000 (2014: £41,000) arising in the ordinary course of business.

The ageing of trade receivables that were not impaired at the balance sheet date was:

	Group and Parent Company	
	2015 £'000	2014 £'000
Not past due date	6,089	5,398
Past due 1–30 days	3,283	1,765
Past due 31–90 days	80	148
Past due over 90 days	44	–
	9,496	7,311

The Group believes that the unimpaired amounts that are past due by more than 30 days are still collectable in full based on historic payment behaviour and extensive analysis of customer credit risk. Based on the Group's monitoring of customer credit risk, the Group believes that no impairment allowance is necessary in respect of trade receivables not past due.

16 Assets held for sale

The asset held for sale at 3 January 2015 was land at Southall which had been identified as no longer required for supply chain expansion. An offer for the site was received in 2014 and negotiations to finalise the sale were ongoing. The sale of the site was completed during 2015.

17 Cash and cash equivalents

	Group and Parent Company	
	2015 £'000	2014 £'000
Cash and cash equivalents	42,915	43,615

18 Trade and other payables

	Group		Parent Company	
	2015	2014	2015	2014
	£'000	£'000	£'000	£'000
Trade payables	42,405	40,865	42,405	40,865
Amounts owed to subsidiary undertakings	–	–	7,807	7,807
Other taxes and social security	5,912	5,767	5,912	5,767
Other payables	27,085	24,753	27,085	24,753
Accruals and deferred income	16,910	18,101	16,910	18,101
Deferred government grants	468	468	468	468
	92,780	89,954	100,587	97,761

19 Current tax liability

The current tax liability of £9,580,000 in the Group and the Parent Company (2014: Group and Parent Company £8,056,000) represents the estimated amount of income taxes payable in respect of current and prior years.

20 Non-current liabilities – other payables

	Group and Parent Company	
	2015	2014
	£'000	£'000
Deferred government grants	6,071	6,555

The Group has been awarded five government grants relating to the extension of existing facilities and construction of new facilities. The grants, which have all been recognised as deferred income, are being amortised over the weighted average of the useful lives of the assets they have been used to acquire.

21 Employee benefits

Defined benefit plan

Scheme background
The Company sponsors a funded final salary defined benefit pension plan (the 'scheme') for qualifying employees. The scheme was closed to future accrual in 2008 and all remaining employees who are still members of the scheme are now members of the Company's defined contribution scheme.

The scheme is administered by a separate Board of Trustees which is legally separate from the Company. The Trustees are composed of representatives of both the employer and employees. The Trustees are required by law to act in the interest of all relevant beneficiaries and are responsible for the investment policy with regard to the assets plus the day-to-day administration of the benefits.

UK legislation required that pension schemes are funded prudently. The last funding valuation of the scheme was carried out by a qualified actuary as at 6 April 2014 and showed a surplus. The Company is currently not required to pay contributions into the scheme.

Profile of the scheme
The defined benefit obligation includes benefits for former employees and current pensioners. Broadly, 60 per cent of the liabilities are attributable to former employees and 40 per cent to current pensioners.

The scheme duration is an indicator of the weighted average time until benefit payments are made. For the scheme as a whole, the duration is approximately 20 years.

Investment strategy
The Company and Trustees have agreed a long-term strategy for reducing investment risk as and when appropriate. This includes a policy to hold sufficient cash and bond assets to cover the anticipated benefit payments for at least the next five years so as to improve the cashflow matching of the scheme's assets and liabilities.

	Group and Parent Company	
	2015	2014
	£'000	£'000
Defined benefit obligation	(102,918)	(106,201)
Fair value of plan assets	99,008	97,683
Net defined benefit liability	(3,910)	(8,518)

Liability for defined benefit obligation

Changes in the present value of the defined benefit obligation are as follows:

	Group and Parent Company	
	2015 £'000	2014 £'000
Opening defined benefit obligation	106,201	95,597
Interest cost	3,751	4,142
Re-measurement (gains)/losses:		
– changes in demographic assumptions	1,384	–
– changes in financial assumptions	(2,519)	10,610
– experience	(1,854)	(882)
Benefits paid	(4,045)	(3,266)
	102,918	106,201

Changes in the fair value of plan assets are as follows:

	Group and Parent Company	
	2015 £'000	2014 £'000
Opening fair value of plan assets	97,683	95,652
Net interest on plan assets	3,444	4,144
Re-measurement gains	1,926	1,153
Benefits paid	(4,045)	(3,266)
Closing fair value of plan assets	99,008	97,683

The costs (charged)/credited in the income statement are as follows:

	Group	
	2015 £'000	2014 £'000
Interest (expense)/income on net defined benefit liability	(307)	2

The amounts recognised in other comprehensive income are as follows:

	Group	
	2015 £'000	2014 £'000
Re-measurement gains/(losses) on defined benefit pension plans	4,915	(8,575)

Cumulative re-measurement gains and losses reported in the consolidated statement of comprehensive income since 28 December 2003, the transition date to adopted IFRSs, for the Group and the Parent Company are net losses of £21,219,000 (2014: net losses of £26,134,000).

The fair value of the plan assets is as follows:

	Group and Parent Company	
	2015 £'000	2014 £'000
Equities – UK	40,320	39,432
– overseas	32,381	30,878
Bonds – corporate	16,547	16,765
– government	3,405	3,512
Absolute return funds	6,125	–
Property	–	2,592
Cash and cash equivalents/other	230	4,504
	99,008	97,683

Principal actuarial assumptions (expressed as weighted averages):

	Group and Parent Company	
	2015	2014
Discount rate	**3.85%**	3.6%
Future salary increases	**n/a**	n/a
Future pension increases	**1.7% - 2.45%**	1.6% - 2.4%

Mortality assumption

Mortality in retirement is assumed to be in line with the S2PXA tables using CMI_2013 projections and a long-term rate of 1.25 per cent per annum. Under these assumptions, pensioners aged 65 now are expected to live for a further 22.5 years (2014: 22.1 years) if they are male and 24.4 years (2014: 24.4 years) if they are female. Members currently aged 45 are expected to live for a further 24.3 years (2014: 23.4 years) from age 65 if they are male and for a further 26.4 years (2014: 25.9 years) from age 65 if they are female.

The sensitivities regarding the principal assumptions used to measure the scheme liabilities are set out below:

	Change in assumption	Impact on scheme liabilities
Discount rate	0.1% increase	Reduction of £2m
Inflation	0.1% decrease	Reduction of £1.4m
Mortality rates	1 year increase	Increase of £3.1m

The other demographic assumptions have been set having regard to latest trends in the scheme.

The Group expects to contribute £nil to its defined benefit plan in 2016.

Defined contribution plan

The Company also operates defined contribution schemes for other eligible employees. The assets of the schemes are held separately from those of the Group. The pension cost represents contributions payable by the Group and amounted to £10,302,000 (2014: £9,901,000) in the year.

Share-based payments – Group and Parent Company

The Group has established a Savings Related Share Option Scheme, an Executive Share Option Scheme and a Performance Share Plan.

The terms and conditions of the grants for these schemes are as follows, whereby all options are settled by physical delivery of shares:

	Date of grant	Employees entitled	Exercise price	Number of shares granted	Vesting conditions	Contractual life
Executive Share Option Scheme 12	August 2006	Senior employees	407p	1,028,000	Three years' service and EPS growth of 3-5% over RPI on average over those three years	10 years
Executive Share Option Scheme 13	April 2008	Senior employees	457p	618,500	Three years' service and EPS growth of 3-5% over RPI on average over those three years	10 years
Executive Share Option Scheme 14	April 2009	Senior employees	356p	2,012,000	Three years' service and EPS growth of 3-7% over RPI on average over those three years	10 years
Savings Related Share Option Scheme 12	April 2011	All employees	453p	697,609	Three years' service	3.5 years
Executive Share Option Scheme 15	August 2011	Senior employees	482p	707,000	Three years' service and EPS growth of 3-7% over RPI on average over those three years	10 years

	Date of grant	Employees entitled	Exercise price	Number of shares granted	Vesting conditions	Contractual life
Performance Share Plan 3	March 2012	Senior executives	£nil	248,922	Three years' service, EPS annual compound growth of 3–8% over RPI over those three years and TSR position relative to an appropriate comparator group	10 years
Savings Related Share Option Scheme 13	April 2012	All employees	468p	703,332	Three years' service	3.5 years
Executive Share Option Scheme 16	March 2013	Senior employees	480p	693,000	Three years' service and EPS growth of 3–7% over RPI on average over those three years	10 years
Transitional bonus share award	March 2013	Chief Executive	£nil	60,000	Continuous service of two and three years	3 years
Performance Share Plan 4	March 2013	Senior executives	£nil	305,592	Three years' service, EPS annual compound growth of 3–8% over RPI over those three years and TSR position relative to an appropriate comparator group	10 years
Savings Related Share Option Scheme 14	April 2013	All employees	414p	699,989	Three years' service	3.5 years
Recruitment share award	February 2014	Senior executive	£nil	5,517	Continuous service of two years	2 years
Performance Share Plan 5	March 2014	Senior executives	£nil	224,599	Three years' service, EPS annual compound growth of 1–4% over RPI over those three years and average annual ROCE of 15.5–17% over those three years	10 years
Executive Share Option Scheme 17	April 2014	Senior employees	500p	598,225	Three years' service and EPS growth of 1–4% over RPI on average over those three years	10 years
Savings Related Share Option Scheme 15	April 2014	All employees	465p	696,344	Three years' service	3.5 years
Executive Share Option Scheme 18	March 2015	Senior employees	1022p	298,045	Three years' service and EPS growth of 1–7% over RPI on average over those three years	10 years
Executive Share Option Scheme 18a	May 2015	Senior employee	1056p	3,285	Three years' service and EPS growth of 1–7% over RPI on average over those three years	10 years
Performance Share Plan 6	March 2015	Senior executives	£nil	146,174	Three years' service, EPS annual compound growth of 1–7% over RPI over those three years and average annual ROCE of 19–21.5% over those three years	10 years
Savings Related Share Option Scheme 16	April 2015	All employees	818p	391,979	Three years' service	3.5 years

The number and weighted average exercise price of share options is as follows:

	2015		2014	
	Weighted average exercise price	Number of options	Weighted average exercise price	Number of options
Outstanding at the beginning of the year	369p	4,333,526	382p	5,155,631
Lapsed during the year	291p	(257,187)	406p	(1,151,544)
Exercised during the year	401p	(882,263)	404p	(1,264,132)
Granted during the year	749p	839,483	391p	1,593,571
Outstanding at the end of the year	446p	4,033,559	369p	4,333,526
Exercisable at the end of the year	365p	331,380	384p	640,812

The options outstanding at 2 January 2016 have an exercise price in the range of £nil to £10.56 and have a weighted average contractual life of 5.2 years. The options exercised during the year had a weighted average market value of £11.38 (2014: £5.33).

The fair value of services received in return for share options granted is measured by reference to the fair value of share options granted. The estimate of the fair value of the services received is measured based on the Black–Scholes model for all Savings Related Share Option Schemes and Executive Share Option Schemes and for Performance Share Plan options granted from 2014 onwards. The Monte Carlo option pricing model was used for Performance Share Plans granted prior to 2014. The fair value per option granted and the assumptions used in these calculations are as follows:

	2015				2014			
	Performance Share Plan 6 March 2015	Executive Share Option Scheme 18 March 2015	Executive Share Option Scheme 18a April 2015	Savings Related Share Option Scheme 16 April 2015	Performance Share Plan 5 March 2014	Recruitment share award February 2014	Executive Share Option Scheme 17 April 2014	Savings Related Share Option Scheme 15 April 2014
Fair value at grant date	971p	140p	145p	230p	443p	499p	48p	68p
Share price	1035p	1022p	1056p	818p	498p	499p	500p	517p
Exercise price	nil	1022p	1056p	1023p	nil	nil	500p	465p
Expected volatility	23.9%	23.9%	23.8%	23.9%	20.6%	–	20.6%	20.7%
Option life	3 years	3 years	3 years	3 years	3 years	2 years	3 years	3 years
Expected dividend yield	2.13%	2.15%	2.08%	2.15%	3.92%	–	3.92%	3.92%
Risk-free rate	0.69%	0.64%	0.69%	0.76%	1.07%	–	1.07%	1.07%

The expected volatility is based on historical volatility, adjusted for any expected changes to future volatility due to publicly available information. The historical volatility is calculated using a weekly rolling share price for the three-year period immediately prior to the option grant date.

The costs charged to the income statement relating to share-based payments were as follows:

	2015 £'000	2014 £'000
Share options granted in 2011	–	(453)
Share options granted in 2012	91	(38)
Share options granted in 2013	1,573	524
Share options granted in 2014	1,321	496
Share options granted in 2015	677	–
Total expense recognised as employee costs	3,662	529

22 Provisions

	2015 Dilapidations £'000	2015 Onerous leases £'000	2015 Total £'000	2014 Dilapidations £'000	2014 Onerous leases £'000	2014 Total £'000
			Group and Parent Company			
Balance at start of year	3,456	3,155	6,611	1,689	3,672	5,361
Additional provision in the year	1,422	581	2,003	3,330	1,232	4,562
Utilised in year	(1,135)	(1,059)	(2,194)	(1,249)	(1,369)	(2,618)
Provisions reversed during the year	(400)	(388)	(788)	(314)	(380)	(694)
Balance at end of year	3,343	2,289	5,632	3,456	3,155	6,611
Included in current liabilities	2,632	1,043	3,675	2,474	1,635	4,109
Included in non-current liabilities	711	1,246	1,957	982	1,520	2,502
	3,343	2,289	5,632	3,456	3,155	6,611

Provisions relate to onerous leases, dilapidations and other commitments associated with properties. Included within the provision is £704,000 in respect of possible recourse on leases which have been conditionally assigned.

The provision for onerous leases is held in respect of leasehold properties for which the Group is liable to fulfil rent and other property commitments for shops from which either the Group no longer trades or for which future trading cash flows are projected to be insufficient to cover these costs. Amounts have been provided for the shortfall between projected cashflows and property costs up to the lease expiry date or other appropriate estimated date. The majority of this provision is expected to be utilised within four years such that the impact of discounting would not be material.

The Group provides for property dilapidations, where appropriate, based on estimated costs of the dilapidation repairs. £2,078,000 of the additional provision made in the prior year in respect of dilapidations was exceptional and relates to the dilapidation costs arising from the removal of in-store bakeries from shops as described in Note 4. £555,000 of this is expected to be utilised after more than one year. The remainder of the dilapidations provision is expected to be utilised within one year.

The provisions reversed or utilised during the year do not contain any items that were included as exceptional costs in the prior year.

23 Capital and reserves

Share capital

	Ordinary shares	
	2015 Number	2014 Number
In issue and fully paid at start and end of year – ordinary shares of 2p	101,155,901	101,155,901

The holders of ordinary shares are entitled to receive dividends as declared from time to time and are entitled to one vote per share at meetings of the Company.

Capital redemption reserve

The capital redemption reserve relates to the nominal value of issued share capital bought back by the Company and cancelled.

Own shares held

Deducted from retained earnings is £13,998,000 (2014: £6,750,000) in respect of own shares held by the Greggs Employee Benefit Trust. The Trust, which was established during 1988 to act as a repository of issued Company shares, holds 857,882 shares (2014: 805,034 shares) with a market value at 2 January 2016 of £11,273,000 (2014: £5,841,000) which have not vested unconditionally in employees. During the year the Trust purchased 940,687 shares for an aggregate consideration of £11,125,000 and sold 887,839 shares for an aggregate consideration of £3,876,000.

The shares held by the Greggs Employee Benefit Trust can be purchased either by employees on the exercise of an option under the Greggs Executive Share Option Schemes, Greggs Savings Related Share Option Scheme and Greggs Performance Share Plan or by the trustees of the Greggs Employee Share Scheme. The trustees have elected to waive the dividends payable on these shares.

Dividends

The following tables analyse dividends when paid and the year to which they relate:

	2015 Per share pence	2014 Per share pence
2013 final dividend	–	13.5p
2014 interim dividend	–	6.0p
2014 final dividend	16.0p	–
2015 interim dividend	7.4p	–
2015 special dividend	20.0p	–
	43.4p	19.5p

The proposed final dividend in respect of 2015 amounts to 21.2 pence per share (£21,264,000). This proposed dividend is subject to approval at the Annual General Meeting and has not been included as a liability in these accounts.

	2015 £'000	2014 £'000
2013 final dividend	–	13,530
2014 interim dividend	–	6,040
2014 final dividend	16,090	–
2015 interim dividend	7,463	–
2015 special dividend	20,161	–
	43,714	19,570

24 Operating leases

Non-cancellable operating lease rentals are payable as follows:

	2015 Property £'000	2015 Equipment £'000	2015 Total £'000	2014 Property £'000	2014 Equipment £'000	2014 Total £'000
Less than one year	36,136	1,928	38,064	36,887	2,031	38,918
Between one and five years	73,881	2,588	76,469	73,630	3,048	76,678
More than five years	13,443	–	13,443	12,210	247	12,457
	123,460	4,516	127,976	122,727	5,326	128,053

The Group leases the majority of its shops under operating leases. The leases typically run for a period of ten years, with an option to renew the lease after that date. Lease payments are generally increased every five years to reflect market rentals. For a small number of the leases the rental is contingent on the level of turnover achieved in the relevant unit; these amounts are immaterial.

The inception of the shop leases has taken place over a long period of time and many date back a significant number of years. They are combined leases of land and buildings. It is not possible to obtain a reliable estimate of the split of the fair values of the lease interest between land and buildings at inception. Therefore, in determining lease classification the Group evaluated whether both parts are clearly an operating lease or a finance lease. Firstly, title does not pass for the land or buildings. Secondly, because the rent paid to the landlord for the buildings is increased to market rent at regular intervals, and the Group does not participate in the residual value of the land or buildings it is judged that substantially all the risks and rewards of the land and buildings are with the landlord. Based on these qualitative factors it is concluded that the leases are operating leases.

25 Capital commitments

During the year ended 2 January 2016, the Group entered into contracts to purchase property, plant and equipment and intangible assets for £2,010,000 (2014: £6,454,000). These commitments are expected to be settled in the following financial year.

26 Related parties

Identity of related parties

The Group has a related party relationship with its subsidiaries (see Note 12) and its Directors and executive officers.

Trading transactions with subsidiaries – Group

There have been no transactions between the Company and its subsidiaries or associates during the year (2014: £nil).

Trading transactions with subsidiaries – Parent Company

	Amounts owed to related parties		Amounts owed by related parties	
	2015 £'000	2014 £'000	2015 £'000	2014 £'000
Dormant subsidiaries	7,807	7,807	–	–

The Greggs Foundation is also a related party and during the year the Company made a donation to the Greggs Foundation of £700,000 (2014: £520,000).

Transactions with key management personnel

The Directors are the key management personnel of the Group. The Company has been notified of the following interests of the Directors who served during the year (including those of their connected persons but excluding interests in shares pursuant to unexercised share options) in the share capital of the Company as follows:

	Ordinary shares of 2p (beneficial interest)		Ordinary shares of 2p (Trustee holding with no beneficial interest)	
	2015 (or date of cessation if earlier)	2014 (or date of appointment if later)	2015 (or date of cessation if earlier)	2014 (or date of appointment if later)
Roger Whiteside	75,998	72,253	–	–
Richard Hutton	77,923	55,787	400,000	600,000
Raymond Reynolds	59,244	53,224	–	–
Ian Durant (Non-Executive)	11,700	11,700	–	–
Allison Kirkby (Non-Executive)	1,600	1,600	–	–
Helena Ganczakowski (Non-Executive)	1,000	1,000	–	–
Peter McPhillips (Non-Executive)	500	–	–	–
Sandra Turner (Non-Executive)	1,000	–	–	–

Details of Directors' share options, emoluments, pension benefits and other non-cash benefits can be found in the Directors' Remuneration report on pages 49 to 65. Summary information on remuneration of key management personnel is included in Note 5.

There have been no changes since 2 January 2016 in the Directors' interests noted above.

27 Events after the reporting period

As noted in the Chief Executive's report on page 19 the Group has completed a detailed review of its manufacturing and distribution operations. As a result of this, subsequent to the year end, the Board has agreed a proposal to invest substantially to reshape its supply chain over the next five years, which includes the proposed closure of three bakery sites. Alongside an increased level of capital expenditure the proposals would lead to one-off costs of around £7 million in 2016, of which £6 million would be a cash cost. No liability for costs arising from this plan has been recognised in these accounts in accordance with IAS 10.

[Any page references within these extracts refer to Greggs annual report as opposed to this book.]

Glossary

Abridged accounts Accounts that can be filed by small companies at Companies House (UK). Abridged accounts contain fewer financial disclosures. See also *statutory accounts.*

Accounting standards Rules and guidelines that set out how transactions should be recorded and presented in financial statements.

Accounts payable Process purchase invoices and pay suppliers.

Accounts receivable Process sales invoices and collect payments from customers.

Accruals Goods or services which have been received, but not yet invoiced or paid. Also known as accrued expenses.

Accrued income Income from the provision of goods or services to a third party which has not yet been invoiced.

Amortisation Another word for depreciation. Amortisation is an accounting expense that reflects the usage, wearing-out or 'consumption' of (intangible) fixed assets.

Angel investors Wealthy individuals who invest their own capital in early stage companies in return for an equity stake in the business. Also known as business angels.

Asset-based finance Source of debt finance for smaller businesses that are unable to access debt finance through more traditional routes, e.g. banks.

Budget A financial and operational business plan.

Capex Payments to purchase or improve long-term assets. Also known as capital expenditure.

Capital allowances An apportionment of the cost of an asset over its life, which can be deducted from taxable profit.

Capital and reserves Owners' equity in a business. Numerically, it is equivalent to net assets in a balance sheet.

Capital employed Total assets less current liabilities. Also known as *TALCL*.

Capital gain If a company sells an asset or investment for more than its original cost, it is subject to tax on the 'capital gain' which arises.

Capital reserves Surpluses arising from activities other than trading.

Confirmation statement An annual return that every company must submit to Companies House (UK) to confirm information held about the company.

Contribution Sales revenue less variable costs.

Corporate governance System by which companies are managed (i.e. directed and controlled).

Corporation tax Tax on a company's profits.

Cost of capital Cost of financing an investment over the long term, which is the discount rate used in NPV and IRR calculations.

Covenant Financial performance limit or target that must be met as a condition of debt finance.

Credit control Managing and collecting amounts owed by credit customers (debtors).

Crowd (or peer) lending Online lending directly to small and medium-sized businesses (see also *equity crowdfunding*). Also known as peer-to-peer (P2P) lending.

CVP analysis Cost-Volume-Profit (or breakeven) analysis.

DCF Discounted cash flow. Cash flow discounted to present value recognising the time value of money.

Debt factoring Outsourcing the collection of debt to a third party, which has specific expertise in managing and collecting debts.

Debt finance Money raised from debtholders (banks, finance houses, individuals, etc.).

Debtor and creditor days Average number of days of outstanding debtors and creditors for all customers and suppliers.

Deferred income Prepayment (or deposit) from a third party.

Deferred tax Timing differences between accounting and tax regulations.

Depreciation Cost of using fixed assets. It is an accounting expense that reflects the usage, wearing-out or 'consumption' of (tangible) fixed assets.

Double taxation Where a company resident in two (or more) countries is potentially subject to tax in both those countries.

EBITDA Earnings before interest, tax, depreciation and amortisation.

Equity Capital and reserves that belong to shareholders.

Equity crowdfunding Source of funding in which the public invest money in return for an equity stake in companies. Investors are sought through online platforms.

Equity finance Money ('capital') raised through the sale of shares to investors.

ERP Enterprise resource planning. A system of integrated IT applications used to manage a business and automate many back office functions.

External audit Examination of a company's financial statements carried out by independent auditors. Auditors are qualified professionals, appointed annually by shareholders to provide an independent opinion on whether the financial statements present a 'true and fair' view.

Financial risk Volatility in profit due to high leverage.

Financing activities Changes to funding from either equity finance or debt finance, identified within the cash flow statement.

Fixed charge Form of security in which particular assets are charged or held as security against debt finance.

Forecast An estimation of an organisation's financial performance for specific periods in the future.

Fraud Intentional deception with a view to gaining personal advantage.

GAAP Generally accepted accounting practice.

Gearing Measure of a company's long-term financing structure. It compares a company's borrowings (debt) with its funding from shareholders (equity).

Going concern A state of operating and financial capability in which a business is expected to continue operations into the future, for a period of at least 12 months from the date the accounts are signed.

Goodwill Difference in value between what a company is worth and the 'sum of its parts'.

Gross profit Revenue less 'cost of sales' (direct costs) from revenue.

Gross profit margin Margin between price and direct costs.

Group A parent company and at least one subsidiary.

Group accounts A single set of financial statements showing consolidated financial information of a group of companies.

HMRC Her Majesty's Revenue and Customs.

Impairment A permanent loss in income-generating potential of an asset.

Incremental budgets Budgets based on the previous year's budget plus or minus a set percentage.

Initial public offering (IPO) First sale of shares to outside investors by a private company.

Insolvency Legal term used where a company is unable to repay the debts that it owes.

Intangible assets Fixed assets that have no physical form and include development costs, patents, trademarks and software.

Interest cover Measure of the affordability of debt to a company. An indication of how many 'times' a company could theoretically afford to pay its interest charges.

Investing activities Acquisition and disposal of long-term assets and other investments, identified within the cash flow statement.

IRR Internal Rate of Return. The 'rate of return' of an investment.

Journals Accounting adjustments to reflect timing differences.

Leverage Utilisation of debt to obtain more finance than would otherwise be possible using equity finance.

Margin Profit as a percentage of the sales price.

Margin of safety Amount by which sales have to fall before a product or service makes a loss.

Market to book ratio Business value divided by net asset value.

Mark-up Profit as a percentage of direct costs.

Mixed costs Costs which include an element of both fixed and variable costs.

NBV Net book value. Difference between cost and accumulated depreciation.

Net assets Fixed assets + current assets − current liabilities − debt.

Net working capital Difference between current assets and current liabilities.

NIC National Insurance Contributions.

Nominal ledger Central repository for all accounting transactions.

Non-controlling interest Proportion of a company not owned by parent, i.e. held by third parties. Non-controlling interests exist when a subsidiary is less than 100 per cent owned.

NPV Net Present Value. The value or contribution of an investment.

Operating activities Principal revenue generating activities of the business, identified within the cash flow statement.

Operating profit Revenue less 'cost of sales' and 'operating expenses'.

Operating profit margin Margin between price and all operating costs, both direct and indirect overheads.

Operating risk Volatility in profit due to a high level of fixed costs compared to variable costs. Also known as *operating gearing*.

Opex Expenses incurred in running a business. Also known as *operating expenditure* or *revenue expenditure*.

Payback period A measure of the time required to pay back an investment.

PAYE Pay As You Earn.

Pre-emption rights Rights protecting existing shareholders against dilution of their percentage shareholding in a company.

Prepayments Goods or services which have been invoiced and paid, but not yet received. Also known as *deferred expense*.

Price customisation Setting different prices for different customers based on their relative perceptions of value. Also known as 'dynamic' or 'demand yield' pricing or price discrimination.

Private equity Funds typically used to 'buy out' shareholders of existing companies rather than providing a source of new finance for companies.

Provision A known yet imprecise liability. A present obligation as a result of a past event where payment is probable and the amount can be reliably estimated.

Public offering Regulated issue of shares to investors.

Retained profit Distributable profit (the profit remaining in the business after all other expenses) less dividends paid to shareholders.

Return on investment 'Return' as a percentage of the 'investment' required to run the business which generated the 'return'.

Revenue reserves Trading profit retained in the business for future investment.

Rights issue Shares issued to existing shareholders typically at a discount and in proportion to shareholders' holding of existing shares.

Rolling budgets Budgets which are re-budgeted on a regular basis, usually monthly or quarterly.

Solvency The ability of a business to pay its long-term debts.

Statutory accounts Accounts prepared and filed by all companies (except dormant companies) at Companies House (UK). See also *abridged accounts*.

Stock Inventory comprising raw materials, work in progress and finished goods.

TALCL Total assets less current liabilities. Also known as *capital employed*.

Tangible fixed assets Assets that possess physical substance.

Tax gap Measure of the difference between the amount of tax collected by a country's tax authorities and the amount that should be collected.

Trial balance List of every account in the *nominal ledger* and its associated 'balance' (or total), categorised into profit and loss account (and balance sheet items).

True and fair Legal term interpreted to mean that accounts are free from material misstatements and faithfully represent the financial performance and position of an entity.

VAT Value added tax.

Venture capital (VC) Funds raised from institutional investors and wealthy individuals (as well as their own monies) available to invest in business. VCs typically buy minority stakes in businesses and expect a 'seat on the board'.

Whistleblowing Reporting of wrong-doing (fraud, illegality or unethical practice) in an organisation.

Working capital Difference between current assets (stock, debtors and cash) and current liabilities (creditors and bank overdrafts).

Zero-based budgets Budgets which are calculated from a 'zero base', i.e. starting from scratch.

Further resources

For supporting resources please visit:

www.financebook.co.uk

Index